Ludwig Wittgenstein

Ludwig Wittgenstein

The Meaning of Life

Edited by Joaquín Jareño-Alarcón

This edition first published 2023
© 2023 John Wiley & Sons Ltd.

All rights reserved. No part of this publication may be reproduced, stored in a retrieval system, or transmitted, in any form or by any means, electronic, mechanical, photocopying, recording or otherwise, except as permitted by law. Advice on how to obtain permission to reuse material from this title is available at http://www.wiley.com/go/permissions.

The right of Joaquín Jareño-Alarcón to be identified as the author of the editorial material in this work has been asserted in accordance with law.

Registered Office
John Wiley & Sons, Inc., 111 River Street, Hoboken, NJ 07030, USA
John Wiley & Sons Ltd, The Atrium, Southern Gate, Chichester, West Sussex, PO19 8SQ, UK

For details of our global editorial offices, customer services, and more information about Wiley products visit us at www.wiley.com.

Wiley also publishes its books in a variety of electronic formats and by print-on-demand. Some content that appears in standard print versions of this book may not be available in other formats.

Trademarks: Wiley and the Wiley logo are trademarks or registered trademarks of John Wiley & Sons, Inc. and/or its affiliates in the United States and other countries and may not be used without written permission. All other trademarks are the property of their respective owners. John Wiley & Sons, Inc. is not associated with any product or vendor mentioned in this book.

Limit of Liability/Disclaimer of Warranty
While the publisher and authors have used their best efforts in preparing this work, they make no representations or warranties with respect to the accuracy or completeness of the contents of this work and specifically disclaim all warranties, including without limitation any implied warranties of merchantability or fitness for a particular purpose. No warranty may be created or extended by sales representatives, written sales materials or promotional statements for this work. The fact that an organization, website, or product is referred to in this work as a citation and/or potential source of further information does not mean that the publisher and authors endorse the information or services the organization, website, or product may provide or recommendations it may make. This work is sold with the understanding that the publisher is not engaged in rendering professional services. The advice and strategies contained herein may not be suitable for your situation. You should consult with a specialist where appropriate. Further, readers should be aware that websites listed in this work may have changed or disappeared between when this work was written and when it is read. Neither the publisher nor authors shall be liable for any loss of profit or any other commercial damages, including but not limited to special, incidental, consequential, or other damages.

Library of Congress Cataloging-in-Publication Data
Names: Jareño Alarcón, Joaquín, 1963– editor.
Title: Ludwig Wittgenstein : the meaning of life / Joaquín Jareño-Alarcón.
Other titles: Ludwig Wittgenstein (John Wiley & Sons)
Description: Hoboken, NJ, USA : John Wiley & Sons, Ltd., 2023. | Includes index.
Identifiers: LCCN 2022054088 (print) | LCCN 2022054089 (ebook) | ISBN 9781394162888 (paperback) | ISBN 9781394162895 (adobe pdf) | ISBN 9781394162901 (epub)
Subjects: LCSH: Wittgenstein, Ludwig, 1889–1951. | Life. | Meaning (Philosophy)
Classification: LCC B3376.W564 L79 2023 (print) | LCC B3376.W564 (ebook) | DDC 113/.8—dc23/eng/20230211
LC record available at https://lccn.loc.gov/2022054088
LC ebook record available at https://lccn.loc.gov/2022054089

Cover Design: Wiley
Cover Image: © Mike Newton

Set in 9.5/12.5pt STIXTwoText by Straive, Pondicherry, India
SKY10049177_061623

To my family
A.M.G.D.

Contents

Introductory Note *ix*
Acknowledgements *xviii*
List of Sources *xix*
Abbreviations *xxiv*

1 **1910–1920** *1*

2 **1921–1930** *43*

3 **1931–1940** *79*

4 **1941–1951** *153*

   Other Sources *199*
   Index *227*

Introductory Note

1

Ludwig Wittgenstein is considered by many to be the greatest philosopher of the twentieth century. There are probably enough reasons to regard the Austrian thinker as one of the most charismatic intellectual giants of the last century. His work has proved sufficiently enduring and robust that it has crossed the boundaries of two centuries, and its vigour remains untouched. What appears surprising is how little he published while he was alive. But this circumstance has helped to maintain the intellectual tension in all those who have tried to navigate his philosophy, in search of the appropriate connections to provide an accurate interpretation of it.

Wittgenstein has been one of the major advocates of the so-called "linguistic turn", stressing the close relationship between language and philosophical problems. Such a view of philosophy has exerted a lasting influence still present today, even touching seemingly distant domains as that of political theory. If we consider all that has been published on Wittgenstein from an academic point of view, there is little room dedicated to matters concerning religion and the meaning of life. This could make us believe that that kind of issues scarcely interested Wittgenstein. However, in view of the considerable amount of material where the philosopher shapes his views on those topics, it is clearly evident that they were of special importance to him. As a matter of fact, it has been pointed out that the principal intention of his best known work, the *Tractatus* – and his only published philosophical book throughout his lifetime – is but to demonstrate the relevance of matters concerning religion and the meaning of life, and the *absolute* position of moral action.

2

This study presents a compilation of those texts revealing Wittgenstein's thoughts and attitudes on the central issues within the closely connected domains of religion and ethics. Nevertheless, from the outset a compilation such as this raises certain doubts and also faces many obstacles. The first problem is the reason to choose such subjects. Traditionally, very different questions have had a specific weight for studies on Wittgenstein's philosophy. As we said before, the texts where he deals with such issues from an academic point of view are not many.

While working on my doctoral dissertation on Wittgenstein and religion, I wrote to Elizabeth Anscombe hoping to meet her in Cambridge and discuss Wittgenstein's views on that matter. As one of Wittgenstein's favourite students, I thought she should be aware of her master's personal interests. The answer I received was very kind and showed Anscombe's generous character, but it ended with a laconic, and categorical: "If I am in Cambridge when you are, I shall be glad to talk with you, though *I don't think I have much to contribute to your topic*"[1] (my italics).

An old letter from G.E. Moore to Norman Malcolm shows a sort of sceptical surprise at the relationship that Wittgenstein had towards religion. After the Catholic burial Wittgenstein received, Moore, who had been present, wrote in a worried tone: "The burial was conducted by a Roman Catholic priest: I don't know why. Had Wittgenstein himself become a Catholic? I should have thought it very unlikely. The most I ever heard him saying in favour of Catholicism was that the fact that such a first-rate person as Smythies had become a Catholic shewed that there was much more to be said for it than one would have thought".[2] Also, in his brief biographical sketch, G.H. von Wright, one of Wittgenstein's literary executors, merely says:

> It seems to me that there are two forms of seriousness of character. One is fixed in 'strong principles'; the other springs from a passionate heart. The former has to do with morality and the latter, I believe, is closer to religion. Wittgenstein was acutely and even painfully sensitive to considerations of duty, but the earnestness and severity of his personality were more of the second kind. Yet *I do not know whether he can be said to have been 'religious' in any but a trivial sense of the word*". (Emphasis added)

Such comments could lead us to think that, actually, Wittgenstein was not particularly interested in religious matters or that he at least did not pay any great attention to them. Textual evidence, however, can force us to reconsider. Not only can we read many testimonies from those who knew him personally, which corroborate the permanent tension between Wittgenstein and religion, but we also

---

1 Something that is in direct contrast to the fact that, just after Anscombe's arrival in Cambridge, she would go for walks with Wasfi Hijab and Wittgenstein and argue about questions related to the philosophy of religion during his tutorials.
2 Add. MS. A. 310 (7); 30.04.1951.

have access to an interesting number of texts in which it is clearly evident that he lived in an ongoing state of preoccupation regarding the basic and fundamental issues dealt with by religious discourse. In spite of the ambiguity he occasionally manifested, there is ample evidence that Wittgenstein was deeply concerned with the significance of religion and ethics in his personal – first person – experience, something that can clearly be seen in "A Lecture on Ethics", to cite a typical example. Theodore Redpath's testimony may also serve as a good instance of what we are talking about. In his book *Ludwig Wittgenstein. A Student's Memoir*, Redpath – a friend of Wittgenstein in the 1930s and a Fellow of Trinity College – writes:

> Wittgenstein said to me on more than one occasion: 'The trouble with you and me, old man, is that we have no religion'. I don't think I ever plumbed the full depth of this statement, either as applied to himself or as applied to me, though I think I have a somewhat better insight into his meaning now than I ever did in those days [c.1936]. As far as he was concerned, I can remember that more than once on going to his rooms for a talk or for tea I found him reading the Bible. One day he said he thought it would be a good thing if we would read the Book of Job together. We never did, but I think I now understand why it might have been good for both of us. We were certainly both impatient people, and I still am. Wittgenstein also once took me along one afternoon to Little St. Mary's Church, a very 'High' Church, which he was much attached to, though I do not know whether he ever attended any services there. He simply took me into the church and we sat down in a pew near the back, on the south side, and just continued to sit there in silence. While we were sitting there a middle-aged woman came into the church, went into one of the pews about halfway up on the north side, and knelt down to pray. Wittgenstein leant over to me and whispered: '*That* is what a church is for!'"[3]

But the domain of the meaning of life does not end there. That is, it is clearly arguable that Wittgenstein had an ethical point of view on religion. Not only because both religion and ethics belong to the domain of the *unspeakable*, or because Wittgenstein had an un-intellectualist view on them, but because they are indissolubly related, as religion speaks of both *good life* and *happy life*, and religious beliefs show in how one manages one's own life. Questions on values, or on what good is or means, and so on, are issues which directly affect the meaning of life or,

---

3 Theodore Redpath, *Ludwig Wittgenstein: A Student's Memoir*. Duckworth, London 1990, pp. 43–4 (italics in the original).

in other words, the problem of life, which is none other than the search for its meaning and how it appears in our daily existence. This properly justifies the presence in this compilation of "A Lecture on Ethics", but also of any notes, remarks and discussions that deal with the basic topics of ethics. There is also a specific, related interest in aesthetics ("Ethik und Aesthetik sind Eins" (**TLP** 6.421)), but such a subject will not be present in our compilation.

3

To the explanation of *why* we have chosen the topics, another of no less importance must be added: the kind of criteria which have been used to select the texts. Any work trying to highlight some elements with respect to others is unavoidably conditioned by the subjective aspects of the selection. This compilation would possibly have been somewhat different if another compiler had carried out the work, or if the compilation had been made at a different time or under different circumstances. Assuming the inevitable risks any selection is to face, the criteria used for ours have attempted to clearly settle Wittgenstein's opinions on the topics under discussion. The chosen texts are large enough for the paragraphs to contain their full meaning and for the context in which they were written to be basically understood, and we have done our best to omit any lines which do not further any such understanding.

In cases such as the *Tractatus*, for instance, we had to deal with the problem of trying to delimit the scope of the selection due to its logical sequence characteristic. Solipsism is mentioned in connection with the metaphysical subject and this – in due turn – in connection with the ethical subject, but we have avoided making the discussion concerning solipsism more explicit. Following that path could have led us to quote almost the whole *Tractatus* in our compilation. Given that many connections can be established between the different areas of that book, we could have made use of the existence of highly elaborated academic reflections as criterion for choosing paragraphs, but that would have led us to select a substantial part of Wittgenstein's entire body of work. A good example of this is the identity Eddy Zemach established between God and the *logical form* in his classic essay "Wittgenstein's Philosophy of the Mystical".[4]

Even so, the idea of quoting a text long enough for it to be fully meaningful could have been misleading given that it contains an explicit interpretive and then subjective value. It has proved effective, however, in separating significant texts from those less so. In Wittgenstein's most personal writings, this task has proved

---

4 Eddy Zemach, Wittgenstein's Philosophy of the Mystical, *The Review of Metaphysics*, vol. 18, n. 1 (1964), pp. 38–57.

difficult but it is clearly justified in examples such as the following, taken from the *Notebooks 1914–1916* entry of 25.05.1915. What appears in the compilation is:

> The urge towards the mystical comes of the non-satisfaction of our wishes by science. We *feel* that even if all *possible* scientific questions are answered *our problem is still not touched at all*. Of course in that case there are no questions any more; and that is the answer.

The text is clearly of importance for our work but comes after an entry which is connected to quite different interests, and *for this reason* has not been included:

> Does the visual image of a *minimum visible* actually appear to us indivisible? What has extension is divisible. Are there parts in our visual image that have no extension? E.g., the images of the fixed stars?

We have given priority to those paragraphs which clearly show Wittgenstein's points of view on our topics. This, in turn, explains why, generally speaking, we have not presented Wittgenstein's full-length letters. Sometimes, our interest falls on but a short sentence or expression without specific continuity, or appears at the end of comments that do not add any significant information for our aims with this book. Let us take the entry of 05.09.1913, a letter to Bertrand Russell, which begins:

> Dear Russell,
>
> I am sitting here in a little place inside a beautiful fiord and thinking about the beastly theory of types. There are still some *very* difficult problems (and very fundamental ones too) to be solved and I won't begin to write until I have got some sort of a solution for them. However I don't think that will in any way affect the Bipolarity business which still seems to me to be absolutely untangible. Pinsent is an enormous comfort to me here. We have hired a little sailing boat and go about with it on the fiord, or rather Pinsent is doing all the sailing and I sit in the boat and work".

What follows is what actually matters here. Wittgenstein complains about the viability of his work and ends his letter using an expression that – knowing Russell's points of view and his relationship with Wittgenstein – is not a mere exclamation:

> Shall I get anything out??! It would be awful if I did not and all my work would be lost. However I am not losing courage and go on thinking. Pray for me!

In this case, we have highlighted the text for the peculiar and surprising character of Wittgenstein's request. It is not a cliché like "God only knows" but shows a specific emotional situation, and the religious expression is consciously used as such. Textual selection, therefore, is manifestly justified by the interest stemming from Wittgenstein's use of specific terminology. In another letter to Russell, in November 1913 – following a long discussion of logic by Wittgenstein – the final paragraph reads:

> Would you do me a great favour: I have promised last year to book *two* serial tickets for the C. U. M. S.[5] Chamber Concerts. Would you kindly book them for me, keep one of them for yourself, give the other to somebody else and charge me for both. If you let me know the price I shall send you the money *at once*.
> Pray for me and God bless you! (If there is such a thing).
>
> Yours as long as
> $(\exists x).x = $ L. W.

Here, the expression "Pray for me and God bless you! (If there is such a thing)" plays a quite specific role. That is, it has a proper religious meaning and that is why it has been used.

4

It is important to note that most of the selected texts are of a private nature (letters, remarks and brief notes). Such writings have been given priority in this compilation. As they were not meant to be published, they have a special importance for our work precisely because we are able to reliably know more about how Wittgenstein discussed matters concerning the meaning of life, including nuances that allow us to adequately locate texts. They are mostly unpolished paragraphs, written directly and without any kind of rhetoric – something which deprives them of any special formal literary value – but their spontaneity offers us a better testimony of Wittgenstein's *spiritual beat* and helps us to discern his personal views on those matters of interest to us. Sometimes, entries are composed of only one sentence that seems to resume the existential problems Wittgenstein is facing at a specific moment of his life – "A confession has to be part of one's new life" (**CV** 1931) – or they densely resume Wittgenstein's view on a given subject: "If Christianity is the truth, then all the philosophy about it is false" (**CV** 1949).

---

5 Cambridge University Musical Society.

On other occasions, as may be the case of manuscripts 101, 102 and 103, Wittgenstein described everything that happened in his military life during the First World War, of which only a part is of interest here. It is true that the special circumstances of a military conflict exert a strong influence on people's character, habits and fears, but that would not justify a complete reproduction of personal notes. In the case of the entry of 25.08.1914, Wittgenstein starts speaking of the difficulties he has had to endure that day but the compilation text begins when Wittgenstein asks himself what his attitude should be when faced with such difficulties, and ends with an assertion which is connected to what in the end will be his conception of ethics: "Only one thing is necessary: to be able to contemplate everything that happens; stay composed! God help me!"

One must remember that Wittgenstein's way of working was quite peculiar. He would take copious notes that were of use to him both in his teaching and to reflect on thoughts as they had come to him. He frequently reviewed what he had written down but was rarely sure of the validity of "final version", which meant that the larger part of his writings never saw the light of day as books. The *Tractatus* itself, for example, is the result of many arguments and much reworking of first thoughts on logic and philosophy. Bear in mind that numerous conversations with Russell or Moore influenced the book, as well as annotations and revisions of them made during the First World War. It is very significant that when he finally finishes the *Tractatus* he says that the problems of philosophy have been definitively resolved. Likewise, there are prior versions of the book that were not published. All of this allows us to comprehend the existence of differences between those texts that were not prepared for later publication and those that were personal commentaries or annotations that served as a form of personal discussion.

Another important source for the work has been the testimony of those closest to Wittgenstein. Literary executors, friends and students have all become essential tools for discovering more about Wittgenstein's personality and thoughts. That is the reason why many of their writings have been used to give a more accurate description of how the philosopher understood matters concerning the meaning of life. Consider, for example, the comment made by Johann Scheibenbauer, one of Wittgenstein's students at Trattenbach in 1921–2, who, although he was unable to go into details, remembered – in the closing years of the last century – that in his classes Wittgenstein "spoke a lot about religion".[6] This compilation tries, therefore, to establish a balanced view between what Wittgenstein himself wrote and the memories of those who were closely connected to him.

---

6 Personal comment to the compiler.

We have also included the full texts where the intention to reflect upon the topics we deal with in this work is clear enough. Unfortunately, there are not many of these texts and they originate mainly as notes from Wittgenstein's students or works they published using such notes. This is the case both in regard to his lectures and also in regard to the comments and remarks Wittgenstein made on topics which interested him or on his readings. Cyril Barrett's "Lectures on Religious Belief" are just notes taken by Wittgenstein's pupils, what Barrett clearly states in his preface to the 1966 edition. This is something we have to bear in mind in order to understand the limits of accuracy in our knowledge of Wittgenstein's thought. All this does not lessen the reliability of the texts but demands a certain critical attitude towards evaluating their actual value. Barrett himself writes:

> The first thing to be said about this book is that nothing contained herein was written by Wittgenstein himself. The notes published here are not Wittgenstein's own lectures notes but notes taken down by students, which he neither saw nor checked. It is even doubtful if he would have approved of their publication, at least in their present form. Since, however, they deal with topics only briefly touched upon in his other published writings, and since for some time they have been circulating privately, it was thought best to publish then in a form approved by their authors.

From the rest of the notes which make up the other lectures, we have chosen only some brief paragraphs which directly mention the topics we are dealing with. Their value may well be minor but, though they have to be treated with the same aforementioned caution, we believe they also clearly reflect how Wittgenstein conceptualised those matters.

5

The exposition of the material has been carried out following the chronological sequence of the texts. Our intention has been to clearly lay out how Wittgenstein's interests were reflected in terms of his own personal and intellectual evolution. This criterion may allow us to better understand the existential dimension of the texts because – despite the way time and experience unavoidably change anyone's points of view – we must not forget that, as Mrs Joan Bevan[7] clearly stated, Wittgenstein never said what he did not want to say[8] and this gives his testimony

---

7 Dr Bevan's wife. He was in charge of Wittgenstein during the last days of the philosopher.
8 Cf. Joan Bevan: "Wittgenstein's Last Year"; in: F.A. Flowers III (ed.): *Portraits of Wittgenstein*, vol. 4. Thoemmes Press, Bristol 1999, p. 137.

a special value. In this sense, the only problem is that not every text is accurately dated – though in the case of letters and diaries this problem was almost non-existent. However, whenever we are certain of a date – even an approximate one – the text has been included at the end of its appropriate year or decade. "Lectures on Religious Belief", for example, appears at the end of the temporal sequence for 1938, given that the basic reference we have is the year in which they were delivered, and the fact that they were not delivered on a single day. The same goes for the Cambridge Lectures between 1930 and 1935. As they cannot be dated with the same accuracy as the letters or diaries, we have chosen to place their excerpts at the end of the year they were delivered.

The case of the "Remarks on Frazer's *Golden Bough*" is a special one. Wittgenstein started writing of Frazer on 19.06.1931, though Rush Rhees believes it possible that he had written some other notes prior to that date. But the second set of remarks belongs to a later stage. Rhees suggests "not earlier than 1936 and probably after 1948", which has led us to place the "Remarks" in the final section of the work, together with all of the excerpts whose dates are imprecise, despite our being able to locate them at a specific moment in Wittgenstein's life.

The brief extracts from the "Remarks on the Philosophy of Psychology" (vols I and II), were written between 1946 and 1949 and appear at the end of the "1941–1951" section. "On Certainty" contains Wittgenstein's remarks belonging to the last year and a half of his life, though the excerpts which appear here cannot be properly dated. In the case of "Zettel", we have fragments from very different dates. As the editors remind us, the first fragment is from 1929 but the vast majority of the texts come from writings dictated between 1945 and 1948. The brief paragraphs we have chosen are undated.

6

Those paragraphs taken directly from the Nachlass appear with their specific denomination, that is, the manuscript they belong to and the pages of the original collection. MS 102, 5v–6v, for instance, means: Manuscript 102, pages 5 *verso* and 6 *verso* (the opposite to *recto*, depending on the place they occupied in the original notebook). All of the items appearing with manuscript characterisation – when originally in German – have been translated into English by Margaret Breugelmans. The same goes for the letters Wittgenstein wrote to Ludwig von Ficker on 24.07.1915 and 20.10.1919, as well as for the texts from "Licht und Schatten".

Acknowledgements

This book is the result of a lasting interest in Wittgenstein's thought and personality. But the work could have not been possible if not for the ongoing support of people and institutions that have helped it to grow and be consistent. First, I must mention the Department of Philosophy at the University of Oxford, which accepted me as Academic Visitor. Thanks to its Visitors' Programme I could make use of enormous bibliographical funds and huge databases, without which I would have been unable to properly accomplish this task. However, I have to make a special mention of Mrs Catriona Hopton, Assistant Administrator of the Department, who has been of invaluable help to me, always ready to give me clues to move easily throughout the whole university. The superb cultural, historic and intellectual environment of Oxford has also helped me to concentrate in my work, constantly stimulating my research interest.

To mention people, there have been many friends and colleagues who have contributed in different ways to this work. I am indebted to Professor Enrique Bonete, from the Universidad de Salamanca, in Spain. His ideas, advice and encouragement have walked along with me since the very beginning of this project. I must also thank Professor José López Martí, from the Universidad de Murcia, in Spain, for the many conversations on Wittgenstein and religion we have had along all these years.

I also want to acknowledge Nazareth and Antonio Javier Jareño, Fergal Martin, Andrej Turk, Imelda Brady, Diana Hernández Pastor and Doctors Miguel Ángel García Olmo and José Jesús García Hourcade for their interesting comments on earlier drafts of this work. I am indebted to Dr Jeff Dean and Dr Liam Cooper, who showed interest in this project from the beginning, making important and fruitful suggestions that have helped the work to improve.

Finally, I want to emphasize my gratitude to Dr P.M.S. Hacker, Emeritus Fellow of St John's College, Oxford, and one of the last gentlemen of philosophy. Without his support, counselling, criticism and patience with me – mainly in our long conversations during lunchtime – this book would have never become what it is today.

List of Sources

A Lecture on Ethics
Edoardo Zamuner, Emerlinda Valentina Di Lascio and D.K. Levy (ed.), *Lecture on Ethics* (Oxford: Wiley-Blackwell, 2014). Reproduced with permission of John Wiley & Sons.

Culture and Value
G.H. von Wright (ed.), in collaboration with Heikki Nyman, *Ludwig Wittgenstein, Culture and Value* (Oxford: Blackwell, 1998), revised edition of the text by Alois Pichler, translated by Peter Winch. Reproduced with permission of John Wiley & Sons.

Last Writings on the Philosophy of Psychology, Vol. I
G.H. von Wright and Heikki Nyman (ed.), *Last Writings on the Philosophy of Psychology, Vol. I*, translated by C.G. Luckhardt and Maximilian A.E. Aue (Oxford: Basil Blackwell, 1982). Reproduced with permission of John Wiley & Sons.

Last Writings on the Philosophy of Psychology, Vol. II
G.H. von Wright and Heikki Nyman (ed.), *The Inner and the Outer: Last Writings on the Philosophy of Psychology, Vol. II*, translated by C.G. Luckhardt and Maximilian A.E. Aue (Oxford: Basil Blackwell, 1992). Reproduced with permission of John Wiley & Sons.

Lectures on Religious Belief
Cyril Barrett (ed.), *Lectures on Religious Belief*, compiled from notes of Wittgenstein's lectures taken by Yorick Smythies, Rush Rhess and James Taylor (Oxford: Basil Blackwell, 1993; first printed in 1966). Reproduced with permission of Trinity College Cambridge.

Lectures on the Foundations of Mathematics. Cambridge 1939
Cora Diamond (ed.), *Lectures on the Foundations of Mathematics. Cambridge 1939*, compiled from notes of Wittgenstein's lectures taken by R.G. Bosanquet, Norman Malcolm, Rush Rhees and Yorick Smythies (Hassocks, Sussex: Harvester Press, 1976). Reproduced with permission of University of Chicago Press.

Letters from Ludwig Wittgenstein with a Memoir
Paul Engelmann, *Letters from Ludwig Wittgenstein with a Memoir*, translated by L. Furtmüller, edited by B.F. McGuinness (Oxford: Basil Blackwell, 1967). Reproduced with permission of John Wiley & Sons.

Licht und Schatten
Ilse Somavilla (ed.), *Ludwig Wittgenstein, Licht und Schatten: Ein nächtliches (Traum)Erlebnis und ein Brief-Fragment* (Innsbruck: Haymon, 2004).

Ludwig Hänsel-Ludwig Wittgenstein: A Friendship, 1929–1940
James C. Klagge and Alfred Nordmann (ed.), *Ludwig Wittgenstein: Public and Private Occasions* (Lanham, Maryland: Rowman & Littlefield, 2003). Reproduced with permission of Rowman & Littlefield.

Ludwig Wittgenstein
G.E.M. Anscombe, "Cambridge Philosophers II: Ludwig Wittgenstein," *Philosophy*, Vol. 70, no. 273 (July 1995), 395–407.

Ludwig Wittgenstein: A Memoir
Norman Malcolm, *Ludwig Wittgenstein: A Memoir*, with a biographical sketch by G.H. von Wright (London: Oxford University Press, 1958). Reproduced with permission of Oxford University Press.

Ludwig Wittgenstein: Personal Recollections
Rush Rhees (ed.), *Ludwig Wittgenstein: Personal Recollections* (Oxford: Basil Blackwell, 1981). Reproduced with the permission of University of Cambridge.

Movements of Thought: Diaries 1930–1932, 1936–1937
James C. Klagge and Alfred Nordmann (ed.), *Movements of Thought: Ludwig Wittgenstein's Diary, 1930–1932 and 1936–1937*, translated by Alfred Nordmann (Lanham, Maryland: Rowman & Littlefield, 2003). Reproduced with permission of Rowman & Littlefield.

Notebooks 1914–1916
G.H. von Wright and G.E.M. Anscombe (ed.), *Ludwig Wittgenstein, Notebooks, 1914–1916* (second edition), translated by G.E.M. Anscombe (Oxford: Basil Blackwell, 1979; first edition 1961). Reproduced with permission of Trinity College Cambridge.

On Certainty
G.E.M. Anscombe and G.H. von Wright (ed.), *On Certainty*, translated by Denis Paul and G.E.M. Anscombe (Oxford: Blackwell, 1995). Reproduced with permission of John Wiley & Sons.

Philosophical Investigations
Ludwig Wittgenstein, *Philosophical Investigations,* second edition, translated by G.E.M. Anscombe (Oxford: Basil Blackwell, 1958). Reproduced with permission of John Wiley & Sons.

Remarks on Colour
G.E.M. Anscombe (ed.), *Remarks on Colour*, translated by Linda L. McAlister and Margarete Schättle (Oxford: Basil Blackwell, 1977). Reproduced with permission of John Wiley & Sons.

Remarks on Frazer's Golden Bough
Rush Rhees (ed.), *Ludwig Wittgenstein, Remarks on Frazer's* Golden Bough, translated by A.C. Miles, revised by Rush Rhees (Brynmill Press / Humanities Press, 1979).

Remarks on the Philosophy of Psychology, Vol. I
G.E.M. Anscombe and G.H. von Wright (ed.), *Remarks on the Philosophy of Psychology, Vol. I*. translated by G.E.M. Anscombe (Oxford: Basil Blackwell, 1988). Reproduced with permission of John Wiley & Sons.

Remarks on the Philosophy of Psychology, Vol. II
G.H. von Wright and Heikki Nyman (ed.), *Remarks on the Philosophy of Psychology, Vol. ll*, translated by C.G. Luckhardt and Maximilian A.E. Aue (Oxford: Basil Blackwell, 1990). Reproduced with permission of John Wiley & Sons.

Tractatus Logico-Philosophicus
Ludwig Wittgenstein, *Tractatus Logico-Philosophicus*, translated by D.F. Pears and B.F. McGuinness (London: Routledge & Kegan Paul, 1981). Reproduced with permission of Taylor and Francis.

Wittgenstein and the Vienna Circle
Friedrich Waismann, *Ludwig Wittgenstein and the Vienna Circle: Conversations*, edited by Brian McGuinness, translated by Joachim Schulte and Brian McGuinness. Oxford: Basil Blackwell, Oxford 1979. Reproduced with permission of John Wiley & Sons.

Wittgenstein: Conversations 1949-1951
O.K. Bouwsma, *Wittgenstein: Conversations 1949-1951*, edited by J.L. Craft and Ronald E. Hustwit (Indianapolis: Hackett, 1986).

Wittgenstein in Cambridge. Letters and Documents 1911-1951
Brian McGuinness (ed.), *Wittgenstein in Cambridge: Letters and Documents* (Oxford: Blackwell, 1995). Reproduced with permission of John Wiley & Sons.

Wittgenstein's Lectures. Cambridge 1930-1932
Desmond Lee (ed.), *Wittgenstein's Lectures: Cambridge 1930-1932*, from the notes of John King and Desmond Lee (Oxford: Basil Blackwell, 1980).

Wittgenstein's Lectures. Cambridge 1930-1933
James C. Klagge and Alfred Nordmann (ed.), *Philosophical Occasions, 1912-1951*, from the notes of G.E. Moore (Indianapolis: Hackett, 1993).

Wittgenstein's Lectures. Cambridge 1932-1935
Alice Ambrose (ed.), *Wittgenstein's Lectures. Cambridge 1932-1935*, from the notes of Alice Ambrose and Margaret Macdonald (Oxford: Basil Blackwell, 1979). Reproduced with permission of Rowman & Littlefield.

Wittgenstein: Tagebücher und Briefe
Ludwig Wittgenstein, Tagebücher und Briefe (Charlottesville, Virginia: InteLex Corporation, 2002). Reproduced with permission of InteLex Technologies, Inc.

Wittgenstein: The Duty of Genius
Ray Monk, *Ludwig Wittgenstein: The Duty of Genius* (London: Jonathan Cape, 1991). Reproduced with permission of Simon & Schuster and Penguin Random House.

Wittgenstein's Nachlass. The Bergen Electronic Edition
Ludwig Wittgenstein, Nachlass (Charlottesville, Virginia: InteLex Corporation, 2003).

Zettel
G.E.M. Anscombe and G.H. von Wright (ed.), *Zettel*, translated by G.E.M. Anscombe (Oxford: Basil Blackwell, 1981). Reproduced with permission of John Wiley & Sons.

Abbreviations

CB	*Wittgenstein: Conversations 1949–1951.* O.K. Bouwsma
CV	*Culture and Value*
NB	*Notebooks 1914–1916*
LC 1930–1932	*Wittgenstein's Lectures. Cambridge 1930–1932*
LC 1930–1933	Wittgenstein's Lectures. Cambridge (by G.E. Moore)
LC 1932–1935	*Wittgenstein's Lectures. Cambridge 1932–1935*
LFM	*Lectures on the Foundations of Mathematics Cambridge 1939*
LH	*Ludwig Hänsel-Ludwig Wittgenstein: A Friendship, 1929–1940*
LPE	*Paul Engelmann. Letters from Ludwig Wittgenstein with a Memoir*
LS	*Licht und Shatten*
LWPPI	*Last Writings on the Philosophy of Psychology*, vol. I
LWPPII	*Last Writings on the Philosophy of Psychology*, vol. II
MT	*Movements of Thought: Diaries 1930–1932, 1936–1937*
NML	*Ludwig Wittgenstein. A Memoir.* Norman Malcolm
PR	*Ludwig Wittgenstein: Personal Recollections*
ROC	*Remarks on Colour*
TDG	*The Duty of Genius.* Ray Monk
TLP	*Tractatus Logico-Philosophicus*
VC	*Wittgenstein and the Vienna Circle*
WCB	*Wittgenstein in Cambridge. Letters and Documents 1911–1951*
WTB	*Wittgenstein: Tagebücher und Briefe*

1
1910–1920

Ludwig Wittgenstein was born in Vienna on 26 April 1889, into one of the wealthiest families in the Austro-Hungarian Empire, as the youngest of eight children. Ludwig's father Karl was an authoritarian, for whom the only worthwhile mission in life was business. The family was strongly influenced by Karl's Protestant asceticism, leading Ludwig to develop a strong sense of duty, from which many of his inner conflicts were to originate.

Ludwig was baptized in the Catholic faith of his mother Leopoldine, despite the fact that the majority of his paternal ancestors were Protestants converted from Judaism. This rupture with their original creed was strongly encouraged and continued in the family as, although his mother's parents belonged to well-known Catholic families, they had also had Jewish ancestors on her father's side. However, even though Karl and Leopoldine were married in the Catholic Cathedral of Vienna and Ludwig received a Catholic education, there is no particular evidence that his family attended religious services. What actually exerted influence in Wittgenstein's home was a moral view of life where honesty and consistent fulfilment of obligations played an outstanding role. As B. McGuinness recalls: "Formal religion, in comparison, played little part in their lives. Moral and cultural and material superiority to those that surrounded them (or the consciousness of each of the three) were inextricably interwoven and formed the atmosphere in which they lived."[1] This way of understanding life is exemplified in Karl's attitude – and also in that of the rest of his family – on the death of his son Rudi, who committed suicide. As this kind of death supposedly revealed a cowardly attitude towards life, Rudi was buried without honours. Immediately after the

---

1 B. McGuinness: *Wittgenstein: A Life. Young Ludwig (1989–1921)*. Duckworth, London 1988, p. 25.

Ludwig Wittgenstein: The Meaning of Life, First Edition. Edited by Joaquín Jareño-Alarcón.
© 2023 John Wiley & Sons Ltd. Published 2023 by John Wiley & Sons Ltd.

burial, Karl took his family and left the cemetery, forbidding his wife to look back at Rudi's grave. Rudi was never again to be mentioned in his father's presence.

Although Karl Wittgenstein approved of education at home, the young Ludwig attended Realschule Linz (1903–6). At this school, which mainly specialized in technical subjects, he failed to obtain high marks, except on two occasions – both in religious studies.[2] Nevertheless, it appears that he lost his childhood faith relatively early, perhaps as a result of his conversations with his sister Margarethe – suggested by R. Monk, and told to Arvid Sjögren by Wittgenstein himself – or as Elizabeth Anscombe states in her portrait of Wittgenstein, as a result of reflections shared with his brother Paul at the tender age of 9.

Ludwig's struggles with religion, however, did not stop at these discussions with Paul, although they did remain under the surface for some time. It was a particular event in Ludwig's life that seems to have renewed his spiritual concerns, enabling further contemplation of religious issues. This event is mentioned by Norman Malcolm in his *Ludwig Wittgenstein: A Memoir*. Around 1910 Wittgenstein attended the performance of *Die Kreuzelschreiber*, a play written by Ludwig Anzengruber, not a renowned author. The play's main character, Johann, was a somewhat stoic character imbued with a mysticism that could be summed up in the following words: "You are part of everything, and everything is part of you. Nothing can happen to you!"[3] This idea strongly influenced Wittgenstein provoking a clear change in his behaviour. He became an avid reader of mystic authors and fond of religious psychology and authorities such as Saint Augustine. In a letter, dated as early as 22 June 1912,[4] Wittgenstein informs Russell that he is reading William James's book *The Varieties of Religious Experience*. Some years later, in a letter to Lady Ottoline Morrell[5] at the end of 1919, and after commenting on the *Tractatus*, Russell himself wrote:

> I had felt in his book a flavour of mysticism, but was astonished when I found that he has become a complete mystic. He reads people like Kierkegaard and Angelus Silesius, and he seriously contemplates becoming a monk. It all started during the winter he spent alone in Norway before the war, when he was nearly mad.

The First World War proved a crucial experience in Wittgenstein's life and his psychological make-up. Though unfit for active military service owing to his two

---

2 Cf. R. Monk: *Ludwig Wittgenstein. The Duty of Genius*. Jonathan Cape, London 1991, p. 15.
3 B. McGuinness: op. cit., p. 94.
4 Wittgenstein had been admitted as a member of Trinity College on 1 February 1912.
5 Ottoline Morrell (1873–1938), English aristocrat and patron of the arts. She was a friend and lover of Bertrand Russell.

hernias, he wanted to participate in the Great War and enlisted as a volunteer. He undertook this participation as a personal challenge – a vital test which he had to overcome. Much later he admitted that he had actually volunteered in an attempt to seek death. Wittgenstein was certainly deeply marked by the First World War. It was precisely during those years that he wrote the *Tractatus*, and his notes taken at the time allow us to understand the intensity of his inner life. It was then that he read Tolstoy's work *The Gospel in Brief*, which made a real impression on him. Although, later on, Wittgenstein found Tolstoy's interpretation of the Gospels quite subjective and inaccurate, the Russian writer deeply influenced his attitude at the end of the war. Wittgenstein read Tolstoy's tales with great interest. For him, they clearly showed the ideal of austerity and moral simplicity he strongly praised.

In many texts from this period Wittgenstein clearly expounds his inner dialogue on the meaning of life, as exemplified in a remark of 11 June 1916: "What do I know about God and the purpose of life?" This question is not merely rhetorical; it emerges as a corollary of the personal and intellectual debate he was facing. The vicissitudes of the war probably led him to consider the importance and meaning of life as an ongoing and open question we must face from a moral perspective. In the light of the *Tractatus*, we can coherently interpret the letter he wrote to Ludwig von Ficker on 20 October 1919 (concerning the *Tractatus* itself): "The sense of the book is a work on morals [...] I wanted to write that my work consists of two parts: one is what is presented here and the other is what I haven't written. And it's precisely this second part which is the important part."

If it is true, as the *Tractatus* seems to state, that a moral act[6] is something absolute, then we can understand why, after finishing his book, Wittgenstein gave up philosophy in order to teach children in small villages of Lower Austria. At the end of the war he had told his fellow captive, Franz Parak, that, while he liked the idea of becoming a priest, he was attracted to the idea of teaching the Gospels to children.[7] Many years later, at the end of the 1980s, Johann Scheibenbauer, Wittgenstein's pupil in Trattenbach in the year 1921–2, told the compiler that, at school, his professor had spoken a great deal about religion. This is, however, matter for the next chapter.

---

6 Cf. J. Vicente Arregui: *Acción y Sentido en Wittgenstein*. Eunsa, Pamplona 1984, pp. 92–3. See *Movements of Thought*, 06.05.1931: "But an ethical proposition is a personal act. Not a statement of fact."
7 Cf. Franz Parak: "Ludwig Wittgensteins Verhältnis Zum Christentum"; in: H. Berghel *et al.* (eds), *Wittgenstein und sein Einfluss die Gegenwärtige Philosophie*. Hölder-Pichler-Tempsky, Vienna 1978, p. 91.

Letter to B. Russell[8]
22.06.1912
Cambridge

Whenever I have time I now read James's[9] "Varieties of religious exp[erience]". This book does me a *lot* of good. I don't mean to say that I will be a saint soon, but I am not sure that it does not improve me a little in a way in which I would like to improve *very much*: namely I think that it helps me to get rid of the *Sorge* (in the sense in which Goethe used the word in the 2nd part of Faust).[10]

WCB

Letter to B. Russell
05.09.1913

Shall I get anything out??! It would be awful if I did not and all my work would be lost.[11] However I am not losing courage and go on thinking. Pray for me! If you see the Whiteheads[12] please remember me to them.

WCB

---

8 Wittgenstein arrived in England in the spring of 1908 to study aeronautical engineering. There, he began to take an interest in mathematics and his intellectual curiosity took him further into that field. His interest grew on reading Russell's book *The Principles of Mathematics* (*Principia Mathematica*) and Frege's *Grundgesetze*, after which he contacted both authors. Frege encouraged Wittgenstein to study with Russell in Cambridge, and they met for the first time in 1911. Wittgenstein was officially admitted as a member of the university and of Trinity College on 1 February 1912.

9 William James (1842–1910), American psychologist and philosopher in the Pragmatist tradition. His main contribution to psychology was his work *Principles of Psychology* (1890). *The Varieties of Religious Experience* was published in 1902, as a result of a conference previously given. It must be made clear that James himself dedicates a section of the book to Tolstoy – the Russian author about whom more will be said later on – during the conferences dedicated to the idea of the 'sick soul' (VI & VII). In James's eyes, Tolstoy was suffering from what could be termed an attack of 'religious melancholy', from which he derived an anhedonist attitude, losing interest in normal life values. Wittgenstein appears to have discovered in James's book the formula for understanding the varied and multiple character of religious experience, highlighting the importance of religious feeling over the existence of creeds or theoretical developments, something that enhanced the importance and value of mystical experience. By distinguishing between optimistic and pessimistic religions, James opens the way for Wittgenstein to self-identify in some way with the second kind, characterized by 'rebirth' and conversion, and in which a special role is given to the feelings of sin and guilt that were so important for the philosopher.

10 Wittgenstein is referring here to an existential unease that will return again and again during his lifetime.

11 This passage shows the tense relationship between Wittgenstein and his work, given how demanding the philosopher was with himself and his need to find a definitive solution to the problems he was faced with. At this time, he was working with a logical theory of types.

12 Alfred North Whitehead (1861–1947). A British mathematician who worked with Russell to write one of the most influential works in the field of logic, *Principia Mathematica*, in which he develops the task of providing a solid mathematical foundation to the discipline.

Letter to B. Russell,
[25.10 or 28.11, November 1913 (?)]
[Skjolden, Sogn, Norway]¹³

Would you do me a great favour: I have promised last year to book *two* serial tickets for the C.U.M.S.¹⁴ Chamber Concerts. Would you kindly book them for me, keep one of them for yourself, give the other to somebody else and charge me for both. If you let me know the price I shall send you the money *at once*.

Pray for me and God bless you! (If there is such a thing).

Yours as long as
$(\exists x).x = $ L.W.

WCB

Letter to B. Russell,
[February 1914]
[Skjolden, Sogn, Norway]

Dear Russell,

Thank you for your friendly letter. It was very good of you to answer me in such a way. But I can't possibly carry out your request to behave as if nothing had happened: that would go clean contrary to my nature. So FORGIVE *me for this long letter* and remember that I have to follow my nature just as much as you. During the last week I have thought a lot about our relationship and I have come to the conclusion that we really don't suit one another. THIS IS <u>NOT</u> MEANT AS A REPROACH! either for you or for me. But it is a fact. We've often had uncomfortable conversations with one another when certain subjects came up. And the uncomfortableness was not a consequence of ill humour on one side or the other but of enormous differences in our natures. I beg you most earnestly not to think I want to reproach you in any way or to preach you a sermon. I only want to put our relationship in clear terms *in order to draw a conclusion*. – Our latest quarrel, too, was certainly not simply a result of your sensitiveness or my inconsiderateness. It came from deeper – from the fact that my letter must have shown you how totally different our ideas are, E.G. of the value of a scientific work. It was, of course, stupid of me to have written to you at such length about this matter: I ought to have told myself that such

---

13 Wittgenstein chose Norway as the most suitable place to retire and complete his work on logic. He first chose David H. Pinsent, who has been thought of as Wittgenstein's best friend, to accompany him, but that trip ended on 1 October. On the eleventh of that very same month, however, Wittgenstein chose to return to Norway and was visited by G.E. Moore in March 1914. Out of this two-week stay with Wittgenstein would come the text known as "Notes Dictated to Moore in Norway".
14 Cambridge University Musical Society.

fundamental differences cannot be resolved by a letter. And this is just ONE instance out of *many*. Now, as I'm writing this in complete calm, I can see perfectly well that your value-judgments are just as good and just as deep-seated in you as mine in me, and that I have no right to catechize[15] you. But I see equally clearly, now, that for that very reason there cannot be any real relation of friendship between us. *I shall be grateful to you and devoted to you* WITH ALL MY HEART *for the whole of my life, but I shall not write to you again and you will not see me again either*. Now that I am once again reconciled with you I want to part from you *in peace* so that we shan't sometime get annoyed with one another again and then perhaps part as enemies. I wish you everything of the best and I beg you not to forget me and to think of me often *with friendly feelings*. Goodbye!

Yours *ever*
Ludwig Wittgenstein

WCB

25.08.1914[16]

There is not one[17] single decent chap in the whole unit. How will I behave towards them all in the future? Should I simply endure? And what if I don't want to? I'd be

---

15 Wittgenstein and Russell ended having enormously different points of view on matters concerning morality and values. In a letter dated 3 March of that year, Wittgenstein once more acknowledged to Russell that their differences over value judgments were irreconcilable.

16 The First World War began for Austria on 28 July 1914 after Serbia refused to accept the demands of the Austrian ultimatum following the assassination of the heir to the Hapsburg throne, Archduke Franz Ferdinand, in Sarajevo whilst on an official visit. The declaration of war was accompanied by an intense patriotic fervour amongst the Austrian population. Wittgenstein volunteered to fight. His brothers Kurt and Paul also enlisted, whilst his sisters Hermine and Gretl did their patriotic duty by working on hospital support tasks.

17 All excerpts from manuscripts 101, 102 and 103 are originally in code. They are "War Diaries", where Wittgenstein wrote down everything that happened during his life in the First World War. These are the left-hand pages in the Notebooks that Wittgenstein wrote during the war. In these diaries, Wittgenstein described both personal affairs and purely philosophical questions. He did so, however, in a very special way: on the right-hand pages he worked out all of the logical and philosophical issues and on the left-hand pages he noted down all his personal experiences. The fact that they represented his private reflections meant that he wrote them down in code, although his code was quite simple: the first letter of the alphabet corresponded to the last, and so on. It is therefore enormously interesting to read both diaries (note groups) side by side in order to get to know Wittgenstein's philosophy and personality. The most interesting aspect of all is that the *Tractatus Logico-Philosophicus* will mature in the light of these notes – preliminary annotations used to develop the ideas laid out in the later work. The *Tractatus* is, to a large extent, a "work of the trenches". The philosophical annotations begin almost at the same time as the personal notes on the opposite page. Specifically, the first annotation is made on 22 August 1914: "Logic must take care of itself". In this sense, please refer to statement 5.473 of the *Tractatus*.

living a continuous battle. Which is better? If I choose the second option I would <u>certainly</u> wear myself out. With the first one I <u>might not</u>. This is going to be an <u>immensely</u> difficult time for me because I have landed myself well and truly in the same kind of situation as when I was at school in Linz. Only one thing is necessary: to be able to contemplate everything that happens; stay composed! God help me![18]
MS 101, 10–11v

02.09.1914

Yesterday I started reading Tolstoy's[19] *The Gospels in Brief*. It's a marvellous piece of work but so far it hasn't been what I was expecting.
MS 101, 12v

12.09.1914

The news is getting worse and worse. The unit will be on high alert this evening. I am working more or less every day and relatively confidently. I keep repeating Tolstoy's words to myself: "Man is <u>powerless</u> in the flesh but <u>free</u> through the Spirit."[20] May the Spirit be in me! This afternoon the lieutenant heard shots nearby. I became very agitated. We will probably be called out. How will I react if we have to start shooting? I'm not afraid of being shot. I'm afraid of not having carried out my duties properly. God give me strength! Amen. Amen. Amen.
MS 101, 20v–21v

---

18 References with a religious theme will be very frequent during the war. They highlight the acute internal tension that Wittgenstein was under right at the time he was writing his *Tractatus*.

19 Tolstoy was excommunicated by the Orthodox Church in 1901; such decision was surely influenced by the publication in 1899 of his work *Resurrection*, though he had previously written some other controversial works. As a response to his excommunication, Tolstoy also wrote a pamphlet where he rejected the dogmas of the Orthodox Church as well as the value of sacraments. Although the book on the Gospels impressed Wittgenstein enormously at first, it is also clear that he would end up distancing himself from it on perceiving that Tolstoy had made a very subjective interpretation of the sacred texts, and had eliminated those references which did not fit into his interpretative wishes. Wittgenstein not only read Tolstoy's work but was also a keen reader of Russian literature more generally, and it was Tolstoy's tales that he both most enjoyed and that had the profoundest affect upon him.

20 Ideas which reflect the dispute that St Paul openly talks of in his epistles. The struggle between flesh and spirit is a constant element in Wittgenstein's personal texts during the course of the war. In them, a clearly ascetic concept of the relationship with God is reflected. St Paul wrote in his Epistle to the Romans that flesh and spirit are two antagonistic principles. The 'works of the flesh' are works of human nature, and certainly not 'works of eternal life'. We wrong when we intend not to and do not do as much good as we would wish. In the Gospel of Matthew (26:41) we read: "the spirit indeed is willing, but the flesh is weak".

15.09.1914

Dreadful scenes two nights ago: almost everyone was drunk. Back on the Goplana[21] again yesterday which was steered into the Dunajec. Didn't work yesterday or the day before. Tried in vain but I couldn't get my head around the whole situation. The Russians are hot on our heels![22] We are extremely close to the enemy. I'm in a good mood as I worked again. I now work best whilst peeling potatoes. I always volunteer willingly. This for me is what grinding lenses was for Spinoza. Things are cooler than before between the lieutenant and me. But courage! "As long as the genius doesn't abandon me –!" God be with me! This is my opportunity to be a decent person because I am face to face with death. May the Spirit enlighten me.
MS 101, 22v–23v

16.09.1914

The night was calm. Heard strong artillery and rifle fire this morning. In all likelihood this will be the end for us. The Spirit is still with me but will he leave me in my greatest hour of need? I hope not! All I need is to keep myself together now and be brave! (9 p.m.). Torrential rain. Man is powerless in the flesh and <u>free through the Spirit</u>. And only through the Spirit. Didn't work at all during the night.
MS 101, 23v–24v

18.09.1914

In post from 1–3. Slept very little. Didn't work yesterday. It is <u>enormously</u> difficult to resist the Devil all the time. It is difficult to serve the Spirit on an empty stomach and when suffering from lack of sleep! But what would be become of me otherwise? The one to be served (with very few exceptions). Travelling to Krakow with galleys. It was a calm and not unpleasant day. Worked a little.
MS 101, 25v–26v

21.09.1914

This evening I received news that upset me terribly. The lieutenant, our former commandant, had been transferred. The news depressed me deeply. I can't explain

---

21 Wittgenstein had enlisted himself as a volunteer in the First World War on 7 August 1914. The same month, on the 13th, he joined the crew of the *Goplana*, a ship captured from the Russians patrolling the Dunajec, a tributary of the river Vistula. His military tasks began as an artillery soldier in the First Army, on the border between Hapsburg Poland and Russia (in the Galicia region).
22 The Austrians were retreating following a successful Russian attack which had forced a partial defeat on the Central Powers.

exactly why but I feel a deep sense of dejection and have been deeply sad since then. I am free through the Spirit but the Spirit has abandoned me! Was able to work a little in the evening and felt better for it. ----
MS 101, 27v–28v

30.09.1914

Last night I began to feel unwell (stomach and head). Thy Will be done.[23]
MS 101, 31v

05.10.1914

Have been thinking a lot about Russell these last few days.[24] Wonder whether he still thinks of me. Wasn't our meeting <u>indeed</u> quite remarkable? When we feel well externally we don't think of the powerlessness of the flesh; yet we become aware of it when we think of times of need. And we turn to the Spirit.
MS 101, 33v–34v

06.10.1914

Did quite a lot of work yesterday.[25] A person shouldn't depend on chance – whether it is favourable or unfavourable. The new commandant boarded the ship yesterday. ---Now they are sending people from the lighting department onto the ship, and they fiddle around with the reflector. Don't worry!! Have just received the order to leave for Russia. So it's serious again! God be with me.
MS 101, 34v

07.10.1914

Travelled through the night to Russia; hardly slept at all. Was on searchlight duty,[26] etc. We will soon come under fire. May the Spirit be with me. [...] I still haven't understood why I should do my duty merely because it is my duty and preserve my whole being for the spiritual life. I could die in an hour, in two hours.

---

23 A typical expression for a believer. It appears in the Lord's Prayer, a prayer that Wittgenstein would tell his friend M.O'C. Drury was the most beautiful he had known (see R. Rhees, "Personal Recollections").

24 Russell was in favour of England remaining neutral during the war. His firm pacifist posture entailed certain consequences: he spent six months in prison thanks to his anti-military activities and he was removed from his post at Trinity College.

25 Wittgenstein was immersed in his work on the picture theory of language.

26 During this first part of the war, Wittgenstein would man the searchlight at night, a solitary task which allowed him to distance himself for a while from his militia colleagues, with whom he did not exactly get on famously.

I could die in a month or in a few years. I don't know when I will die and can do nothing about it. That's how life is. So how can I live in such a way that I really exist in every moment? By living in what's good and beautiful until life comes to its natural end.
MS 101, 34v–35v

08.10.1914
Unfortunately, when I'm cold and tired, I quickly lose the will to endure life as it is. But I make an effort not to go astray. ---Every hour of physical wellbeing is a grace.
MS 101, 36v

09.10.1914
Order: all line up on deck, armed. God be with me! – Travelled to Sandomierz.[27] We hear the incessant roar of heavy gunfire. We see grenades exploding. I am in a very good mood.
MS 101, 36v–37v

11.10.1914
Calm night. ---Carry Tolstoy's "Gospels in brief" around with me all the time like a Talisman. I overheard a conversation between our commandant and his counterpart on another ship: we are to remain here in Nabzesze and may not travel down until the morning. Have just heard that Antwerp has fallen!![28] And our troops have won a substantial battle somewhere. The grace I enjoy now that I am able to think and write is indescribable. I must become indifferent to the difficulties of the external life. We are to travel to Zawichost[29] this evening to land troops and supplies and have to drive right in front of the Russian positions. May God be with me.---
MS 101, 37v–38v

---

27 Polish city.
28 On 25 August a German zeppelin bombed Antwerp, but the German offensive proper on the city did not begin until October. Resistance continued until 10 October when the city's defences could hold the German onslaught no more, following several days of destruction. One of the soldiers who was able to return to Great Britain, despite the Germans entering the city, was Rupert Brooke, the English poet who had studied at King's College, Cambridge.
29 Polish village in the Sandomierz area.

12.10.1914
I find myself fluctuating between periods of indifference towards external fate and periods of yearning for outer freedom and calm when I am tired of having to blindly carry out any order. Stepping into the <u>complete</u> unknown! In short, there are times when I cannot live <u>purely</u> in the present or only by the spirit. We should be grateful and enjoy the good times in life as a grace and be indifferent to life at other times. [...] It seems we are to shoot with automatic weapons and machine-guns, more to create noise than to fire at anyone. I also gather that the whole situation will be very dangerous. It will <u>surely</u> be the end of me if I have to turn on the searchlight. But that doesn't matter. Only one thing is necessary![30] We set off in an hour. <u>God is with me</u>!
MS 101, 39v–40v

13.10.1914
We are already on the move. I am spirit therefore free. We are near to Lopiza and the grenades are whistling past over our heads.
MS 101, 40v–41v

20.10.1914
Unwell. Worked <u>ever so hard</u>. Felt better this afternoon, but am not really happy; I long to see David:[31] if only I could write to him. But my spirit is speaking within me against the depressions. God be with me.
MS 101, 45v

25.10.1914
Russian gunfire has suddenly ...
   God is with me!---It was nothing but a Russian aeroplane.
MS 101, 48v

---

30 Jesus Christ's answer to Martha in his dialogue with Martha and Mary at Lazarus' house (the Gospel According to Luke): "But the Lord answered: 'Martha, Martha', he said 'you worry and fret about so many things, and yet few are needed, indeed only one. It is Mary who has chosen the better part; it is not to be taken from her.'" (10:41-2) (*The Jerusalem Bible*. Philippine Bible Society, 1966). A month before, Wittgenstein had expressed the same idea in another entry of his Diary (together with comments on war): "Nur *eines* ist von Nöten!" (17/09/1914, MS 101, 24v).
31 David Hume Pinsent (1891-1918). One of Wittgenstein's best friends (soon after Pinsent's death, Wittgenstein wrote to his friend's mother: "David was my first and my only friend. I have indeed known many young men of my own age and have been on good terms with some, but only in him did I find a real friend, the hours I have spent with him have been the best in my life, he was to me a brother and a friend"). Pinsent died in a plane crash on 8 May 1918. Wittgenstein's *Tractatus* is dedicated to Pinsent's memory.

28.10.1914

I keep thinking about poor Paul[32] who <u>lost his occupation</u> so suddenly! How terrible. Which philosophy would one need to apply to get over that, if it's even possible to get over something like that with anything other than suicide!![33] – Didn't do much work; but I am working confidently. – Thy Will be done. –.–.
MS 101, 50v

04.11.1914

Calm night. Heading off early. Worked very hard. We are to be in Krakow tomorrow. I hear we can probably expect a siege from Krakow. I'll need a lot of strength to preserve my spirit. –. I just shouldn't be dependent on the outside world. That way you need be afraid of nothing that happens in it. Watch duty last night. It's easier to be detached from things than from people. But the latter must be possible too!
MS 102, 4v–5v

05.11.1914

Have been somewhat tired all day and inclined to depression. Didn't do much work. Am in Krakow. It's too late to visit Trakl[34] today.---May the Spirit give me strength.
MS 102, 5v–6v

---

32 Paul Wittgenstein (1887–1961). Wittgenstein's brother, a gifted pianist, lost his right arm during the First World War. Josef Labor, Richard Strauss, Maurice Ravel and Sergei Prokofiev wrote works for him.

33 Suicide is a frequent topic in Wittgenstein's life. Two of his brothers, Rudi and Kurt, committed suicide, and the disappearance of his elder brother Hans is believed to be a suicide as well. Wittgenstein himself had suicidal thoughts from time to time, especially in 1920. David Pinsent, in his *Diary (1913–1914)*, tells how from approximately from 1902 to 1911 Wittgenstein had frequently thought of dying due to his strong feeling of loneliness, but that he felt ashamed for not being courageous enough to commit suicide (entry of 1 June 1912). During the First World War, on February 1915, Wittgenstein had suicidal thoughts again. In this compilation there are some texts alluding to such issue. See: MS 103, 1v (28.03.1916 [?]); NB 10.01.1917; LPE 21.06.1920. McGuinness recalls a moment in Wittgenstein's life that reflects his existential tension quite well. It is dated July 1918: "Wittgenstein's uncle Paul came across him unexpectedly at a railway station (Salzburg is the obvious possibility) in a state of great mental anguish. In fact Ludwig was on his way to commit suicide somewhere in the mountains (of the Salzkammergut, one supposes). Paul, the man of the World, frowned on by severer aunts, had a genial liking for his nephew and even his nephew's philosophy, which is perhaps what made it possible for him to persuade Ludwig to come instead to Hallein, where Paul had a house. Useless to ask for the suicide plan. Wittgenstein felt alone in the World" (op. cit., p. 264).

34 Georg Trakl (1887–1914), Austrian Expressionist poet. One of the most renowned poets of his time. Deeply affected by the horrors of war, he committed suicide dying from an overdose of cocaine. However, this particular has been discussed and disputed (McGuinness states that he died after having "taken poison which was available to him as a hospital orderly", op. cit., p. 223). He died on 3 November 1914. Wittgenstein had thought of visiting him on 5 November, but arrived at the hospital to which Trakl had been sent on the following day, and was met with news of the poet's death. In 1913 Trakl had published the book *Der Jüngste Tag*.

06.11.1914
Didn't work. Poor Trakl.---. Thy Will be done.--
MS 102 6v

07.11.1914
We suddenly received orders at nine o'clock in the evening to shine the searchlight[35] for a job on another ship yesterday. So I got out of bed and shone the searchlight until 3½ in the morning. Am consequently very tired. I bought some provisions in town this afternoon. The siege in Krakow is awaited with a great sense of determination. I yearn to leave my ship. Didn't work. I long to meet someone decent for I am surrounded by immorality here. May the Spirit stay with me and remain steadfast in me.
MS 102, 6v–7v

09.11.1914
... I have been so inclined to depression these past few days!! I take no real pleasure in anything and I live in fear of the future because I can no longer find peace within. Every act of indecency that surrounds me – and there are plenty – wounds me deeply, and as soon as one wound heal, another appears! Even when I'm not depressed – like this evening – I still don't feel truly free. Only seldom do I feel like working and when I do, it's only for short periods as I cannot feel any sense of contentment. I feel I am depending on the world and must consequently fear it even if nothing bad is happening to me at the moment. I see myself, the I, in which I was able to find rest, as a distant island, one that I yearn to reach but one that has been snatched from me.---The Russians are rapidly advancing towards Krakow.[36] The civilians must all leave town. The situation here looks very bad! God come to my aid!! Did a little work.
MS 102, 9v–10v

13.11.1914
I think a lot about my life – which is another reason why I can't do any work.[37] Or is it the other way round? [...] On duty this evening. I visit a coffee-house every

---

35 One of Wittgenstein's tasks during the war was to be in charge of the searchlight. He was sometimes called upon to act in order to light ships as they were being repaired, but in combat the job of searchlight commander was especially dangerous, given how easy a target it represented for enemy action.

36 The Russian Army invaded Silesia by mid-October that year, but the German Army under Ludendorff counter-attacked across the Lodz-Warsaw area (11–25 November 1914) causing the Russian retreat to the Bzura and Rawka rivers.

37 The only thing he had written that day in the right-hand pages of his diary was: "In this work more than any other it is rewarding to keep on looping at questions, which one considers solved, from another quarter, as if they were unsolved."

evening now and drink 2 glasses of coffee and the respectable ambiance does me good. Did <u>very little</u> work!---! God give me good sense and strength!!
MS 102, 14v–15v

24.11.1914
Ficker[38] sent me poems written by poor Trakl today which I thought were brilliant without fully understanding them. They did me good. God is with me!
MS 102, 27v

26.11.1914
It now seems we'll be moving into winter quarters and if we do I may have to sleep with the others; God forbid!! ---Whatever happens, may I not lose the presence of the Spirit. God be with me!
MS 102, 29v–30v

28.11.1914
I believe I <u>will</u> come to a miserable end in the midst of such crude, vulgar people who are unrestrained by any kind of danger, unless by some miracle I am given considerably more strength and wisdom than I currently have. Yes, I will need a miracle if I am to survive!! I am living in fear of my future. Did very little work.[39] A miracle! A miracle!
MS 102, 30v–31v

30.11.1914
I was in the Personnel division this afternoon and spoke to an artificer about whether it would be possible for me to work in the balloon division. He said I should speak about it with artificer Wlcek who works there. I hope to be able to do this. ---Didn't work much, but still had some inspirations. [...] We should live by one's own Spirit alone and leave everything to God!
MS 102, 33v

---

38 Ludwig von Ficker (1880–1967), publisher of *Der Brenner*, received 100,000 crowns from Wittgenstein to help artists in need. A. Loos, G. Trakl or R.M. Rilke were among the beneficiaries.

39 For that day, on the right-hand page of his notebook, where he wrote down his philosophical annotations, there is the following phrase: "Negation combines with the ab-functions of the elementary proposition. And the logical functions of the elementary proposition must mirror their reference, just as much as all the others."

01.12.1914
I went looking for the artificer Wlcek this afternoon but couldn't find him. I was directed to the artillery division and will no doubt go there in two days after watch duty. Did very little work.[40] May the Spirit protect me whatever happens!
MS 102, 34v–35v

02.12.1914
We're going on watch duty this afternoon: thank God our commandant is coming with us so at least there will be <u>one</u> decent person with us. Terrible thunder heard from the work plants last night. And it started again this morning at 8 o'clock. We are to sleep out in the open evening. I probably won't manage to work. I mustn't forget God.
MS 102, 35v

05.12.1914
I'm leaving here tomorrow or the following day. Where I am to live has not yet been decided. I certainly don't want to be attached to such things. Didn't work much; but I'm not standing idle. I think <u>a lot</u> about <u>dear</u> David![41] May God protect him! And me!
MS 102, 37v

06.12.1914
This ship will be on field duty again tomorrow, and if I'm not summoned tomorrow, I'll have to go too which will be very unpleasant for me because my leg still hasn't healed after my fall. It's raining and the loamy paths here are terrible. May the Spirit protect me!
MS 102, 38v

07.12.1914
My leg has got worse. Probably won't go with them on watch duty. I have received no orders regarding my transfer. Heavy thunder nearby. ---. Have just heard that I'll be leaving here tomorrow. Can't go on watch duty because of my foot.

---

40 Wittgenstein continues to develop his picture theory. That day, the philosophical annotation reads: "The proposition says as it were: This picture cannot (or can) present a situation in this way." Compare this to paragraphs 4.021, 4.023 and 4.024 of the *Tractatus*, for example.
41 David Pinsent.

Didn't work much. Spoke to our commandant; he was very nice. Am tired. Everything is in God's hands.
MS 102, 38v–39v

08.12.1914
Bought and started reading Nietzsche volume 8.[42] Am deeply disturbed by his hatred of Christianity for there is also some truth in his writings. Certainly, Christianity is the only certain path to happiness. But how can this be, if someone rejects this happiness?! Would it not be better to perish unhappy, in a hopeless struggle against the outside world? But this kind of life is pointless. So why not lead a pointless life? Is it undignified? How does it fit in with a strongly solipsistic point of view? What must I do to ensure I don't lose my life? I must always be aware of Him – of the Spirit.
MS 102, 39v–41v

30.12.1914[43]
Didn't work. Mustn't lose my way.
MS 102, 48v

13.01.1915
Worked a little. Still don't work with great enthusiasm. My thoughts are weary. Instead of seeing things clearly I see them as routine and lifeless. It's as if a flame has been extinguished and I have to wait until it reignites itself again. And yet my spirit is active. I think ...
MS 102, 50v–51v

25.01.1915
Worked but without much success. I am completely in the dark as to how my work will go ahead.[44] It will only be successful by way of a miracle. Only by way of a miracle as the veil is lifted from my eyes from outside of me. I must abandon

---

42 This volume, possibly from the Naumann's Leipzig Edition, includes one of Nietzsche's hardest diatribes against Christianity: *The Anti-Christ*. The subtitle is especially violent: *Fluch auf das Christentum (Curse on Christianity)*. Wittgenstein felt really impressed by its hardness.
43 On Christmas Eve, Wittgenstein was promoted to officer rank.
44 We must not forget that Wittgenstein is working systematically on logic by that time. He is also giving shape to what in the end will be the *Tractatus*. The philosophical annotation that day reads: "We can also say: ~p is false, when p is true."

myself <u>fully</u> to my fate. Whatever fate decrees for me, is how it will be. I am living in the hands of fate. (Just don't be small.) And I can't become small like that.
MS 102, 53v–54v

03.02.1915
Didn't work. Was uninspired. I'm to take on the supervision of our forge. How will that be? May the Spirit come to my aid! It will be very difficult. But: courage!
MS 102, 56v

10.02.1915
Didn't work. Had a nice letter from Ficker and a dedication from Rilke.[45] If only I could get back to work again!! Then everything else would fall into place. When will I be inspired again??! It all remains in God's hands. I just have to desire it and hope for it! That way no time is wasted.
MS 102, 57v–58v

11.02.1915
Didn't work. – I'm now on less than friendly terms with one of the officers-cadet Adam. It could easily come to blows between us. That's why one should still live well and according to your conscience, may the spirit be with me! Now and in the future! – !
MS 102, 58v

13.02.1915
I didn't work. May the spirit be with me.
MS 102, 58v–59v

07.03.1915
=. The situation remains unchanged and uncomfortable. Am still completely unclear about a suitable change. A severe frost has descended at a most inopportune moment! Don't feel well. My soul is weary, so weary. What's to be done about it?? I am exhausted by these repulsive circumstances. I am besieged by my whole outer life with all its nastiness. And inside I am full of hatred and am unable to let

---

45 Rainer M. Rilke (1875–1926). Though born in Prague, he was one of the best German writers of the twentieth century. He published his first collection of poems in 1894: *Leben und Lieder* ("Life and Songs"), and in 1922 his most renowned work: *Duino Elegies*, and his *Sonnets to Orpheus*. Amongst his prose works, *Letters to a Young Poet* and *The Notebooks of Malte Laurids Brigge* were the most notorious of all.

the Spirit enter within me. God is love. –. I am like a burned out oven, full of cinders and rubbish. –
MS 102, 64v–65v

23.05.1915[46]
The limits of my language mean the limits of my world (**TLP** 5.6).

There really is only one world soul, which I for preference call *my* soul and as which alone I conceive what I call the souls of others.

The above remark gives the key for deciding the way in which solipsism is a truth (cf. **TLP** 5.62).

I have long been conscious that it would be possible for me to write a book: "The world I found" (cf. **TLP** 5.631).

(...)

In the book "The world I found" I should also have to report on my body and say which members are subject to my will, etc. For this is a way of isolating the subject, or rather of shewing that in an important sense there is no such a thing as the subject; for it would be the one thing that could *not* come into this book (cf. **TLP** 5.631).
NB

25.05.1915
The urge towards the mystical comes of the non-satisfaction of our wishes by science. We *feel* that even if all *possible* scientific questions are answered *our problem is still not touched at all*. Of course in that case there are no questions any more; and that is the answer (cf. **TLP** 6.52).
NB

27.05.1915
I can only speak *of* them [the objects], I cannot express them.

"But might there not be something which cannot be expressed by a *proposition* (and which is also not an object)?" In that case this could not be expressed by means of *language*; and it is also impossible for us to *ask* about it.[47]

Suppose there is something outside the *facts*? Which our propositions are impotent to express? But here we do have, e.g., *things and we feel no demand at all* to express them in propositions.

---

46 Remember that the texts known here as *Notebooks 1914–1916* are the right (recto) page of manuscripts 101, 102 and 103. In the case of the *Notebooks* the original text is uncoded German. The left (verso) pages are in code.

47 Here begins what in the *Tractatus* will be known as the "Theory of the inexpressible", in which the mystical problem will finally appear.

What cannot be expressed we do not express-. And how try to *ask* whether THAT can be expressed which cannot be EXPRESSED?
Is there no domain outside the facts?
NB

Letter to Ludwig von Ficker
24.07.1915

Dear Mr. von Ficker!

I received your letter of the 11th a week ago. That same day I suffered an electric shock and a few minor injuries following an explosion in the workshop. I was consequently unable to reply immediately. I am writing this from the hospital.[48] I didn't receive your letter from Brixen. I understand your sad news only too well. You are living in darkness so to speak and have found no words of comfort. It might seem stupid that I offer you advice, I who am so fundamentally different from you. I willtake the risk all the same. Do you know Tolstoy's "Gospel in Brief"? This book has kept me alive during this time. Would you buy this book and read it?! If you haven't heard of it you can't imagine what an effect it has on people. There is so much I'd want to say to you if you were here now. I may be leaving for Vienna in a week's time for 14 days or so. If only we could meet up there! Do write back.

Your devoted
Ludwig Wittgenstein

WTB

28.03.1916(?)
... and should take my own life. I have suffered <u>torments of hell</u>. And yet the image of life was so enticing I wanted to live again. I won't poison myself until I really want to poison myself.
MS 103, 1v

29.03.1916
Am <u>forced</u> to do so much that I am unaccustomed to doing. I need so much to endure them. Often I am so close to dispair. I haven't worked for more than a week. <u>I</u> don't have <u>any time!</u> God! But that's natural of course because I won't have

---

48 Wittgenstein spent a week in the hospital.

time to work when I am dead either. Inspection now. My soul is shrivelling up. Enlighten me God! Enlighten me God! God, enlighten my soul.[49]
MS 103, 1v

06.04.1916
Life is a
MS 103, 3v

07.04.1916
form of torture from which one is only occasionally finds relief so as to remain receptive to subsequent agonies. What terrible agonies. An exhausting march, coughing all through the night, the company of drunkards, the company of nasty, stupid people. Do good and rejoice in your virtues. Am sick and my life is bad. I am a poor unhappy person. Save me God and grant me peace! Amen.
MS 103, 3v

13.04.1916
I am staggering and still fall in the dark and have not yet returned to life.
MS 103, 4v

18.04.1916
Going to the firing position tomorrow or the following day. <u>Take courage!</u> God will help me.
MS 103, 4v

20.04.1916
Improve me God! And then I will be more content too. Probably going into our firing positions today. God help me.
MS 103, 5v

23.04.1916
Have been in a new post for a few days. Involves <u>heavy</u> manual work all day long; am now unable to think. God help me. I have so much to put up with. I tried to get

---

[49] At the end of this month Wittgenstein was sent to the Russian front.

onto the observation post today. Everyone hates me here because they don't understand me. And because I'm no saint!⁵⁰ God help me!
MS 103, 5v

26.04.1916
The officers from the battery seem to get on very well with me. I am consequently spared much unpleasantness. Thanks be to God. Your will be done! You go your way! May <u>your</u> will be done!
MS 103, 6v

27.04.1916
Almost everyone in the unit hates me volunteering which means I am now almost constantly surrounded by people who hate me. And this is the only thing I haven't yet come to terms with. What evil, heartless people there are here. It is almost impossible for me to find any trace of humanity in them. God help me to live. Had a feeling today that there would be a state of alert this evening. And there really is strict duty this evening. God be with me! Amen.
MS 103, 6v–7v

28.04.1916
It was quiet at night. Wrote to Russell. Had a bad dream last night. May God protect me.
MS 103, 7v

29.04.1916
Stayed with the aircraft this afternoon. We were shot at. I thought of God. May your will be done! God be with me.
MS 103, 7v

30.04.1916
Am returning to the aircraft today during a raid: man needs God <u>alone</u>.
MS 103, 7v

---

50 This statement, as with so many during the war, will highlight the tense ascetic struggle that Wittgenstein is experiencing internally.

03.05.1916

Everything is so hard for me! May God protect me and stay beside me. Amen. May the heaviest chalice be taken from me, but may <u>Your</u> will be done.[51] The work is still turning around in my head.
MS 103, 8v

04.05.1916

At my request I may go out to the aircraft tomorrow. That's when the war really begins for me. And maybe – life too! Perhaps being close to death will bring me the light of life.[52] May God enlighten me. I am a worm but I'll become a man by the grace of God.[53] God be beside me. Amen.
MS 103, 8v–9v

05.05.1916[54]

On the aircraft stand I feel like a prince in a bewitched castle. Now, by day, everything is calm, but it will be <u>terrible</u> tonight! Will I be able to stand it???? Tonight will reveal all. God be beside me!!
MS 103, 9v

06.05.1916

I'm in constant danger of my life. We got through the night by the grace of God. I occasionally feel despondent. That's what is taught at the school of the false concept of life! Understand the people! Every time you want to hate them, try instead to understand them. Live with inner peace! But how can inner peace be attained? <u>Only</u> when I am living in a way that is pleasing to God! <u>Only</u> then is it possible to endure life.
MS 103, 9v–10v

---

51 Remember that this is the petition Christ makes to the Father in Gethsemane, as told in Matthew 26:39, Mark 14:36 and Luke 22:42.

52 Wittgenstein was awarded several war medals for his courageous behaviour at the front: the Silver Medal for Valour and the Band of the Military Service Medal with Swords, though he was initially promoted for the Gold Medal for Valour.

53 Wittgenstein is referring here to Psalm 22, in which the humiliation of Christ and his exaltation of God the Father is foreshadowed: "Ich aber bin ein Wurm und kein Mensch."

54 By 5 June, Wittgenstein had gone into combat on the front line, defending the ground won against Brusilov's forces. In this battle, the philosopher proved his enormous bravery and was later recommended for a medal not normally awarded to soldiers. That same day, his friend Bertrand Russell was tried for publishing a pamphlet in which he supported conscientious objection to the army. The two friends had ended up occupying very different positions during the war, but this would not prevent them from staying in touch, even after the end of the war.

07.05.1916
The night was calm. Thanks be to God. It's only me who's feeling wretched.
MS 103, 11v

08.05.1916
A calm night. God be with me! The people I am with are not so much vulgar as <u>incredibly</u> narrow-minded! This makes any kind of dialogue with them almost impossible because they are forever misunderstanding me. These people are not stupid, just narrow-minded. They are clever enough in their own field. But they lack character and consequently have no desire to broaden their horizons. "The orthodox heart understands everything." Can't do any work now.
MS 103, 11v–12v

09.05.1916
I would have enough time and peace to work now but nothing is happening. My subject matter is far from me. Life only acquires meaning through death.
MS 103, 12v

10.05.1916
I feel very well now by the grace of God. Unfortunately I cannot work. But may Your will be done! Amen. He will not abandon me in moments of danger!!
MS 103, 12v–13v

11.05.1916
I change post in two days' time. <u>Most</u> unpleasant! But Thy will be done.
MS 103, 13v

16.05.1916
I'm in my third post. There is much toil as usual. But also much grace. Am weak as usual! I cannot work. Am sleeping in the infantry today and will probably be destroyed. God be with me! In eternity. Amen. I am a weak person, but He has spared me so far. Praise God for all eternity. Amen. I surrender my soul to the Lord.
MS 103, 13v–14v

21.05.1916
God make me a better person!
MS 103, 14v

25.05.1916
We're being shot at. Whatever God wills!
MS 103, 14v

27.05.1916
I received letters from Mining[55] and mother. There is to be a Russian attack today or tomorrow. Whatever God wills. Have fallen heavily into sin. But God will forgive me.
MS 103, 14v

28.05.1916
Today we'll be on high alert. My commandant is very kind to me. I'm thinking of the meaning of life. That's still the best you can do. I should be happier. Oh, if only my spirit were stronger!!! God be with me now! Amen.
MS 103, 15

29.05.1916
God be with me.
MS 103, 15v

11.06.16[56]

> What do I know about God and the purpose of life?
> I know that this world exists.

---

55 Hermine Wittgenstein (1874–1950), Wittgenstein's eldest sister.

56 The fearsome Brusilov offensive – the Russians' greatest victory during the war – took place in June 1916. Wittgenstein's work had hitherto focused on logic. In fact, by the end of 1915 a first draft of the *Tractatus* was ready. In this version there were no remarks on ethical or religious issues. On 11.06.1916, the notebooks began abruptly with the comments appearing here. These paragraphs already belong to the right-hand pages of the war notebooks. Here one can start to appreciate the influence of Schopenhauer, and especially of his work *The World as Will and Representation*. Wittgenstein read Schopenhauer interestedly as a young man. Regarding the importance of the influence of this author on Wittgenstein, it has been said – perhaps with a little exaggeration – that the entire conceptual framework of the *Tractatus* is Schopenhauerian. From now until the beginning of July, no new annotations are made. The division Wittgenstein belonged to was in combat incessantly. In fact, they took part in the battle of Kolomea, during which the Russians took more than ten thousand Austrian prisoners. Russian troops entered the city on June 29.

That I am placed in it like my eye in its visual field.
That something about it is problematic, which we call its meaning.
That this meaning does not lie in it but outside it (cf. **TLP** 6.41).
That life is the world (cf. **TLP** 5.621).
That my will penetrates the world.[57]
That my will is good or evil.
Therefore that good and evil are somehow connected with the meaning of the world.
The meaning of life, i.e. the meaning of the world, we can call God. And connect with this the comparison of God to a father.
To pray is to think about the meaning of life.
I cannot bend the happenings of the world to my will: I am completely powerless.
I can only make myself independent of the world – and so in a certain sense master it – by renouncing any influence on happenings.

NB

05.07.16
The world is independent of my will (**TLP** 6.373).

Even if everything that we want were to happen, this would still only be, so to speak, a grace of fate, for what would guarantee it is not any logical connexion between will and world, and we could not in turn will the supposed physical connexion (**TLP** 6.374).

If good or evil willing affects the world it can only affect the boundaries of the world, not the facts, what cannot be portrayed by language but can only be shewn[58] in language (cf. **TLP** 6.43).

In short, it must make the world a wholly different one (see **TLP** 6.43).

The world must, so to speak, wax or wane as a whole. As if by accession or loss of meaning (cf. **TLP** 6.43).

As in death, too, the world does not change but stops existing (**TLP** 6.431).
NB

---

57 Wittgenstein begins to discuss the enormously complex issue of the will as an ethical subject from the relationships between the 'self' and the 'world'. Here we have those discussions that will be aphoristically shortened in the *Tractatus*, from paragraph 5.63 onwards: "Ich bin meine Welt (*Der Mikrokosmos*)".

58 Here one can appreciate a taste of what will become the fundamental distinction Wittgenstein proposes in the *Tractatus* between *saying* and *showing*.

06.07.1916
Everything felt enormously difficult last month. I have thought considerably about all kinds of things yet surprisingly am unable to establish a connection with my mathematical thought processes.[59]
MS 103, 15v–16v

06.07.16
And in this sense Dostoievsky is right when he says that the man who is happy is fulfilling the purpose of existence.

Or again we could say that the man is fulfilling the purpose of existence who no longer needs to have any purpose except to live. That is to say, who is content.

The solution of the problem of life is to be seen in the disappearance of this problem (see **TLP** 6.521).

But is it possible for one so to live that life stops being problematic? That one is *living* in eternity and not in time?
NB

07.07.16
Isn't this the reason why men to whom the meaning of life had become clear after long doubting could not say what this meaning consisted in? (see **TLP** 6.521).
NB

08.07.16.[60]
To believe in a God means to understand the question about the meaning of life.

To believe in a God means to see that the facts of the world are not the end of the matter.

To believe in God means to see that life has a meaning.

The world is *given* me, i.e. my will enters into the world completely from outside as into something that is already there.

(As for what my will is, I don't know yet.)

That is why we have the feeling of being dependent on an alien will.

However this may be, at any rate we *are* in a certain sense dependent, and what we are dependent on we can call God.

---

59 Wittgenstein points out here that he had been meditating on the divine and the human, wondering how to establish a connection with his philosophical reflections. The day after making this annotation, he would write that sooner or later he would unveil such a connection.
60 That was the day Russian troops reached Delatyn, close to the Hungarian border.

In this sense God would simply be fate, or, what is the same thing: The world – which is independent of our will.

I can make myself independent of fate.

There are two godheads: the world and my independent I.

I am either happy or unhappy, that is all. It can be said: good or evil do not exist.

A man who is happy must have no fear. Not even in face of death.

Only a man who lives not in time but in the present is happy.

For life in the present there is no death.[61]

Death is not an event in life. It is not a fact of the world (cf. **TLP** 6.4311).

If by eternity is understood not infinite temporal duration but non-temporality, then it can be said that a man lives eternally if he lives in the present (see **TLP** 6.4311).

In order to live happily I must be in agreement with the world. And that is what "being happy" *means*.

I am then, so to speak, in agreement with that alien will on which I appear dependent. That is to say: 'I am doing the will of God'.

Fear in face of death is the best sign of a false, i.e. a bad, life.

When my conscience upsets my equilibrium, then I am not in agreement with Something. But what is this? Is it *the world*?

Certainly it is correct to say: Conscience is the voice of God.

For example: it makes me unhappy to think that I have offended such and such a man. Is that my conscience?

Can one say: "Act according to your conscience whatever it may be"?

Live happy!

NB

14.7.16.

Man cannot make himself happy without more ado.

Whoever lives in the present lives without fear and hope.

NB

16.07.1916

Terrible thunder and lightning. I'm in the rocks, it's bad, am most inadequately protected, it's as cold as ice, raining and foggy. A miserable life. It will be terribly difficult not to lose one's life. For I am indeed weak but the Spirit is helping me. It would be best if I were already ill then I would at least get some rest.

MS 103, 16v

---

61 From paragraph 6.431 onwards, one can read the *Tractatus's* discussion of the meaning of death.

20.07.1916
Work hard to be good.
MS 103, 17v

21.07.16
What really is the situation of the human will? I will call "will" first and foremost the bearer of good and evil.

Let us imagine a man who could use none of his limbs and hence could, in the ordinary sense, not exercise his *will*. He could, however, think and *want* and communicate his thoughts to someone else. Could therefore do good or evil through the other man. Then it is clear that ethics would have validity for him, too, and that he in the *ethical sense* is the bearer of a *will*.

Now is there any difference in principle between this will and that which sets the human body in motion?

Or is the mistake here this: even *wanting* (thinking) is an activity of the will? (And in this sense, indeed, a man *without* will would not be alive.)

But can we conceive a being that isn't capable of Will at all, but only of Idea (of seeing for example)? In some sense this seems impossible. But if it were possible then there could also be a world without ethics.
NB

24.07.16
The World and Life are one [**TLP** 5.621].

Physiological life is of course not "Life". And neither is psychological life. Life is the world.

Ethics does not treat of the world. Ethics must be a condition of the world, like logic.

Ethics and aesthetics are one [see **TLP** 6.421].
NB

26.07.1916
Received a moving letter from David. He writes that his brother has been hit in France. Dreadful! This kind friendly letter has opened my eyes to how I am living in exile here. It might be a salutary exile but it is still exile. I am banished to live amongst scum and have to live with them under the most repugnant conditions. And I am supposed to lead a good life and purify myself in this environment. But it's terribly difficult! I am too weak. I am too weak! God help me.
MS 103, 17v–18v

29.07.1916

Was shot at yesterday. Felt despondent. I was afraid of dying. My wish now is to live! And it is difficult to sacrifice life when you have grown to like it. Even that is a "sin", to live a senseless life, to have a false concept of life. I occasionally behave like an <u>animal</u> where I can think of nothing but eating, drinking and sleeping. Terrible! And then I suffer like an animal, without any hope of inner salvation. I am exposed to my lusts and aversions. And then it becomes impossible to think about living a true life.
MS 103, 18v–19v

29.07.16

For it is a fact of logic that wanting does not stand in any logical connexion with its own fulfilment. And it is also clear that the world of the happy is a *different* world from the world of the unhappy [cf. **TLP** 6.43].

Is seeing an activity?

Is it possible to will good, to will evil, and not to will?

Or is only he happy who does *not* will?

"To love one's neighbour"[62] would mean to will!

But can one want and yet not be unhappy if the want does not attain fulfilment? (And this possibility always exists.)

Is it, according to common conceptions, good to want *nothing* for one's neighbour, neither good nor evil?

And yet in a certain sense it seems that not wanting is the only good.

Here I am still making crude mistakes! No doubt of that!

It is generally assumed that it is evil to want someone else to be unfortunate. Can this be correct? Can it be worse than to want him to be fortunate?

Here everything seems to turn, so to speak, on *how* one wants.

It seems one can't say anything more than: Live happily!

The world of the happy is a different world from that of the unhappy [see **TLP** 6.43].

The world of the happy is *a happy world*.

Then can there be a world that is neither happy nor unhappy?
NB

---

62 It is a central commandment of Christian faith. In the New Testament it appears in the gospels: Mark: 12:33; Matthew: 22:39; 19:19; Luke: 10:27; John: 13:34; and the epistles: Epistle to Romans: 13:9; Epistle to Galatians: 5:4; Epistle of St. James: 2:8. It is a specific version of the golden rule.

30.07.16

When a general ethical law of the form "Thou shalt..." is set up, the first thought is: Suppose I do not do it?

But it is clear that ethics has nothing to do with punishment and reward. So this question about the consequences of an action must be unimportant. At least these consequences cannot be events. For there must be something right about that question after all. There must be a *kind* of ethical reward and of ethical punishment but these must be involved in the action itself.

And it is also clear that the reward must be something pleasant, the punishment something unpleasant [**TLP** 6.422].

I keep on coming back to this! simply the happy life is good, the unhappy bad. And if I *now* ask myself: But why should I live *happily*, then this of itself seems to me to be a tautological question; the happy life seems to be justified, of itself, it seems that it *is* the only right life.

But this is really in some sense deeply mysterious! *It is clear* that ethics *cannot* be expressed! [cf. **TLP** 6.421].

But we could say: The happy life seems to be in some sense more *harmonious* than the unhappy. But in what sense??

What is the objective mark of the happy, harmonious life? Here it is again clear that there cannot be any such mark, that can be *described*.

This mark cannot be a physical one but only a metaphysical one, a transcendental one.

Ethics is transcendental [see **TLP** 6.421].
NB

01.08.16

How things stand, is God.

God is, how things stand.

Only from the consciousness of the *uniqueness of my life* arises religion – science – and art.
NB

02.08.16

And this consciousness is life itself.

Can there be any ethics if there is no living being but myself?

If ethics is supposed to be something fundamental, there can.

If I am right, then it is not sufficient for the ethical judgment that a world is given.

Then the world in itself is neither good nor evil.

For it must be all one, as far as concerns the existence of ethics, whether there is living matter in the world or not. And it is clear that a world in which there is only dead matter is in itself neither good nor evil, so even the world of living things can in itself be neither good nor evil.

Good and evil only enter through the *subject*. And the subject is not part of the world, but a boundary of the world [cf. **TLP** 5.632].

It would be possible to say (à la Schopenhauer): It is not the world of Idea that is either good or evil; but the willing subject.

I am conscious of the complete unclarity of all these sentences.[63]

Going by the above, then, the willing subject would have to be happy or unhappy, and happiness and unhappiness could not be part of the world.

As the subject is not a part of the world but a presupposition of its existence, so good and evil which are predicates of the subject, are not properties in the world.

Here the nature of the subject is completely veiled.

My work has extended from the foundations of logic to the nature of the world.

NB

04.08.1916

Isn't the thinking subject in the last resort mere superstition?

Where in the world is a metaphysical subject to be found? [see **TLP** 5.633].

NB

05.08.16

The thinking subject is surely mere illusion. But the willing subject exists [cf.**TLP** 5.631].

If the will did not exist, neither would there be that centre of the world, which we call the I, and which is the bearer of ethics.

What is good and evil is essentially the I, not the world.

The I, the I is what is deeply mysterious!

NB

06.08.1916

We are now marching toward our firing position after a 3 day train journey. Am not in the best of health and feel mentally exhausted with all the vulgarity and

---

63 This whole discussion will occupy the final part of the *Tractatus*. From paragraph 6.41 onwards.

narrowmindedness that surrounds me. God give me strength, inner strength, to defy mental illness. God keep me in good spirits.
MS 103, 20v–21v

07.08.16[64]
The I is not an object.
NB

11.08.1916
Am living my life in sin, ie unhappy. Am morose and cheerless. Am living in a state of strife because of all that surrounds me.
MS 103, 21v

11.08.16
I objectively confront every object. But not the I.

So there really is a way in which there can and must be mention of the I in a *non-psychological sense* in philosophy [cf. **TLP** 5.641].
NB

12.08.1916
You know what you have to do to be happy; so why don't you do it? Because you are foolish. A bad life is a foolish life. What's important is not to get annoyed.
MS 103, 21v–22v

13.08.1916
Still struggling in vain with my bad nature. God give me strength!
MS 103, 22v

13.08.16
Suppose that man could not exercise his will, but had to suffer all the misery of this world, then what could make him happy?

How can man be happy at all, since he cannot ward off the misery of this world? Through the life of knowledge.

The good conscience is the happiness that the life of knowledge preserves.

---

64 That day, General Brusilov took Stanislawów, to the east of Galicia, and captured 7,000 Austrian prisoners and around 3,500 Germans. Even so, there was considerable slaughter on both sides.

The life of knowledge is the life that is happy in spite of the misery of the world.

The only life that is happy is the life that can renounce the amenities of the world.

To it the amenities of the world are so many graces of fate.

NB

19.08.1916[65]

Surrounded by vulgarity! I am to leave soon for the cadre in the hinterland. I'm pleased about it. Surrounded by vulgarity. God will help me.

MS 103, 22v

02.09.1916

Here we can see that solipsism coincides with pure realism, if it is strictly thought out.

The I of solipsism shrinks to an extensionless point and what remains is the reality coordinate with it [**TLP** 5.64].

What has history to do with me? Mine is the first and only world!

I want to report how *I* found the world.

What others in the world have told me about the world is a very small and incidental part of my experience of the world.

I have to judge the world, to measure things.

The philosophical I is not the human being, not the human body or the human soul with the psychological properties, but the metaphysical subject, the boundary (not a part) of the world. The human body, however, my body in particular, is a part of the world among others, among beasts, plants, stones etc., etc. [cf. **TLP** 5.641].

Whoever realizes this will not want to procure a pre-eminent place for his own body or for the human body.

He will regard humans and beasts quite naïvely as objects which are similar and which belong together.

NB

12.10.16

A stone, the body of a beast, the body of a man, my body, all stand on the same level.

---

65 On 27 August, Romania declared war on Austria. This is the last annotation that appears on the left-hand page of his war diaries.

That is what happens, whether it comes from a stone or from my body is neither good nor bad.

[...]

It is true: Man *is* the microcosm:
I am my world.
NB

15.10.16

What cannot be imagined cannot even be talked about [cf. **TLP** 5.61].

Things acquire "significance" only through their relation to my will.

For "Everything is what it is and not another thing."

One conception: As I can infer my spirit (character, will) from my physiognomy, so I can infer the spirit (will) of each thing from *its* physiognomy.

But can I *infer* my spirit from my physiognomy?

Isn't this relationship purely empirical?

Does my body really express anything?

Is it itself an internal expression of something?

Is, e.g., an angry face angry in itself or merely because it is empirically connected with bad temper?

But it is clear that the causal nexus is not a nexus at all [cf. **TLP** 5.136].[66]

Now is it true (following the psycho-physical conception) that my character is expressed only in the build of *my* body or brain and not equally in the build of the whole of the rest of the world?

This contains a salient point.

This parallelism, then, really exists between my spirit, i.e. spirit, and the world.

Only remember that the spirit of the snake, of the lion, is *your* spirit. For it is only from yourself that you are acquainted with spirit at all.

Now of course the question is why I have given a snake just this spirit.

And the answer to this can only lie in the psycho-physical parallelism: If I were to look like the snake and to do what it does then I should be such-and-such.

The same with the elephant, with the fly, with the wasp.

But the question arises whether even here, my body is not on the same level with that of the wasp and of the snake (and surely it is so), so that I have neither inferred from that of the wasp to mine nor from mine to that of the wasp.

Is this solution of the puzzle why men always believed that there was *one* spirit common to the whole world?

---

66 This proposition from the *Tractatus* will be broadened with paragraph 5.1361, which ends by saying: "Belief in the causal nexus is superstition."

And in that case it would, of course, also be common to lifeless things too.

This the way I have travelled: Idealism singles men out from the world as unique, solipsism singles me alone out, and at last I see that I too belong with the rest of the world, and so on the one side *nothing* is left over, and on the other side, as unique, *the world*. In this way idealism leads to realism if it is strictly thought of [cf. **TLP** 5.64].
NB

17.10.16

And in this sense I can also speak of a will that is common to the whole world.

But this will is in a higher sense *my* will.

As my idea is the world, in the same way my will is the world-will.
NB

20.10.16

It is clear that my visual space is constituted in length from breadth.

The situation is not simply that I everywhere notice where I see anything, but I also always find myself at a particular point of my visual space, so my visual space has as it were a shape.

In spite of this, however, it is true that I do not see the subject.

It is true that the knowing subject is not in the world, that there is no knowing subject [cf. **TLP** 5.631].

At any rate I can imagine carrying out the act of will for raising my arm, but that my arm does not move (e.g., a sinew is torn). True, but, it will be said, the sinew surely moves and that just shews that the act of will related to the sinew and not to the arm. But let us go farther and suppose that even the sinew did not move, and so on. We should then arrive at the position that the act of will does not relate to a body at all, and so that in the ordinary sense of the word there is no such thing as the act of the will.

Aesthetically, the miracle is that the world exists. That there is what there is.

Is it the essence of the artistic way of looking at things, that it looks at the world with a happy eye?

Life is grave, art is gay.
NB

21.10.16

For there is certainly something in the conception that the end of art is the beautiful.

And the beautiful *is* what makes happy.
NB

04.11.16
Is the will an attitude towards the world?

The will seems always to have to relate to an idea. We cannot imagine, e.g., having carried out an act of will without having detected that we have carried it out.

Otherwise there might arise such a question as whether it had yet been *completely* carried out.

It is clear, so to speak, that we need a foothold for the will in the world.

The will is an attitude of the subject to the world.

The subject is the willing subject.

Have the feelings by which I ascertain that an act of the will takes place any particular characteristic which distinguishes them from other ideas?

It seems not!

In that case, however, I might conceivably get the idea that, e.g., this chair was directly obeying my will.

Is that possible?

In drawing the square ⊠ in the mirror one notices that one is only able to manage it if one prescinds completely from the visual datum and relies only on muscular feeling. So here after all there are two quite different acts of the will in question. The one relates to the visual part of the world, the other to the muscular-feeling part.

Have we anything more than empirical evidence that the movement of the same part of the body is in question in both cases?

Then is the situation that I merely accompany my actions with my will?

But in that case how can I predict – as in some sense I surely can – that I shall raise my arm in five minutes' time? That I shall will this?

This is clear: it is impossible to will without already performing the act of the will.

The act of the will is not the cause of the action but is the action itself.

One cannot will without acting.

If the will has to have an object in the world, the object can be the intended action itself.

And the will does have to have an object.

Otherwise we should have no foothold and could not know what we willed.

And could not will different things.

Does not the willed movement of the body happen just like any unwilled movement in the world, but that it is accompanied by the will?

Yet it is not accompanied just by a *wish*! But by will.

We feel, so to speak, responsible for the movement.

My will fastens on to the world somewhere, and does not fasten on to other things.

Wishing is not acting. But willing is acting.

(My wish relates, e.g., to the movement of the chair, my will to a muscular feeling.)

The fact that I will an action consists in my performing the action, not in my doing something else which causes the action.

When I move something I move.

When I perform an action I am in action.

But: I cannot will everything. –

But what does it mean to say: "I cannot will *this*"?

Can I try to will something?

For the consideration of willing makes it looks as if one part of the world were closer to me than another (which would be intolerable).

But, of course, it is undeniable that in a popular sense there are things that I do, and other things not done by me.

In this way then the will would not confront the world as its equivalent, which must be impossible.

The wish precedes the event, the will accompanies it.

Suppose that a process were to accompany my wish. Should I have willed the process?

Would not this accompanying appear accidental in contrast to the compelled accompanying of the will?

NB

09.11.16

Is belief a kind of experience?

Is thought a kind of experience?

All experience is world and does not need the subject.

The act of will is not an experience.

NB

19.11.16

What kind of reason is there for the assumption of a willing subject?

Is not *my world* adequate for individuation?

NB

02.12.16

The correct method in philosophy would really be to say nothing except what can be said, i.e. what belongs to natural science, i.e. something that has nothing to do with philosophy, and then whenever someone else tried to say something metaphysical to shew him that he had not given any reference to certain signs in his sentences [see **TLP** 6.53].

This method would be unsatisfying for the other person (he would not have the feeling that we were teaching him philosophy) but it would be the only correct one [see **TLP** 6.53].

NB

10.01.17

If suicide is allowed then everything is allowed.

If anything is not allowed then suicide is not allowed.

This throws a light on the nature of ethics, for suicide is, so to speak, the elementary sin.

And when one investigates it it is like investigating mercury vapour in order to comprehend the nature of vapours.

Or is even suicide in itself neither good nor evil?

NB

Letter to Paul Engelmann
16.01.1918

Dear friend,

Many thanks for your letter of 8.1. If I only understood it! But I do not understand it. It is true there is a difference between myself as I am now and as I was when we met in Olmütz. And, as far as I know, the difference is that I am now *slightly* more decent. By this I only mean that I am slightly clearer in my own mind about my lack of decency. If you tell me now that I have no faith, you are *perfectly right*, only I did not have it before either. It is plain, isn't it, that when a man wants, as it were, to invent a machine for becoming decent, such a man has no faith. But what am I to do? *I am clear about one thing*: I am far too bad to be able to theorize about myself; in fact I shall either remain a swine or else I shall improve, and that's that! Only let's cut out the transcendental twaddle when the whole thing is as plain as a sock on the jaw.

It is not impossible that I may soon be transferred to Olmütz!

I am sure you are quite right in all you say.

Think of
Yours sincerely
L. Wittgenstein

LPE

Letter to Ludwig von Ficker
(after 20.10.1919)
Vienna

Dear Mr Ficker!

I'm sending you the manuscript with this letter. Why didn't I think of you <u>straight away</u>? Yes, you're thinking, I <u>did</u> think of you straight away; but that was at a time when the book[67] couldn't be published because it wasn't ready yet. At that point the war broke out and I couldn't even think about asking for your help. Now however I am hoping for your help. And it might help you if I write a few words about my book: when you read it I don't think you will gain much from it. Because you won't understand it; the material will seem quite strange to you. In reality it isn't strange to you because the sense of the book is a work on morals. At one time I wanted to add a sentence in the foreword which is actually not in it now but I would like to send it to you anyway because it might provide a key to understanding it: I wanted to write that my work consists of two parts: one is what is presented here and the other is what I haven't written. And it's precisely this second part which is the important part.[68] The ethical part will be restricted through my book from within so to speak; and I am convinced that <u>strictly speaking</u> it can **only** be limited in that way. In short I believe: everything that is <u>criticised</u> by <u>many</u> today, is set out in my book by me saying nothing about it. And that's why the book, if I am not very mistaken, will say much that you want to say yourself but perhaps you don't see that it has been said in the book. I recommend that you read the <u>foreword</u> and the <u>conclusion</u> as these highlight the sense of the book in the most direct way. –

---

67 The *Tractatus Logico-Philosophicus*.
68 This is the well-known letter in which Wittgenstein makes clear the sense in which the *Tractatus* is written; he highlights the point that it must be read from a perspective in which ethics takes absolute first place, although nothing can be *said* about it. Wittgenstein asked von Ficker to publish the Tractatus, but not even the editor of *Der Brenner* would do so. Following several more failed attempts, in 1920, the publishing house Reclam also rejected the book, which caused Wittgenstein to become disinterested in its publication. In the end, it was Russell's valiant efforts that managed to get Wilhelm Ostwald, the publisher of *Annalen der Naturphilosophie*, to publish the *Tractatus*, in the 14th issue in 1921. This was the edition that, interestingly, Wittgenstein would come to see as *pirated*, given the errors Ostwald's edition contained, according to him. There were an incomprehensibly large number of difficulties in publishing such a high-level text. At one point of the – up to then – unfruitful search, Wittgenstein wrote to Russell (27.11.1919): "The difficulties with my book have started up again. Nobody wants to publish it. Do you remember how you were always pressing me to publish something? And now when I should like to, it can't be managed. The devil take it!"

The manuscript I'm sending you now is not the actual printed manuscript but one which I've revised in haste and which will suffice for you to orientate yourself. The printed manuscript needs to be carefully revised; it is currently in England with my friend Russell. I sent it to him when I was in prison. He will send it back to me soon. In the meantime I wish myself lots of luck.

I send you warm greetings

Your devoted Ludwig Wittgenstein

WTB

Letter from B. Russell to Lady Ottoline
20.12.1919
The Hague

I have much to tell you that is of interest. I leave here today, after a fortnight's stay, during a week of which Wittgenstein was here, and we discussed his book every day. I came to think even better of it than I had done; I feel sure it is a really great book, though I do not feel sure it is right.[69] I told him I could not refute it, and that I was sure it was either all right or all wrong, which I considered the mark of a good book; but it would take me years to decide this. This of course didn't satisfy him, but I couldn't say more.

I had felt in his book a flavour of mysticism,[70] but was astonished when I found that he has become a complete mystic. He reads people like Kierkegaard and Angelus Silesius, and he seriously contemplates becoming a monk. It all started with William James's Varieties of Religious Experience, and grew (not unnaturally) during the winter he spent alone in Norway before the war, when he was nearly mad. Then during the war a curious thing happened. He went on duty to the town of Tarnov in Galicia, and happened to come upon a bookshop which however seemed to contain nothing but picture postcards. However, he went

---

69 This would not be the only time Russell would express his doubts on Wittgenstein's philosophy. To give another example, when in 1930 Wittgenstein applied for a fellowship from Trinity College to continue with his research, Russell wrote a report on 8 May that year in support of the application. In that supporting report, he wrote: "The theories contained in this new work of Wittgenstein's are novel, very original, and indubitably important. Whether they are true, I don't know." In his work *My Philosophical Development*, he would come to say Wittgenstein had wasted his talent with what came after the *Tractatus*, that the philosophy Wittgenstein developed in his *Philosophical Investigations* was unintelligible and that, in Russell's eyes, Wittgenstein had tired of serious thought.

70 Russell would once again highlight these thoughts in the obituary he published to Wittgenstein in *Mind* journal (239), pp. 297–8, in which he pointed out that during the First World War, Wittgenstein became a mystic, and that could clearly be seen – according to Russell – in the *Tractatus*.

inside and found that it contained just one book: Tolstoy on the Gospels. He bought it merely because there was no other. He read it and re-read it, and thenceforth had it always with him, under fire and at all times. But on the whole he likes Tolstoy less than Dostoewski (especially Karamazov). He has penetrated deep into mystical ways of thought and feeling, but I think (though he wouldn't agree) that what he likes best is mysticism is its power to make him stop thinking. I don't much think he will really become a monk – it is an idea, not an intention. His intention is to be a teacher. He gave all his money to his brothers and sisters,[71] because he found earthly possessions a burden. I wish you had seen him.
WCB

Letter to Paul Engelmann
09.01.1920
XIII. St. Veitgasse 17, c/o Frau Sjögren

D. Mr. E., – Yesterday I got a letter from one Mr. Viktor Lautsch 'Lautsch' may be a slip of the pen (occasioned by the 'Lachs' which follows) for 'Deutsch': there was a family of that name in Olmütz, who gives Mr. Lachs, Groag, and you as references and begs me to support him. Since I have no money myself and do not know the gentleman, I am sending him for the time being only very little money and some underwear I can spare, and I request you urgently to let me have more information about the petitioner. Perhaps my sister Mining could help him. The sooner you answer me, the better!

It just occurs to me that I myself have not yet answered your last kind letter. However, I was in bed with influenza when it arrived. I will deal another time with your remarks on religion.[72] They are still not clear enough, it seems to me. I, too, feel that I am seeing the matter more clearly than a month ago. It must be possible, I believe, to say all these things much more adequately. (Or not at all, which is even more likely.)

Please give my respects and kind regards to your revered mother.

Yours
Ludwig Wittgenstein

LPE
Letter to Paul Engelmann

---

71 At the end of the war, and as a result of his profound spiritual transformation, Wittgenstein decided to distribute his money (his part of the family's heritage) among his brothers and sisters (except Margarethe), insisting on the fact that nothing could be left for him, what made that the notary in charge of the operation exclaimed: "You want to commit financial suicide."

72 Wittgenstein is answering a letter from Engelmann concerning the dispute on the relationships and connections between the figures of God and Christ.

21.06.1920

D. Mr. E., – Many thanks for your kind letter, which has given me much pleasure and thereby perhaps helped me a little, although as far as the merits of my case are concerned I am beyond any outside help. – In fact I am in a state of mind that it is terrible to me. I have been through it several times before: it is the state of *not being able to get over a particular fact*. It is a pitiable state, I know. But there is only one remedy that I can see, and that is of course to come to terms with that fact. But this is just like what happens when a man who can't swim has fallen into the water and flails about it with his hands and feet and feels that he *cannot* keep his head above water. That is the position I am now. I know that to kill oneself is always a dirty thing to do. Surely one *cannot* will one's own destruction, and anybody who has visualized what is in practice involved in the act of suicide knows that suicide is always a *rushing of one's own defences*. But nothing is worse than to be forced to take oneself by surprise.

Of course it all boils down to the fact that I have no faith!

Well, we shall see! –

Please thank your revered mother in my name for her kind letter. I will certainly come to Olmütz, but I don't know when. I do hope I can make it soon.

Yours
Ludwig Wittgenstein

LPE

Letter to B. Russell
20.09.1920

Dear Russell,

Thank you for your kind letter. I have obtained a position: I am to be an elementary-school teacher in a tiny village called Trattenbach. It's in the mountains, about four hours' journey south of Vienna. It must be the first time the schoolmaster at Trattenbach has ever corresponded with a Professor in Pekin. How are you? And what are you lecturing on? Philosophy? If so, I wish I could attend and could argue with you afterwards. A short while ago I was *terribly depressed* and tired of living, but now I am slightly more hopeful, and one of the things I hope is that we'll meet again.

God be with you! Warmest regards from

Your devoted friend
Ludwig Wittgenstein

WCB

2
1921–1930

Being a soldier of a defeated country, Wittgenstein was only released as a prisoner of war on 21 August 1919. It was then that the complicated path towards the publication of his first work, the *Tractatus Logico-Philosophicus*, began. It is hard to fathom how one of the most important philosophical works of the twentieth century faced such incredible difficulties in finding a willing publisher; nonetheless, thanks to the invaluable help of Russell, the book finally saw the light of day in 1921, in the *Annalen der Naturphilosophie*. The letters exchanged between Wittgenstein and Russell in those years are a good testimony of the many obstacles this publication had to overcome. It should be taken into consideration, though, that the book's contents were quite ambitious, with the prologue ending with those well-known, forceful and slightly shocking sentences:

> Dagegen scheint mir die *Wahrheit* der hier mitgeteilten Gedanken unantastbar und definitiv. Ich bin also der Meinung, die Probleme im Wesentlichen endgültig gelöst zu haben.

In addition, the following comments are particularly intriguing and give the work a certain mysterious tone:

> Und wenn ich mich hierin nicht irre, so besteht nun der Wert dieser Arbeit zweitens darin, daß sie Zeigt, wie wenig damit getan ist, daß die Probleme gelöst sind.

Whatever interpretation is given to the *Tractatus*, the depth of its comments on the role of philosophy and the importance of those questions regarding God and the meaning of life cannot be obviated. It is in this sense that we can interpret Wittgenstein's statement that, in his book, the issues have been analysed in a

Ludwig Wittgenstein: The Meaning of Life, First Edition. Edited by Joaquín Jareño-Alarcón.
© 2023 John Wiley & Sons Ltd. Published 2023 by John Wiley & Sons Ltd.

definitive manner, that is, in their ultimate consequences, which brings us to the domains of ethics and religion. This is what makes Wittgenstein's work a complete system and helps us explain the huge influence of the *Tractatus* in all domains of philosophical discussion.

The English translation by C.K. Ogden and F.P. Ramsey was ready in 1922. By then, Wittgenstein was already a schoolteacher, despite a previous experience which had better suited his religious sensitivity, as during the summer of 1920 he had worked as a gardener at the monastery of Klosterneuburg, on the outskirts of Vienna. It appeared that this labour had helped him alleviate his existential tensions. In a letter to Paul Engelmann (20 August 1920), Wittgenstein wrote: "I am sure the gardening work was the most sensible thing I could have done in my holidays." However, that same year he began his career as a teacher, and, if we are to heed a letter to Engelmann of 11 October 1920, he undertook this task with high expectations and enthusiasm:

> At last I have become a primary-school teacher, and I am working in a beautiful and tiny place called Trattenbach (near Kirchberg-am-Wechsel, Lower Austria). I am happy in my work at school, and I do need it badly, or else all the devils in Hell break loose inside me.

It turned out that Wittgenstein's time as a teacher in small villages in Lower Austria was not a very pleasant one. He became worn out by many problems with the peasants whom he had idealized after reading Tolstoy's works. In real life, however, he found them mean and reluctant to accept his unique, complicated personality.[1] His daily life in Lower Austria was frugal and austere. He resided in very basic lodgings, thus showing his contempt for material goods. This annoyed the inhabitants of the villages of Trattenbach and Otterthal. Wittgenstein is said to have started and finished classes by praying the Our Father. Nevertheless, he became very tired of Tolstoy's "noble servants". His sojourn there was cut short after being accused of ill-treating his pupils in the so-called "Haidbauer case". He continued to work as a schoolteacher until 1926, remaining in Trattenbach until 1922, and from September to November of that year he worked at a secondary school in the village of Hassbach, near Neunkirchen, and afterwards in Puchberg. The final two years of his teaching career were spent in Otterthal. It was in Trattenbach that Wittgenstein befriended Alois Neururer, the local parish priest who could be considered his only genuine friend in that area. Neururer, who left Trattenbach in 1936, used to rebel against the prevailing form of Catholicism in the country throughout the 1920s.

---

1 It has been coherently argued that Wittgenstein suffered from 'Asperger's syndrome'. See: M. Fitzgerald: "Did Ludwig Wittgenstein Have Asperger's Syndrome?"; in: *European Child & Adolescent Psychiatry*, vol. 9 (2000), pp. 61–5.

During Wittgenstein's teaching years in Lower Austria the fame of his *Tractatus* began to spread along the academic circles. He had also spent some time devising ways to improve the vocabulary of his pupils, which resulted in the publication of his *Wörterbuch für Volksschulen*. Apart from the *Tractatus*, this proved to be his only other book published in his lifetime.

In the meantime, the *Tractatus* had become a work of reference. By 1923, Ramsey, the author of a classical review of this work, paid a two-week visit to Wittgenstein in Puchberg. Two more visits followed, but this time in Otterthal. Wittgenstein left the village in May 1926 and spent the summer at the Hospitallers' monastery in Hütteldorf, on the outskirts of Vienna, where he seriously considered becoming a monk. In the end he rejected the idea and, instead, decided to help build a house for his sister Margarethe. In the supervision of the building he was very meticulous, as indeed he was in anything he did. This was a very significant time for Wittgenstein; after giving up rural life, he returned to urban and intellectual milieux and again took part in discussions concerning his own philosophy, which had become a matter of special interest. Braithwaite had lectured on the *Tractatus* at the Moral Science Club of Cambridge as early as 1923, and the Vienna Circle members made of the book an icon – a kind of a *secular gospel*.

Wittgenstein definitively returned to philosophy in 1929. A new stage began, which eventually resulted in a new vision of philosophical thought, radically opposed to that of the *Tractatus*. Nevertheless, his "Lecture on Ethics" given at the end of 1929 was still in the spirit of that work. The following year saw the death of the death of Ramsey, Wittgenstein's best friend at Cambridge after his comeback. Ramsey had also been a tutor to Wittgenstein, who had been admitted as an "advanced student", and was of great help in pointing out to him the mistakes in the *Tractatus*. In December 1930 Wittgenstein was chosen as Research Fellow of Trinity College.

Letter to Paul Engelmann
25.04.1921

D. Mr. E.,

Only a few lines today, as I am physically in poor shape. Perhaps it would be good for us to meet again, though not at the beginning of the summer holidays but at the end, say the beginning of September. My condition – I mean my state of mind – is not as bad as it was when I wrote you last; though it is not really good; in fact, basically it is bad. I can write no more now. Auf Wiedersehen next September! Until then may God help us!

Yours
L. Wittgenstein

LPE

1921
3.031[2]
It is used to be said that God could create anything except what would be contrary to the laws of logic. – The reason being that we could not *say* what an 'illogical' world look like.
TLP

5.6
The limits of my language mean the limits of my world.
TLP

5.61
Logic pervades the world: the limits of the world are also its limits.
 So we cannot say in logic, 'The world has this in it, and this, but not that'.
 For that would appear to presuppose that we were excluding certain possibilities, and this cannot be the case, since it would require that logic should go beyond

---

2 With this entry, the paragraphs corresponding to the *Tractatus* can be seen. From paragraph 6.373 of this compilation onwards, the texts on ethics begin. Nevertheless, the previous paragraphs have been selected in an attempt to clear up how the relationship between the subject and the world – a crucial part of later understanding the role of the willing subject (the ethical subject) – is to be understood.

the limits of the world; for only in that way could it view those limits from the other side as well.

We cannot think what we cannot think; so what we cannot think we cannot *say* either.

TLP

5.62

This remark provides the key to the problem, how much truth there is in solipsism.

For what the solipsist *means* is quite correct; only it cannot be *said*, but makes itself manifest.

The world is *my* world: this is manifest in the fact that the limits of *language* (of that language which alone I understand) mean the limits of *my* world.

TLP

5.621
The world and life are one.
TLP

5.63
I am my world. (The microcosm).
TLP

5.631

There is no such thing as the subject that thinks or entertains ideas.

If I wrote a book called *The World as I found it*, I should have to include a report on my body, and should have to say which parts were subordinate to my will, and which were not, etc., this being a method of isolating the subject, or rather of showing that in an important sense there is no subject; for alone it could *not* be mentioned in that book. –

TLP

5.632
The subject does not belong to the world: rather, it is a limit of the world.
TLP

5.633
Where *in* the world is a metaphysical subject to be found?
TLP

5.634
This is connected with the fact that no part of our experience is at the same time a priori.
    Whatever we see could be other than it is.
    Whatever we can describe at all could be other than it is.
    There is no a priori order of things.
TLP

5.64
Here it can be seen that solipsism, when its implications are followed out strictly, coincides with pure realism. The self of solipsism shrinks to a point without extension, and there remains the reality co-ordinated with it.
TLP

5.641
Thus there really is a sense in which philosophy can talk about the self in a non-psychological way.
    What brings the self into philosophy is the fact that 'the world is my world'.
    The philosophical self is not the human being, not the human body, or the human soul, with which psychology deals, but rather the metaphysical subject, the limit of the world – not a part of it.
TLP

6.373
The world is independent of my will.
TLP

6.374
Even if all that we wish for were to happen, still this would only be a favour granted by fate, so to speak: for there is no *logical* connexion between the will and the world, which would guarantee it, and the supposed physical connexion itself is surely not something that we could will.
TLP

6.41[3]

The sense of the world must lie outside the world. In the world everything is at it is, and everything happens as it does happen: *in* it no value exists – and if it did exist, it would have no value.

If there is any value that does have value, it must lie outside the whole sphere of what happens and is the case. For all that happens and is the case is accidental.

What makes it non-accidental cannot lie *within* the world, since if it did it would itself be accidental.

It must lie outside the world.

TLP

6.42

So too it is impossible for there to be propositions of ethics.

Propositions can express nothing that is higher.

TLP

6.421

It is clear that ethics cannot be put into words.

Ethics is transcendental.

(Ethics and aesthetics are one and the same).

TLP

6.422

When an ethical law of the form, 'Thou shalt ...', is laid down, one's first thought is, 'And what if I do not do it?' It is clear, however, that ethics has nothing to do with punishment and reward in the usual sense of the terms. So our question about the *consequences* of an action must be unimportant. – At least those consequences should not be events. For there must be something right about the question we posed. There must indeed be some kind of ethical reward and ethical punishment, but they must reside in the action itself.

---

3 We can say that it is here where the problem of ethics and the meaning of life properly begins. This final part of the work progressively makes clear that the importance of ethics obliges us to situate it outside the realm of language, so it is entirely coherent to state that the result of the *Tractatus* is to bring out the absolute character of ethics. This is not to be expressed in language but rather, inevitably, in action.

(And it is also clear that the reward must be something pleasant and the punishment something unpleasant).
TLP

6.423

It is impossible to speak about the will in so far as it is the subject of ethical attributes.

And the will as a phenomenon is of interest only to psychology.
TLP

6.43

If the good or bad exercise of the will does alter the world, it can alter only the limits of the world, not the facts – not what can be expressed by means of language.

In short the effect must be that it becomes an altogether different world. It must, so to speak, wax and wane as a whole.

The world of the happy man is a different one from that of the unhappy man.
TLP

6.431

So too at death the world does not alter, but comes to an end.
TLP

6.4311

Death is not an event in life: we do not live to experience death.

If we take eternity to mean not infinite temporal duration but timelessness, then eternal life belongs to those who live in the present.

Our life has no end in just the way in which our visual field has no limits.
TLP

6.4312

Not only is there no guarantee of the temporal immortality of the human soul, that is to say of its eternal survival after death; but, in any case, this assumption completely fails to accomplish the purpose for which it has always been intended. Or is some riddle solved by my surviving for ever? Is not this eternal life itself as much of a riddle as our present life? The solution of the riddle of life in space and time lies *outside* space and time.

(It is certainly not the solution of any problems of natural science that is required).
TLP

6.432

How things are in the world is a matter of complete indifference for what is higher. God does not reveal himself *in* the world.
TLP

6.4321

The facts all contribute only to setting the problem, not to its solution.
TLP

6.44

It is not *how* things are in the world that is mystical, but *that* it exists.
TLP

6.45

To view the world sub specie aeterni is to view it as a whole – a limited whole.
 Feeling the world as a limited whole – it is this that is mystical.
TLP

6.5

When the answer cannot be put into words, neither can the question be put into words.
 The *riddle* does not exist.
 If a question can be framed at all, it is also *possible* to answer it.
TLP

6.52

We feel that even when all *possible* scientific questions have been answered, the problems of life remain completely untouched. Of course there are then no questions left, and this itself is the answer.
TLP

6.521

The solution of the problem of life is seen in the vanishing of the problem.
 (Is not this the reason why those who have found after a long period of doubt that the sense of life become clear to them have been unable to say what constituted that sense?).
TLP

6.522
There are, indeed, things that cannot be put into words. They *make themselves manifest*. They are what is mystical.
TLP

6.53
The correct method in philosophy would really be the following: to say nothing except what can be said, i.e. propositions of natural science – i.e. something that has nothing to do with philosophy – and then, whenever someone else wanted to say something metaphysical, to demonstrate to him that he had failed to give a meaning to certain signs in his propositions. Although it would not be satisfying to the other person – he would not have the feeling that we were teaching him philosophy – *this* method would be the only strictly correct one.
TLP

6.54
My propositions serve as elucidations in the following way: anyone who understands me eventually recognizes them as nonsensical, when he has used them – as steps – to climb up beyond them. (He must, so to speak, throw away the ladder after he has climbed up it).

He must transcend these propositions, and then he will see the world aright.
TLP

7
What we cannot speak about we must pass over in silence.
TLP

13.01.1922[4]
I had a strange experience last night.

It began like this: I dreamt that for some particular reason (which I have since forgotten) my sister Mining made a flattering remark about my intellectuality.[5] (In a way that seemed to praise me she said something like: "This is precisely where you see the difference between great"). I rejected her particular opinion whilst defending others that Mining made on a deeper level but was essentially rather flattered by the remarks and pleased about my apparently superior intellect. Thereupon I awoke and feeling ashamed of my vanity and vulgarity and

---
4 By that time, the *Tractatus* had already been published in German, the previous year. The English version would be translated by C.K. Ogden, with Ramsey's help, in 1922. Wittgenstein was then working in the Austrian hamlet of Trattenbach.
5 One of the 'sins' that Wittgenstein would struggle with his entire life was vanity.

as a form of repentance – I don't remember my exact thoughts – I started to make the sign of the cross. In order to do so, I felt I ought to at least sit up or kneel down but was too lazy to do so and made the sign of the cross in a half-raised position before lying down again. At that point I felt I had to get up – that God was asking this of me. And this is what happened: I suddenly became aware of my complete nothingness and understood that God could ask whatever he wanted of me since my life was <u>immediately</u> meaningless when I disobeyed. I immediately wondered whether I could still consider the whole thing to be an illusion and whether or not this had been a command from God; but it became clear to me that I would then have to consider all religion in me to be an illusion and that I would have to deny the meaning of life. – After some initial reluctance I responded to the command, switched on the light and got up.

Feeling terrified I stood in the room. I went to the mirror and looked at myself. My reflection looked so grey that I hid my face in my hands. I felt completely worn out and in the hands of God who could do with me whatever he wanted at any moment. I felt that God could force me at that moment to confess to my wickedness immediately, that he could force me to agree to accepting that which I feared most but that I wasn't prepared to take on what I feared most, that I wasn't yet willing to give up friendship and all earthly happiness. Would I ever be willing?! I wasn't permitted to go back to bed, but was afraid of being given further commands so, filled with terror, I ignored the command and, like a bad soldier or a deserter, returned to bed. As I switched off the light I had an accident. The electric bulb had unscrewed itself from its holder so when I touched the electric wire I suffered an electric shock. As I flinched I knocked my elbow on the edge of the bed causing me enormous pain. Yet the considerable pain acted as a great relief for me from my situation and distracted me to some degree from my inner feelings. I lay there for a time feeling terrible, fearing I would fall asleep and become aware of this whole situation in all its clarity and have to agree to undertaking that which I most feared or lose my mind. – I then fell asleep and didn't dream about the matter again. Early the next morning I felt relatively normal, but now I am quite weary and exhausted.

As I said I became aware of my complete nothingness during the night. God had chosen to reveal this to me. While this was happening I kept thinking about Kierkegaard and believed that I was in a state of "fear and trembling".[6]
LS

---

[6] S. Kierkegaard's influential book, published in 1843. To publish it, Kierkegaard used the pseudonym Johannes de Silentio. The title is from a sentence appearing in the epistle of St. Paul to the Philippians (2:12): "Work out your own salvation with fear and trembling." Wittgenstein had a special sympathy towards Kierkegaard, mentioning him in some of his most personal writings. On one occasion, Wittgenstein wrote: "Kierkegaard was by far the most profound thinker of the last century. Kierkegaard was a saint" (to Maurice O'Connor Drury; **PR**, pp. 102–3).

Letter to B. Russell[7]
1922

Dear Russell,

[...]

P.S. Do you happen to have among your books the "Religious Controversies" of Lessing?[8] If so, please, read them. I think they will interest you and give you pleasure. I like them very much. Yours L.W.

WCB

1925 (?)[9]

If the purely (spiritual, religious) ideal is compared to white light, then the ideals of other cultures can be compared to coloured lights that appear when pure light passes through coloured glass. Imagine someone who has lived all of his life in a room where light only enters through panes of red glass.

This person probably wouldn't be able to imagine a light different to his own light (the red light) might exist. He will not pay much attention to the red quality of the light. In a certain sense he won't even notice the redness of the light surrounding him. In other words: he will consider his light to be the light and not a dimmer version of the one light (which it is in reality). The person moves around in his room, inspects the objects closely, assesses them, etc.

As his room isn't the room, but only a part of the room restricted by red glass, he will certainly reach the edge of the room if he moves far enough. This is when

---

7 Wittgenstein broke off relations with Russell that year. They would not meet again until 1929, when Russell was a member of the tribunal to judge Wittgenstein's doctoral thesis. Interestingly, the work that Wittgenstein presented was the *Tractatus*.

8 Gotthold Ephraim Lessing (1729–81), German classicist poet. A key figure of German *Aufklärung*, author of the work *Laocoön: An Essay on the Limits of Painting and Poetry* (1766).

9 That year, Wittgenstein would seriously consider whether or not to continue teaching, a job he would finally abandon in April 1926. In a letter to Engelmann in February 1925, he would write: "I suffer much from the human, or rather inhuman, beings whom I live – in short it is as usual!" In October of the same year, in another letter to Keynes, he would write: "I have decided to remain teacher, as long as I feel that the troubles into which I get that way, may do me any good. If one has a toothache it is good to put a hot-water bottle on your face, but it will only be effective, as long as the heat of the bottle gives you some pain. I will chuck the bottle when I find that it no longer gives me the particular kind of pain which will do my character any good. That is, if people here don't turn me out before that time." In reality, his problems as a schoolmaster had begun relatively early on. In a letter to Russell dated 23.10.1921, we wrote the following comment: "I am still at Trattenbach, surrounded, as ever, by odiousness and baseness. I know that human beings on the average are not worth much anywhere, but here they are much more good-for-nothing and irresponsible than elsewhere. I will perhaps stay on in Trattenbach for the present year but probably not any longer, because I don't get on well here even with the other teachers (perhaps that won't be better in another place)."

various things can happen: one person will now see the edge of the room but cannot break through the glass and will therefore give up. He will say: "So my light wasn't the light after all. I/we can only imagine the light and I/we need to be content with our dim light." Such a person will then either be filled with humour or melancholy or alternate between the two. For those who give up react with humour and melancholy. That is why the person doesn't experience these feelings until he has reached the edge of the room, although he can also be funny and sad of course (but funny and sad are not the same as being full of humour and melancholy). Another person will reach the edge of the room but won't quite understand that this is the edge and accepts the situation as if he had just bumped into a body inside the room. Nothing changes for this person and he carries on living as he did before.

Finally, a third person says: I have to go into that room and into that light. He breaks through the glass and steps beyond his boundaries out into the open.

Application: the person in the red glass bell represents humanity from a particular culture, for example the Western culture which more or less began with the migration of people and in the 18th century reached one of its summits – its last, I believe. The light is the ideal and the dimmed light is the cultural ideal. As long as humanity hasn't reached the edges of this culture, that culture will be considered the Ideal. Sooner or later however humanity will reach the edge because each culture is only a limited part of the room. – At the start of the 19th century (of the spiritual century) humanity reached the edge of Western culture.

And now the bitterness sets in: the melancholy and the humour (for both are bitter). And it can now be said that every significant person of that period in the 18/19th century is either a humorist or a melancholic (or both) and the more intensive, the more significant he is; otherwise he goes beyond the limits and becomes religious [and it can happen that someone has already stuck his head out into the open but, blinded by the light, withdraws and carries on living in the glass bell with a bad conscience]. It can therefore be said: the significant person always has something to do with the light (this makes him significant). If he lives in the midst of that culture he associates it with the coloured light. If he reaches the limits of the culture he then has to give serious thought to the type and intensity of the culture that made us interested in it, which moved us with its works. The more intensive the more interested we are, the less intensive, the less interested we are. The talent even if it is still so extraordinary/unusual which has been filled by the border, is only shallow and nebulous. He can come to terms with it through his games, but he cannot move us any more through his games, even through the most beautiful games (they have now lost the substantial part of their beauty and we only like them because they remind us of what was beautiful in the past); except where it reaches a deeper discussion. That – I believe – is the case with Mendelssohn. The strange originality of his work – even the most distinctive originality of his work is not what moves us [otherwise Wagner would move us more than any other] – it is so to speak something merely animal. It is our encounter with the spirit, with the light that moves us. – That's enough for now.
LS

11.10.1929[10]
If a circle is actually what we see – that is, see in the same sense as when we see the blue mark – then we must be able to see it and not merely something similar to it.
   God, keep my ideal straight!
MS 107 161

31.10.1929
I was able to philosophise a little more today. Thanks be to God.
MS 107 179

10.11.1929
What is Good is Divine too. That, strangely enough, sums up my ethics.
   Only something supernatural can express the Supernatural.
CV

15.11.1929
You cannot lead people to the good; you can only lead them to some place or other; the good lies outside the space of facts.
CV

A LECTURE ON ETHICS[11]
17.11.1929
Before I begin to speak about my subject proper let me make a few introductory remarks. I feel I shall have great difficulties in communicating my thoughts to you and I think some of them may be diminished by mentioning them to you

---

10 In 1926, Hölder-Pichler-Tempsky published the only one of Wittgenstein's works to be published in his lifetime, apart from the *Tractatus*. The chosen work was *Vörterbuch für Volkschulen*, a dictionary with which he meant to improve his pupils' vocabulary and pronunciation, placing special emphasis on the local dialect. After retiring as a schoolmaster, Wittgenstein dedicated himself to the design of his sister Margarethe's house in Vienna, although he also worked as a gardener in the monastery at Hütteldorf on the outskirts of Vienna. Following a conference by the mathematician Brouwer in Vienna in 1928, he restarted his philosophical work, although he had corresponded somewhat with Ramsey in this sense in 1927. In 1929, he published the article "Some Remarks on Logical Form" in the *Proceedings of the Aristotelian Society*; this would be the last of his works printed during his lifetime. That same year, Wittgenstein received a fellowship to continue his philosophical research, beginning what would become his path towards the *Philosophical Investigations*. On 19 June of that year, he had presented his doctoral thesis to the tribunal on which Russell and Moore sat.

11 Invited by C.K. Ogden, Wittgenstein gave his only conference ever to a non-academic audience. He lectured before a private society called "The Heretics", a free-thinkers association – in fact a Cambridge students society – with Ogden as president. The "Lecture" is still written in the spirit of the *Tractatus,* and Wittgenstein emphasizes that he is speaking in first person.

beforehand. The first one, which almost I need not mention, is that English is not my native tongue and my expression therefore often lacks that precision and subtlety which would be desirable if one talks about a difficult subject. All I can do is to ask you to make my task easier by trying to get at my meaning in spite of the faults which I will constantly be committing against the English grammar. The second difficulty I will mention is this, that probably many of you come up to this lecture of mine with slightly wrong expectations. And to set you right in this point I will say a few words about the reason for choosing the subject I have chosen: When your former secretary honoured me by asking me to read a paper to your society, my first thought was that I would certainly do it and my second thought was that if I was to have the opportunity to speak to you I should speak about something which I am keen on communicating to you and that I should not misuse this opportunity to give you a lecture about, say, logic. I call this a misuse, for to explain a scientific matter to you it would need a course of lectures and not an hour's paper. Another alternative would have been to give you what's called a popular-scientific lecture, that is a lecture intended to make you believe that you understand a thing which actually you don't understand, and to gratify what I believe to be one of the lowest desires of modern people, namely the superficial curiosity about the latest discoveries of science. I rejected these alternatives and decided to talk to you about a subject which seems to me to be of general importance, hoping that it may help to clear up your thoughts about this subject (even if you should entirely disagree with what I will say about it). My third and last difficulty is one which, in fact, adheres to most lengthy philosophical lectures and it is this, that the hearer is incapable of seeing both the road he is led and the goal which it leads to. That is to say: he either thinks: "I understand all he says, but what on earth is he driving at" or else he thinks "I see what he's driving at, but how on earth is he going to get there". All I can do is again to ask you to be patient and to hope that in the end you may see both the way and where it leads to.

I will now begin. My subject, as you know, is Ethics and I will adopt the explanation of that term which Professor Moore has given in his book *Principia Ethica*. He says: "Ethics is the general enquiry into what is good." Now I am going to use the term Ethics in a slightly wider sense, in a sense in fact which includes what I believe to be the most essential part of what is generally called Aesthetics. And to make you see as clearly as possible what I take to be the subject matter of Ethics I will put before you a number of more or less synonymous expressions each of which could be substituted for the above definition, and by enumerating them I want to produce the same sort of effect which Galton produced when he took a number of photos of different faces on the same photographic plate in order to get the picture of the typical features they all had in common. And as by showing to you such a collective photo I could make you see what is the typical – say – Chinese face; so if you look through the row of synonyms which I will put before you, you will, I hope, be able to see the characteristic features they all have in common and these are the characteristic features of Ethics. Now instead of saying "Ethics is the enquiry into what is good" I could have said Ethics is the enquiry into what is valuable, or, into what is really important, or I could have said Ethics is the enquiry into the meaning of life, or into what makes life worth living, or into the right way of living. I believe if you look at all these phrases you will get a rough idea as to what it is that Ethics is concerned with. Now the first thing that strikes one about all these expressions is that each of them is actually used in two very different senses. I will call them the trivial or relative sense on the one hand and the ethical or absolute sense on the other. If for instance I say that this is a *good* chair this means that the chair serves a certain predetermined purpose and the word good here has only meaning so far as this purpose has been previously fixed upon. In fact the word good in the relative sense simply means coming up to a certain predetermined standard. Thus when we say that this man is a good pianist we mean that he can play pieces of a certain degree of difficulty with a certain degree of dexterity. And similarly if I say that it is *important* for me not to catch a cold I mean that catching a cold produces certain describable disturbances in my life and if I say that this is the *right* road I mean that it's the right road relative to a certain goal. Used in this way these expressions don't present any difficult or deep problems. But this is not how Ethics uses them. Supposing that I could play tennis and one of you saw me playing and said "Well, you play pretty badly" and suppose I answered "I know, I'm playing badly but I don't want to play any better", all the other man could say would be "Ah then that's all right". But suppose I had told one of you a preposterous lie and he came up to me and said "You're behaving like a beast" and then I were to say "I know I behave badly, but then I don't want to behave any better", could then he say "Ah, then that's all right?" Certainly not; he would say "Well, you *ought* to want to behave better." Here you have an absolute judgment of value, whereas the first instance was one of a relative judgment. The essence of this difference seems to be obviously this: Every judgment of relative value is a mere statement of facts and can therefore be put in such a form that it loses all the appearance of a judgment of value: Instead of saying "This is the right way to Granchester", I could equally well have said, "This is the right way you have to go if you want to get to Granchester in the shortest time"; "This man is a good runner" simply means that he runs a certain number of miles in a certain number of minutes, etc. Now what I wish to contend is that, although all judgments of relative value can be shown to be mere statements of facts, no statement of fact can ever be, or imply, a judgment of absolute value. Let me explain this: Suppose one of you were an omniscient person and therefore knew all the movements of all the bodies in the world dead or alive and that he also knew all the states of mind of all human beings that ever lived, and suppose this man wrote all he knew in a big book, then this book would contain the whole description of the world; and what I want to say is, that this book would contain nothing that he would call an *ethical* judgment or anything that would logically imply such a judgment. It would of course contain all relative judgments of value and all true scientific propositions and in fact all true propositions that can be made. But all the facts described would, as it were, stand on the same level and in the same way all propositions stand on the same level. There are no propositions which, in any absolute sense, are sublime, important, or trivial. Now perhaps some of you will agree to that and be reminded of Hamlet's words: "Nothing is either good or bad, but thinking makes it so." But this again could lead to a misunderstanding. What Hamlet says seems to imply that good and bad, though not qualities of the world outside us, are attributes to our states of mind. But what I mean is that a state of mind, so far as we mean by that a fact which we can describe, is in no ethical sense good or bad. If for instance in our world-book we read the description of a murder with all its details physical and psychological, the mere description of these facts will contain nothing we could call an *ethical* proposition. The murder will be on exactly the same level as any other event, for instance the falling of a stone. Certainly the reading of this description might cause us pain or rage or any other emotion, or we might read about the pain or rage caused by this murder in other people when they heard of it, but there will simply be facts, facts, and facts but no Ethics. And now I must say that if I contemplate what Ethics really would have to be if there were such a science, this result seems to me quite obvious. It seems to me obvious that nothing we could ever think or say should be *the* thing. That we cannot write a scientific book, the subject matter of which could be intrinsically sublime and above all other subject matters. I can only describe my feeling by the metaphor, that, if a man could write a book on Ethics which really was a book on Ethics, this book would, with an explosion, destroy all the other books in the world. Our words used as we use them in science, are vessels capable only of containing and conveying meaning and sense, *natural* meaning and sense. Ethics, if it is anything, is supernatural and our words will only express facts; as a teacup will only hold a teacup full of water [even] if I were to pour out a gallon over it. I said that so far as facts and propositions are concerned there is only relative value and relative good, right, etc. And let me, before I go on, illustrate this by a rather obvious example. The right road is the road which leads to an arbitrarily predetermined end and it is quite clear to us all that there is no sense in talking about the right road apart from such a predetermined goal. Now let us see what we could possibly mean by the expression, "the absolute right road". I think it would be the road which *everybody* on seeing it would, *with logical necessity*, have to go, or be ashamed for not going. And similarly the *absolute good*, if it is a describable state of affairs, would be one which everybody, independent of his tastes and inclinations, would *necessarily* bring about or feel guilty for not bringing about. And I want to say that such a state of affairs is a chimera. No state of affairs has, in itself, what I would like to call the coercive power of an absolute judge. Then what have all of us who, like myself, are still tempted to use such expressions as "absolute good", "absolute value", etc., what have we in mind and what do we try to express? Now whenever I try to make this clear to myself it is natural that I should recall cases in which I would certainly use the expressions and I am then in the situation in which you would be if, for instance, I were to give you a lecture on the psychology of pleasure. What you would do then would be to try and recall some typical situation in which you always felt pleasure. For, bearing this situation in mind, all I should say to you would become concrete and, as it were, controllable. One man would perhaps choose as his stock example the sensation when taking a walk on a fine summer's day. Now in this situation I am, if I want to fix my mind on what I mean by absolute or ethical value. And there, in my case, it always happens that the idea of one particular experience presents itself to me which therefore is, in a sense, my experience *par excellence* and this is the reason why, in talking to you now, I will use this experience as my first and foremost example. (As I have said before, this is an entirely personal matter and others would find other examples more striking). I will describe this experience in order, if possible, to make you recall the same or similar experiences, so that we may have a common ground for our investigation. I believe the best way of describing it is to say that when I have it *I wonder at the existence of the world*. And I am then inclined to use such phrases as "how extraordinary that anything should exist" or "how extraordinary that the world should exist". I will mention another experience straight away which I also know[12] and which others of you might be acquainted with: it is, what one might call, the experience of feeling *absolutely* safe. I mean the state of mind in which one is inclined to say "I am safe, nothing can injure me whatever happens". Now let me consider these experiences, for, I believe, they exhibit the very characteristics we try to get clear about. And there the first thing I have to say is, that the verbal expression which we give to these experiences is nonsense! If I say "I wonder at the existence of the world" I am misusing language. Let me explain this. It has a perfectly good and clear sense to say that I wonder at something being the case, we all understand what it means to say that I wonder at the size of a dog which is bigger than anyone I have ever seen before or at any thing which, in the common sense of the word, is extraordinary. In every such a case I wonder at something being the case which I *could* conceive *not* to be the case. I wonder at the size of this dog because I could conceive of a dog of another, namely the ordinary size, at which I should not wonder. To say "I wonder at such and such being the case" has only sense if I can imagine it not to be the case. In this sense one can wonder at the existence of, say, a house when one sees it and has not visited it for a long time and has imagined that it had been pulled down in the meantime. But it is nonsense to say that I wonder at the existence of the world, because I cannot imagine it not existing. I could of course wonder at the world

---

12 Wittgenstein was possibly referring here to the experience he had whilst attending the performance of *Die Kreuzschreiber* which influenced him so much during the First World War.

round me being as it is. If for instance I had this experience while looking into the blue sky, I could wonder at the sky being blue as opposed to the case when it's clouded. But that's not what I mean. I am wondering at the sky being *whatever it is*. One might be tempted to say that what I am wondering at is a tautology, namely at the sky being blue or not blue. But then it's just nonsense to say that one is wondering at a tautology. Now the same applies to the other experience[s] which I have mentioned, the experience of absolute safety. We all know what it means in ordinary life to be safe. I am safe in my room, when I cannot be run over by an omnibus. I am safe if I have had whooping cough and cannot therefore get it again. To be safe essentially means that it is physically impossible that certain things should happen to me and therefore it's nonsense to say that I am safe *whatever* happens. Again this is a misuse of the word "safe" as the other example was of a misuse of the word "existence" or "wondering". Now I want to impress on you that a certain characteristic misuse of our language runs through *all* ethical and religious expressions. All these expressions *seem*, prima facie, to be just *similes*. Thus it seems that when we are using the word *right* in an ethical sense, although, what we mean, is not right in its trivial sense, it's something similar, and when we say "This is a good fellow", although the word good here doesn't mean what it means in the sentence "This is a good football player" there seems to be some similarity. And when we say "This man's life is valuable" we don't mean it in the same sense in which we would speak of some valuable jewelry but there seems to be some sort of analogy. Now all religious terms seem in this sense to be used as similes or allegorically. For when we speak of God and that he sees everything and when we kneel and pray to him all our terms and actions seem to be parts of a great and elaborate allegory which represents him as a human being of great power whose grace we try to win, etc., etc. But this allegory also describes the experience[s] which I have just referred to. For the first of them is, I believe, exactly what people were referring to when they said that God had created the world; and the experience of absolute safety has been described by saying that we feel safe in the hands of God. A third experience of the same kind is that of feeling guilty and again this was described by the phrase that God disapproves of our conduct. Thus in ethical and religious language we seem constantly to be using similes. But a simile must be the simile for *something*. And if I can describe a fact by means of a simile I must also be able to drop the simile and to describe the facts without it. Now in our case as soon as we try to drop the simile and simply to state the facts which stand behind it, we find that there are no such facts. And so, what at first appeared to be a simile now seems to be mere nonsense. Now the three experiences which I have mentioned to you (and I could have added others) seem to those who have experienced them, for instance to me, to have in some sense an intrinsic, absolute value. But when I say they are experiences, surely, they are facts; they have taken place then and there, lasted a certain definite time and consequently are describable. And so from what I have said some minutes ago I must admit it is nonsense to say that they have absolute value. And I will make my point still more acute by saying "It is the paradox that an experience, a fact, should seem to have supernatural value". Now there is a way in which I would be tempted to meet this paradox. Let me first consider, again, our first experience of wondering at the existence of the world and let me describe it in a slightly different way; we all know what in ordinary life would be called a miracle. It obviously is simply an event the like of which we have never yet seen. Now suppose such an event happened. Take the case that one of you suddenly grew a lion's head and began to roar. Certainly that would be as extraordinary a thing as I can imagine. Now whenever we should have recovered from our surprise, what I would suggest would be to fetch a doctor and have the case scientifically investigated and if it were not for hurting him I would have him vivisected. And where would the miracle have got to? For it is clear that when we look at it in this way everything miraculous has disappeared; unless what we mean by this term is merely that a fact has not yet been explained by science which again means that we have hitherto failed to group this fact with others in a scientific system. This shows that it is absurd to say "Science has proved that there are no miracles". The truth is that the scientific way of looking at a fact is not the way to look at it as a miracle. For imagine whatever fact you may, it is not in itself miraculous in the absolute sense of that term. For we see now that we have been using the word "miracle" in a relative and an absolute sense. And I will now describe the experience of wondering at the existence of the world by saying: it is the experience of seeing the world as a miracle. Now I am tempted to say that the right expression in language for the miracle of the existence of the world, though it is not any proposition *in* language, is the existence of language itself. But what then does it mean to be aware of this miracle at some times and not at other times? For all I have said by shifting the expression of the miraculous from an expression *by means of* language to the expression *by the existence* of language, all I have said is again that we cannot express what we want to express and that all we *say* about the absolute miraculous remains nonsense. Now the answer to all this will seem perfectly clear to many of you. You will say: Well, if certain experiences constantly tempt us to attribute a quality to them which we call absolute or ethical value and importance, this simply shows that by these words we *don't* mean nonsense, that after all what we mean by saying that an experience has absolute value *is just a fact like other facts* and that all it comes to is that we have not yet succeeded in finding the correct logical analysis of what we mean by our ethical and religious expressions. Now when this is urged against me I at once see clearly, as it were in a flash of light, not only that no description that I can think of would do to describe what I mean by absolute value, but that I would reject every significant description that anybody could possibly suggest, *ab initio*, on the ground of its significance. That is to say: I see now that these nonsensical expressions were not nonsensical because I had not yet found the correct expressions, but that their nonsensicality was their very essence. For all I wanted to do with them was just *to go beyond* the world and that is to say beyond significant language. My whole tendency and I believe the tendency of all men who ever tried to write or talk Ethics or Religion was to run against the boundaries of language. This running against the walls of our cage is perfectly, absolutely hopeless. Ethics so far as it springs from the desire to say something about the ultimate meaning of life, the absolute good, the absolute value, can be no science. What it says does not add to our knowledge in any sense. But it is a document of a tendency in the human mind which I personally cannot help respecting deeply and I would not for my life ridicule it.

Ludwig Wittgenstein

20.11.1929
Could one say: "I seem to be sad, so I'll become disheartened"?
The God who finds his place in the world and therefore in language would be an idol.
MS 107 202

25.12.1929
I'm a swine[13] and yet I'm not unhappy because of it. I'm in danger of becoming even more superficial. God forbid!
MS 108 38

28.12.1929
Something inside is urging me to write my biography and I would indeed like to give a clear account of my life at some point for others and so as to see it clearly before me. Not so much to make judgements about it but at least for clarity and truth.

This afternoon I was listening to Koder playing piano to me. I urged him to be more serious about the piano playing for in my opinion his performance wasn't serious enough. Then I turned to Helene[14] and whistled Schubert songs to her accompaniment but I wasn't really concentrating on the music. I kept thinking about myself and couldn't really get a feel for the pieces or give myself fully to the task. I wasn't being truly earnest at all. I was doing something but it was never or almost never the right thing. I told myself I was being serious but it was all going straight over my head. I felt like a swine because I too was mixing what was real with what was unreal. May God grant me purity and truth!
MS 108 46-7

---

13 As can be seen by this and some other texts, Wittgenstein's self-accusations were frequent.
14 Helene 'Lenka' Wittgenstein-Salzer (1879–1956). Wittgenstein's sister.

c.1929

My ideal is a certain coolness. A temple providing a setting for the passions without meddling with them.

CV

1929

Wittgenstein asked me this afternoon to come out for a walk with him. We walked to Madingly and back. He asked me about my childhood. I found we had both the same game of inventing an imaginary country and writing its history in a private code we had invented. He said he thought that this was very common among children. He then went on to tell me that as a child he had suffered greatly from morbid fears. In the lavatory of his home some plaster had fallen from the wall and he always saw this pattern as a duck, but it terrified him: it had the appearance for him of those monsters that Bosch painted in his 'Temptations of St. Anthony'. Even when he was a student at Manchester he suffered at times from morbid fears. To get from his bedroom to his sitting room he had to cross over a landing, and sometimes he found himself dreading making this crossing. We were at that time walking quite briskly, but he suddenly stopped still and looked at me very seriously.

> WITTGENSTEIN: "You will think I am crazy, you will think I have gone mad, when I tell you that only religious feelings are a cure for such fears".

I replied that I didn't think that was crazy at all; that coming from Ireland I knew something of the power of religion. He seemed displeased as if I hadn't understood him.

> WITTGENSTEIN: "I am not talking about superstition but about real religious feeling".

After this we walked on in silence for some time.

M. O'C. DRURY,[15] **PR, pp. 115–16**

1929

In view of our conversation on the way back from Madingly I thought it necessary to tell Wittgenstein that, after leaving Cambridge, I intended to be ordained as an Anglican priest.

---

15 Maurice O'Connor Drury (1907–76). A student of Wittgenstein at Trinity College and a close friend until Wittgenstein's death. He later became a psychiatrist.

WITTGENSTEIN: "Don't think I ridicule this for one minute, but I can't approve; no, I can't approve. I would be afraid that one day that collar would choke you".

We went on to talk about the Bible. I said that for me the Old Testament was no more than a collection of Hebrew folk-lore and that whether it was true history didn't matter at all. But I felt quite differently about the New Testament: that lost its significance if it wasn't an account of what really happened.

WITTGENSTEIN: "For me too the Old Testament is a collection of Hebrew folk-lore – yes, I would use that expression. But the New Testament doesn't have to be proved to be true by historians either. It would make no difference if there had never been an historical person as Jesus is portrayed in the Gospels; though I don't think any competent authority doubts that there really was such a person".

M. O'C. DRURY, PR, p. 116

1929

Today a further discussion with Wittgenstein about my intention to be ordained.

WITTGENSTEIN: "Just think, Drury, what it would mean to have to preach a sermon every week; you couldn't do it. I don't mean that there haven't been people in the past who were great preachers, but there are no such people today".

I told him that as a boy I had been greatly influenced by the seriousness and deep piety of an Anglo-Catholic priest in Exeter (Fr. E.C. Long, rector of St. Olave's Church).

WITTGENSTEIN: "I know how impressive such a person can be. I have only one objection: that there is a certain narrowness about them. There are some subjects you feel you can't discuss with them. In one point I do agree with Russell: I like to feel free to discuss anything with anyone I am with".

Then after a pause, he sighed and said: "Russell and the parsons between them have done infinite harm, infinite harm".

I was puzzled by his coupling Russell and the parsons in the one condemnation.

WITTGENSTEIN: "I would be afraid that you would try and give some sort of philosophical justification for Christian beliefs, as if some sort of proof was needed. You have intelligence; it is not the best thing about you, but it is something you mustn't ignore. – The symbolisms of Catholicism are wonderful beyond words. But any attempt to make it into a philosophical system is offensive.

"All religions are wonderful, even those of the most primitive tribes. The ways in which people express their religious feelings differ enormously".

DRURY: "I think I could be happy working as a priest among people whom I felt shared the same beliefs as I have".

WITTGENSTEIN: "Oh, don't depend on circumstances. Make sure that your religion is a matter between you and God only".

After we had talked a little longer he went on to say that there had been only two great religious writers in Europe of recent times, Tolstoy and Dostoievsky. We in the West were inclined to forget the existence of the Eastern Orthodox Church with its millions of members. He advised me to read *The Brothers Karamazov*. When he was a schoolmaster in Austria he read this book constantly, and at one time read it aloud to the village priest.

M. O'C. DRURY, PR, pp. 116–18

Cambridge, after 23 November 1929
Letter from Wittgenstein to Ludwig Hänsel[16]

L.H.!

Thanks for your letter. I don't agree with you, you know that. And I will briefly say why not. I consider both parties[17] indecent. The red one appears less onerous to me <u>only insofar</u> as its indecency is in keeping with the times, whereas that of the others is moreover one that is retrograde. That is I would mention in passing the greens & blacks haven't even gotten so far yet. Further: All of these parties lack religion but the greatest danger for religiosity seems to me to lie with the green party, in roughly the same sense in which the lukewarm is more distant from the warm than is the cold, though that sounds paradoxical; but you also knows where it comes from. Open hostility to religion seems more promising to me than the other disgusting conviction, which is on personal terms with religion & with God & drags it down to its own level. I am not dumb enough to believe that a "noble atheism" rules the red party, instead there too everything is cloaked & false, but by

---

16 Wittgenstein met Hänsel at Cassino, where they were prisoners of war. Their relationship surely begun at the beginning of 1919.

17 'Red' Means Social Democrat Party, the opposition in 1927. 'Black' means the Christian-Social Party, and 'green' the nationalistic Landbund. The last two formed a coalition composing the government together with the Großdeutschen.

a slight degree less well cloaked & therefore less dangerous to the soul than a conviction that manages to be apparently on good terms with the highest ideals. It would be a long matter to explain why the party system in other countries, for example in England, is at least not yet a disgrace to every decent human being; but in our special situation I believe that all parties are hopeless & the only extreme faint hope rests on the few, who do not believe that something good can nevertheless come from supporting an indecent thing. That is, I believe that in this case it is not right to choose between two evils but to repudiate both equally, since all misery here comes about precisely through this that no one has enough character to radically stress the demand of decency & doesn't in the end make a deal after all. Where the situation is as acute as with us, a greater seriousness of decision is also necessary, of course, than elsewhere. It is just as in the life of the individual whose decision in less serious situations can more or less follow tradition, but who must make a nonbourgeois decision if an extraordinary situation occurs. – If the state – like ours – has lost its cultural (secular bourgeois) meaning, its only hope – I believe – rests on those who recognize the seriousness of this situation & now call upon a higher power for a decision where the secular/bourgeois power (the magistrate, so to speak) has lost his divine right. That's how I see the matter. The greater the treasure the better one must guard it & the higher the ideal the more careful one must be in the choice of the means for upholding it. If you believe that you have to wrap your ideal in old rags so that nothing happens to it, then look out that it won't evaporate in the end & you hold nothing but a sack of old rags. But I am not afraid of that in your case; you won't let it evaporate, but you must think of those to whom you hand the package that they won't take the packaging for the ideal. Much more could be said about this but I can't go on anymore.
LH

29.06.1930[18]
If anyone should think he has solved the problem of life & feels like telling himself everything is quite easy now, he need only tell himself, in order to see that he is wrong, that there was a time when this "solution" had not been discovered; but it must have been possible to live *then* too & the solution which has now been discovered appears in relation to how things were then like an accident. And it is the same for us in logic too. If there were a "solution to the problems of logic

---

18 In March of that year, he had written to Moore to tell him how his work was coming along. He was immersed in the development of his *Philosophische Bemerkungen* and wanted to ask for help from Trinity College in order to continue with his research. The Trinity Council commissioned Moore to procure favourable reports from Russell and the mathematician J.E. Littlewood. Finally, on 5 December, the Council would inform Wittgenstein that had been selected for a type-B fellowship.

(philosophy)" we should only have to caution ourselves that there was a time when they had not been solved (and then too it must have been possible to live and think) –
CV

22.08.1930
Similarly when E.[19] looks at this writings and finds them splendid (even though he would not care to publish any of the pieces individually) he is seeing his life as God's work of art, & and as such it is certainly worth contemplating, as is every life & everything whatever. But only the artist can represent the individual thing so that it appears to us as a work of art; those manuscripts *rightly* lose their value if we contemplate them singly & in any case without *prejudice*, i.e. without being enthusiastic about them in advance. The work of art compels us – as one might say – to see it in the right perspective, but without art the object is a piece of nature like any other & the fact that *we* may exalt it through our enthusiasm does not give anyone the right to display it to us. (I am always reminded of one of those insipid photographs of a piece of scenery which is interesting to the person who took it because he was there himself, experienced something, but which a third party looks at with justifiable coldness; insofar as it is ever justifiable to look at something with coldness.)

But now it seems to me too that besides the work of the artist there is another through which the world may be captured sub specie aeterni. It is – as I believe – the way of thought which as it were flies above the world and leaves it the way it is, contemplating it from above in its flight.
CV

04.10.1930
Am saddened by the thought of not being able to help M.[20] I am very weak & moody. If I remain strong, with the help of God, I can perhaps help her through that. It is possible that what she needs most of all is a strong & firm post that remains standing no matter how she flutters. Whether I will have the strength for that? And the necessary loyalty? May God grant me what is necessary.
MT

07.10.1930
Looking for an apartment & feeling miserable & restless. Incapable of collecting myself. Have not received a letter from M. & that too worries me. Terrible that there is no possibility of helping her or that at any rate I don't know how she can

---

19 Engelmann.
20 Marguerite Respinger de Chambrier (1904–2000). A Swiss woman friend of Wittgenstein and allegedly his girlfriend in the early 1930s.

be helped. I don't know what word from me would do her good or whether it would be best for her to hear nothing from me. Which word won't she misunderstand? Which will she need? One can almost always answer both ways & must ultimately leave it to God.

[...]

I asked Moore today whether he is glad when I come to see him regularly (as in the previous year) & said that I will not be offended whatever the answers turns out to be. He said that it wasn't clear to himself, & I: he should thing it over & inform me; which he promised to do. I said I could not promise that his answer will not sadden me, yet, however, that it will not offend me. – And I believe it is God's will with me, That I shall hear & <u>bear</u> it.
MT

18.10.1930
The manner in writing is a sort of mask behind which the heart makes faces as it pleases. Genuine modesty is a religious matter.
MT

05.11.1930
In Renan's[21] Peuple d'Israël I read: "Birth, sickness, death, madness, catalepsy, sleep, dreams, all made an infinite impression and, even nowadays, it is given to only a small number to see clearly that these phenomena have causes within our constitution. <"> On the contrary there is absolutely no reason to marvel at such things; because they are such everyday occurrences. If primitive human beings *must* marvel at them, how much more so dogs & monkeys. Or is it being assumed that human beings suddenly awoke as it were & noticed these things which had always been there & were understandably amazed? Well, one might even assume something like this; not however that they became aware of these things for the first time, but rather that they suddenly began to marvel at them. But that too has nothing to do with their being primitive. Unless we call it primitive not to marvel at things, in which case it is precisely the people of today & Renan himself who are primitive, if he believes that scientific explanation could enhance wonderment.

As though today lightning were more commonplace or less astounding than 2000 years ago.

In order to marvel human beings – and perhaps peoples – have to wake up. Science is a way of sending them off to sleep again.

---

21 Ernst Renan (1823–92). French philosopher and historian of religion. He left the Catholic Church in 1845 because he thought that Church teachings collided with historical criticism.

I.e. it is simply false to say: of course, these primitive peoples *had* to marvel at everything. But perhaps right that these people *did* marvel at everything around them. – To think they had to marvel at them is a primitive superstition. (Like that of thinking that they *had* to fear all the forces of nature & that we of course do not have to fear. On the other hand experience may show that certain primitive tribes are very strongly inclined to fear natural phenomena. – But we cannot exclude the possibility that highly civilized peoples will become liable to this very same fear again & their civilization and the knowledge of science will not protect them from this. All the same it is true that the *spirit* in which science is carried on nowadays is not compatible with fear of this kind).

What Renan calls the bon sens précoce of the semitic races (an idea that I already entertained a long time ago) is their *unpoetic* mentality, which heads straight for what is concrete. Which is characteristic of my philosophy.

Things are right before our eyes, not covered by any veil. – This is where religion & art part company.
CV

06–07.11.1930
Everything ritualistic (everything that, as it were, smacks of the high priest) is strictly to be avoided because is straightaway turns rotten.

Of course a kiss is a ritual too & it isn't rotten; but no more ritual is permissible than is a genuine as a kiss.
CV

08.11.1930
I would like to say "this book has been written for the glory of God", but that would be a misnomer today, ie it wouldn't be correctly understood. It means it has been written with good intentions and in so far as it is not written with good intentions but for reasons of vanity etc., that's the extent by which the writer wishes to have it judged. He cannot purify it further from these ingredients than to the extent that he is purified of it himself.

When one reaches the limits of one's own decency this is where a kind of vortex of thoughts exists, an endless regress: one can say what one wants but it doesn't get one any further.

I am surrendering this book to all those who are well disposed to the spirit in which it is meant.

In my earlier book[22] the solution to problems is presented in a way that is far too unadventurous. It still looks too much as if discoveries are needed to solve

---

22 The *Tractatus*.

our problems and it is all too little the form of grammatical matters of course brought in the usual way of expressing oneself. It still all looks too much like discoveries.
MS 109 212–13

---

26 [11 or 12] 1930
A being that stands in contact with God is strong.
MT

17.12.1930[23]

ON SCHLICK'S ETHICS

Schlick[24] says that in theological ethics there used to be two conceptions of the essence of the good: according to the shallower interpretation the good is good because it is what God wants; according to the profounder interpretation God wants the good because it is good. I think that the first interpretation is the profounder one: what God commands, that is good. For it cuts off the way to any explanation 'why' it is good, while the second interpretation is the shallow, rationalist one, which proceeds 'as if' you could give reasons for what is good.

The first conception says clearly that the essence of the good has nothing to do with facts and hence cannot be explained by any proposition. If there is any proposition expressing precisely what I think, it is the proposition 'What God commands, that is good'.

VALUE

In describing reality I describe what I come upon among men. Similarly, sociology must describe our conduct and our valuations just like those of the Negroes. It can only report what occurs. But the proposition, 'Such-and-such means progress', must never occur in a sociologist's description.

---

23 The *Tractatus* had ended up being a reference work for the Vienna Circle, which represented the maximum expression of logical positivism. The leader of the group was Moritz Schlick. Wittgenstein met Waismann and Schlick several times to talk about his ideas, but they were moving further away from those outlined in the *Tractatus*. The biggest difference at that time, however, was related to the importance Wittgenstein gave to questions of religion and ethics, treated in the *Tractatus* as *nonsense*. For logical positivists – particularly O. Neurath and A.J. Ayer – this special value given to the subject of what was inexpressible was especially irritating.
24 Moritz Schlick (1882–1936). German philosopher, founder of the Vienna Circle. Killed by a Nazi ex-student.

What I can describe is that preferences are stated. Suppose I discovered by experience that of two pictures you always prefer the one containing more green, or a greenish tinge, etc. In this case I have described only *that* but not that the picture in question is more valuable.

What is valuable in a Beethoven sonata? The sequence of notes? No, it is only one sequence among many, after all. Indeed, I would go so far as to say that even the feelings Beethoven had when he was composing this sonata were not more valuable than any other feelings. And the fact of being preferred has equally little claim to be something valuable in itself.

Is value a particular state of mind? Or a form attaching to some data or other of consciousness? I would reply that whatever I was told, I would reject, and that not because the explanation was false but because it was an explanation.

If it were told anything that was a *theory*, I would say, No, no! That does not interest me. Even if this theory were true, it would not interest me – it would not be the exact thing I was looking for.

What is ethical cannot be taught. If I could explain the essence of the ethical only by means of a theory, then what is ethical would be of no value whatsoever.

At the end of my lecture on ethics I spoke in the first person: I think that this is something very essential. Here there is nothing to be stated any more; all I can do is to step forth as an individual and speak in the first person.

For me a theory is without value. A theory gives me nothing.

RELIGION

Is talking essential to religion? I can well imagine a religion in which there are no doctrinal propositions, in which there is thus no talking. Obviously the essence of religion cannot have anything to do with the fact that there is talking, or rather: when people talk, then this itself is part of a religious act and not a theory. Thus it also does not matter at all if the words used are true or false or nonsense.

In religion talking is not *metaphorical* either; for otherwise it would have to be possible to say the same things in prose. Running against the limits of language? Language is, after all, not a cage.

All I can say is this: I do not scoff at this tendency in man; I hold it in reverence. And here it is essential that this is not a description of sociology but I am speaking *about myself*.

The facts of the matter are of no importance for me. But what men mean when they say that '*the world is there*' is something I have at heart.

WAISMANN[25] ASKS: Is the existence of the world connected with what is ethical?

---

25 Friedrich Waismann (1896–1959). Austrian philosopher, member of the Vienna Circle. In 1938 he became a reader in philosophy at Cambridge University, moving to Oxford in 1939.

WITTGENSTEIN: Men have felt that here there is a connection and they have expressed it thus: God the Father created the world, the Son of God (or the Word that comes from God) is that which is ethical. That the Godhead is thought of as divided and, again, as one being indicates that there is a connection here.

OUGHT

What does the word 'ought' mean? A child ought to do such-and-such means that if he does not do it, something unpleasant will happen. Reward and punishment. The essential thing about this is that the other person is brought to do something. 'Ought' makes sense only if there is something lending support and force to it – a power that punishes and rewards. Ought in itself is nonsensical.

'To moralize is difficult, to establish morality impossible'.
VC, pp. 115–17

1930

DRURY: "I find Lotze very heavy going, very dull".

WITTGENSTEIN: "Probably a man who shouldn't have been allowed to write philosophy. A book you should read is William James's *Varieties of Religious Experience*; that was a book that helped me a lot at one time".[26]

DRURY: "Oh yes, I have read that. I always enjoy reading anything of William James. He is such a human person".

WITTGENSTEIN: "That is what makes him a good philosopher; he was a real human being".

M. O'C. DRURY, PR, p. 121

1930

Another book he noticed on my shelves was Schweitzer's[27] *The Quest for the Historical Jesus*.

> WITTGENSTEIN: "The only value of that book is that it shews how many, many different ways people can interpret the Gospel story".

M. O'C. DRURY, PR, p. 121

---

26 See, for instance, the letter to Russell of 22.06.1912; or Russell's letter to Lady Ottoline Morrell of 20.12.1919.

27 Albert Schweitzer (1875–1965). French theologian, philosopher and doctor. Awarded the Nobel Prize for Peace in 1952.

1930
Before going out we sat for a time talking. He had evidently been looking at something of von Hügel's since our conversation of a few days previously.

> WITTGENSTEIN: "von Hügel[28] seems to have been a very pure character, almost a Roman Catholic".
> DRURY: "But von Hügel was a Roman Catholic. He was closely connected with what was called the Modernist movement[29] at the beginning of this century".
> WITTGENSTEIN: "People who call themselves Modernists are the most deceived of all. I will tell you what Modernism is like: in *The Brothers Karamazov* the old father says that the monks in the nearby monastery believe that the devils have hooks to pull people down into Hell; 'Now? says the old father, 'I can't believe in those hooks'. That is the same sort of mistake that Modernists make when they misunderstand the nature of symbolism".

We then set off for our walk.

> WITTGENSTEIN: "I have been reading a German Author, a contemporary of Kant's, Hamman,[30] where he says, commenting on the story of the Fall in Genesis:[31] "How like God to wait until the cool of the evening before confronting Adam with his transgression'. Now I wouldn't for the life of me dare to say, 'how like God'. I wouldn't claim to know how God should act. Do you understand Hamman's remark? Tell me what you think – I would really like to know".
> DRURY: "Perhaps if something terrible had happened to one at a time when you felt strong enough to bear it, then one might say: Thank God this didn't happen before, when I could not have stood up to it".
> Wittgenstein didn't seem pleased with this answer.

---

28 Friedrich von Hügel (1852-1925). Austrian theologian linked to the Modernist movement, though he remained faithful to the Catholic Church. His most important works are: *The Mystical Element of Religion* (1908), *Essays and Addresses* (1921) and *The Reality of God* (1931).

29 The Movement arises within the Catholic Church attempting to combine the developments of modern thinking with Catholic theology, weakening ecclesiastical authority. Modernism ended denying Christ's divinity (the Christ of history would not be the Christ of faith), the divine foundation of Church and of sacraments, clearly attacking the dogmatic aspects of Christian doctrine. Its main supporters were Alfred Loisy (1857-1940) and George Tyrrell (1861-1909). The Movement was condemned by Pope St. Pious X's encyclical *Pascendi Dominici Gregis* (08.09.1907). The Pope states in it that Modernism holds any heresy. The encyclical, which deals with Modernist postulates, stresses that such point of view helps to strengthen agnosticism and immanence in matters of faith and morality.

30 Johann Georg Hamann (1730-88). German philosopher born in Königsberg. A friend of Kant though strongly critical to his work.

31 The story appears in chapter 3 of the Book of Genesis.

WITTGENSTEIN: "For a truly religious man nothing is tragic".
We walked on in silence for a time. Then he said.
WITTGENSTEIN: "It is a dogma of the Roman Church that the existence of God can be proved by natural reason.[32] Now this dogma would make it impossible for me to be a Roman Catholic. If I thought of God as another being like myself, outside myself, only infinitely more powerful, then I would regard it as my duty to defy him".

M. O'C. DRURY, PR, pp. 122–3

1930

On the way back from the walk we passed a street preacher who was proclaiming in a loud, raucous voice all that Jesus Christ had done for him. Wittgenstein shook his head sadly.

WITTGENSTEIN: "If he really meant what he was shouting, he wouldn't be speaking in that tone of voice. This is a kind of vulgarity in which at least you can be sure that the Roman Catholic Church will never indulge. On the other hand, during the war the Germans got Krupps[33] to make a steel, bomb-proof container to convey the consecrated Host to the troops in the front line. This was disgusting. It should have had no protection from human hands at all".

M. O'C. DRURY, PR, p. 126

1930(?)

Wittgenstein presented me with a copy of Dr. Johnson's[34] *Prayers*.
We talked about the ancient Liturgies, particularly the collects in the Latin Mass.

DRURY: "Isn't it important that there should be ordained priests to carry on this tradition? That was my idea in wanting to be ordained".
WITTGENSTEIN: "At first sight it would seem a wonderful idea that there should be in every village someone who stood for these things. But it

---

32 This dogma was defined by Pope Pius IX during the First Vatican Council (1869–70).
33 The Krupp family is notoriously known for its links with steel industry in Germany, earning enormous sums of money manufacturing weapons (for the two world wars) and railway equipment. We might also say that the Wittgenstein family was to Austria more or less what the Krupp family was to Germany.
34 Samuel Johnson (1709–84). Eighteenth-century essayist of Anglican belief. Best known for his work *Prayers and Meditations*.

hasn't worked out that way at all. For all you and I can tell, the religion of the future will be without any priests or ministers. I think one of the things you and I have to learn is that we have to live without the consolation of belonging to a church. If you feel you must belong to some organization, why don't you join the Quakers?"[35]

The very next morning he came to see me, to see that he had been quite wrong to suggest my becoming a Quaker. I was to forget that he ever mentioned it. "As if nowadays any one organization was better than another".

WITTGENSTEIN: "Of one thing I am certain. The religion of the future will have to be extremely ascetic; and by that I don't mean just going without food and drink".

I seemed to sense for the first time in my life the idea of an asceticism of the intellect. That this life of reading and discussing in the comfort of Cambridge society, which I so enjoyed, was something I would have to renounce. Wittgenstein saw that I was troubled.

WITTGENSTEIN: "But remember that Christianity is not a matter of saying a lot of prayers; in fact we are told not to do that. If you and I are to live religious lives, it mustn't be that we talk a lot about religion, but that our manner of life is different. It is my belief that only if you try to be helpful to other people will you in the end find your way to God".

Just as I was leaving he suddenly said, "There is a sense in which you and I are both Christians".

M. O'C. DRURY, PR, pp. 129-30

1930 (?)
We were talking one day about prayer and I mentioned to Wittgenstein how very impressive I found the ancient liturgical prayers of the Latin rite and their translation in the Anglican prayer-book.

WITTGENSTEIN: Yes, those prayers read as if they had been soaked in centuries of worship. When I was a prisoner of war in Italy we were compelled to attend Mass on Sundays. I was very glad of that compulsion.

---

35 Religious group whose official name is "The Religious Society of Friends". Its most prominent figure was George Fox (1624–91), founder of this new dissident Anglican sect. The name "quaker" is from "trembling with fear at the Word of God". They lack a properly established doctrine, rejecting the existence of priest and sacraments. Pennsylvania's founder, William Penn (1644–1718), is another of the illustrious Quakers.

He went on to say that he had at one time begun each day by repeating the Lord's prayer,[36] but that he had not done so now for some time. He did not say why he had discontinued this practice.

> WITTGENSTEIN: It is the most extraordinary prayer ever written. No one ever composed a prayer like it. But remember that the Christian religion does not consist in saying a lot of prayers, in fact we are commanded just the opposite. If you and I are to live religious lives it must not just be that we talk a lot about religion, but that in some way our lives are different.

PR, p. 109

1930 (?)
We were walking in Cambridge and passed a book shop. In the Windows there was a book entitled "The Bible designed to be read as literature".

> WITTGENSTEIN: "Now I wouldn't want to look at that. I don't want some literary gent to make selections from the Bible for me."
> DRURY: "I am at present reading a commentary on the Epistle to the Romans by a Swiss theologian, Karl Barth.[37] It seems to me a remarkable book".
> WITTGENSTEIN: "Moore and I once tried to read the Epistle to the Romans together; but we didn't get very far with it and gave it up".

The next day I asked him if I might read out to him something of Karl Barth's. I had with me the volume called 'The Word of God and the Word of Man'. I had only been reading for a short time when Wittgenstein told me to stop.

> WITTGENSTEIN: "I don't want to hear any more. The only impression I get is one of great arrogance".

M. O'C. DRURY, PR, pp. 133–4

F.R. LEAVIS[38]
(1929–30?)
I will relate a characteristic instance that, in the concrete, was for me profoundly impressive. I had a pupil, R., bearer of a distinguished Victorian name, who insisted on coming to me though he didn't belong to one of "my" colleges. He

---

36 The "Our Father".
37 Karl Barth (1886–1968). Swiss theologian in the Reformed tradition. Studied at the universities of Tübingen, Berlin and Marburg. He strongly questioned the liberal tradition in theology.
38 Leavis was born on 14 July 1895. A fellow of Downing College and university reader in English at Cambridge from 1936 to 1961.

soon got to feel that I didn't sufficiently appreciate his distinction, and I for my part thought that in his own estimate of that distinction, and of the critical authority which that gave him, his sense of the family connexion counted for too much. Anyway, we recognized that we were not congenial to one another, and the things said between us meant that the relation had to come to an end. I can't remember what the young man's status was, but he was certainly not a first-year undergraduate, and I was not altogether surprised when I heard that he had gained admission to Wittgenstein's lectures. I *was*, however, surprised when Wittgenstein, quite inapropos of anything that had passed between us, said: "R. thinks highly of you." I replied: "I don't really care what R. thinks of me". "You ought to care," said Wittgenstein. Thinking this decidedly an instance of the Wittgenstein quality when it deserved rebuke as too like arrogance, or something closely akin, I retorted with marked quietness: "Do you know that R.'s final remark to me was?" Then (for Wittgenstein only looked), reproducing as well as I could R.'s tone and intention: "He said as he turned to go: 'You're like Jesus Christ'". Wittgenstein's reaction to this exemplified a profound characteristic that had its bearing on one's judgment of the "arrogance": "That's an extraordinary thing to say!"
PR, p. 68

3
1931–1940

The beginning of the 1930s found Wittgenstein again deeply immersed in philosophical work. The celebration of his return to Cambridge is illustrated by the famous comment of J.M. Keynes to Lydia Lopokova:[1] "Well, God has arrived. I met him on the 5.15 train". He returned in January and received his doctorate in June. His doctoral dissertation was no less than the *Tractatus*, with both Russell and Moore as examiners. If Wittgenstein returned to philosophy it was because he was convinced that he had something new to say. In spite of the overwhelming words with which he had ended his first philosophical writings, it was his own coherence that led him to reconsider his standpoints and decide to start all over again. He applied for a research fellowship and started working from a new philosophical perspective. Those years were ones of prolificacy and deep discussions on the influence of the *Tractatus*. He entered into most bitter, and, at times, very controversial disputes with some members of the Vienna Circle, owing to what Wittgenstein claimed was their misinterpretation of his work. The main points of controversy were the epistemological role of metaphysic and religious statements. The majority of the Circle members were not only opposed to these statements but also had a disparaging attitude towards them, especially Otto Neurath.

In his conversations with Waismann, Wittgenstein defended the significance of religious and ethical matters, at the same time stressing the impossibility of an appropriate use of language when talking about them. However, their meaning in existential terms did put them in a privileged place, so to speak. This justifies Wittgenstein's statement: "All I can say is this: I do not scoff at this tendency in man; I hold it in reverence. And here it is essential that this is not a description of sociology but I am speaking *about myself*". However, such considerations were not

---

1 Keynes's wife (1892–1981).

Ludwig Wittgenstein: The Meaning of Life, First Edition. Edited by Joaquín Jareño-Alarcón.
© 2023 John Wiley & Sons Ltd. Published 2023 by John Wiley & Sons Ltd.

well received by all members of the Vienna Circle. Many years later, and in some kind of *reckoning* with Wittgenstein, Alfred J. Ayer,[2] clearly indebted to Logical Positivism, still criticized the value of *important nonsense*, that is, of religious and ethical matters as treated by Wittgenstein in his *Tractatus*.

These years saw a gradual emergence of a new, revolutionary concept of philosophy. Wittgenstein started reconsidering his old viewpoints. He became highly critical of them and distanced himself from them. However, despite the changes in his philosophy, the significance given to matters of religion and the meaning of life remained unchanged. Philosophical problems arose due to a misuse of grammar, and once they were cleared, they disappeared. In philosophy, then, we have only tangles and linguistic riddles. Wittgenstein's *Philosophical Grammar* belongs to this period. The so-called *Blue Book* was finished in 1934 and the *Brown Book* in 1935. Both were preliminary works for the development of what was to become Wittgenstein's great second masterpiece – *Philosophical Investigations*, on which he worked during the latter years of the decade.

These years also witnessed extraordinary political upheavals in Europe and worldwide, events in which Wittgenstein, given his particular viewpoints as well as his condition of being an Austrian Jew, was to become personally involved. The 1930s saw an unprecedented confrontation between two opposing political views: communism and fascism. They were marked by terrible Stalinist purges and by the coming to power in Germany of an Austrian called Adolf Hitler and his Nazi party, plunging Europe back to dark ages. Wittgenstein was somehow affected by both extremes of ideological confrontation. He wished to travel to the USSR, presumably motivated by the ascetic ideal of simplicity promoted by the Soviet propaganda. According to Wittgenstein's biographer Monk, this interest could be explained by Keynes's presentation of Soviet Marxism as some kind of religion,[3] although Ludwig's intention had probably arisen prior to that. Wittgenstein's history shows that this idea of his was quite unrealistic, idyllic and utopian. He intended to give up his academic life, move to Russia and work as a manual labourer. While Wittgenstein's political orientation[4] cannot be clearly identified,

---

2 *Wittgenstein*. London: George Weidenfeld & Nicholson Ltd 1985.

3 In this sense, E. Kanterian writes: "This is what Wittgenstein was probably drawn to when reading Keynes's description – the prospect of a radically new life, of religious renewal on Tolstoyan terms. Wittgenstein's reasoning is not entirely transparent, however." *Ludwig Wittgenstein*. London: Reaktion Books 2007, p. 137.

4 However, Monk quotes a comment from Rowland Hutt where Hutt says that Wittgenstein once told him: "I am a communist *at heart*" (op. cit., p. 343). The fact is that Wittgenstein ended his visit to the USSR, coming back to the "bourgeois" Cambridge, and he rarely made a comment on his trip to Russia.

his close friend Piero Sraffa,[5] an Italian economist, held a Marxist viewpoint on economy, which was not uncommon at the time. It is, however, a fact that Wittgenstein studied Russian with Fania Pascal and that he visited the USSR in 1935, although this visit was not politically motivated.

All this gave rise to somewhat fantastic and strange rumours, such as the one placing Wittgenstein at the centre of the famous "Cambridge Spy Ring", a group of intellectuals sympathetic to Communism who became spies for the USSR. Kimberley Cornish – who, among other similarly surprising statements in his book *The Jew of Linz*, also links Wittgenstein with Hitler – claims that the philosopher was the *fifth man*, in charge of recruiting young Cambridge talents: Philby (the *third man*), Burgess, MacLean and Blunt. It is, however, known from Oleg Gordievsky's testimony that the spy who completed the *Circle* was John Cairncross, and that what had been said of Wittgenstein was pure morbid fiction. In any case, Wittgenstein in Russia did not find the *happy Arcadia* he was hoping for, and his second attempt to find the human simplicity and moral depth spoken of by Tolstoy's and Dostoevsky ended in disappointment.

At the other extreme of the political spectrum, Wittgenstein as a Jew suffered the consequences of the Nazi *Anschluss*. As an Austrian citizen he inevitably became part of the "new Arian order". In such a situation he was in real danger – as history has sadly shown with the *Shoah*. Acquiring British citizenship now became a necessity as opposed to the previously considered optional possibility. In those hard times it was obviously a ticket to freedom for European Jews. A letter to Piero Sraffa (12 March 1938), clearly reveals Wittgenstein's anxiety:

> You know, of course, more than I about the recent events in Austria. I take it, it is conceivable that they are the immediate preparation for a war and if a war should break out now, God knows what would happen and I'm not talking about this possibility.
> [...] I needn't say that, being of Jewish de[s]cent I *couldn't* get a job in Austria.

In another letter to G. Pattison (15 March 1938), Wittgenstein continues: "As you know I am automatically becoming a German citizen, i.e. a German Jew. [...] [So I am now| Therefore now I have been] seriously considering the idea of acquiring British citizenship". The same problem will be addressed in a letter to Keynes (18 March 1938): "You know that by the annexation of Austria by Germany I have

---

5 Piero Sraffa (1898–1983), a friend of Antonio Gramsci, criticized Alfred Marshall (1842–1924), founder of the Cambridge School of Economics. Wittgenstein acknowledged his influence in the changes leading to a final rejection of the philosophy of the *Tractatus* and the creation of a new philosophical perspective, that of the *Philosophical Investigations*.

become a German citizen and, by the German laws, a German Jew (as three of my grandparents were baptised only as adults). [...] For all these reasons I have now decided to try 1) to get a University job at Cambridge, 2) to acquire British citizenship". Wittgenstein got his British passport on 2 June 1939, after being appointed Professor of Philosophy in Cambridge on 11 February the same year.

01.01.1931 (?)

What[6] different people expect to get from religion is what they expect to get from philosophy.

I don't want to give you a definition of philosophy but I should like you to have a very lively idea as to the character of philosophic problems. If you had, by the way, I could start lecturing at once.
MS 155 37r–37v

17.01.1931

I find it difficult to work, that is to prepare my lecture – even though it is high time – because my thoughts are with my relationship to Marguerite.[7] A relationship in which I can draw satisfaction just about only from what I give. I must ask God that he lets me work.
MT

27.01.1931

One could conceive a world where the religious people are distinguished from the irreligious ones only in that the former were walking with their gaze turned upwards while the others looked straight ahead. And here the upward gaze is really related to one of our religious gestures, but that is not essential & it could be the other way round with the religious people looking straight ahead etc. What I mean is that in this case religiosity would not seem to be expressed in words at all & these gestures would still say as much & as little as the words of our religious writings.
MT

22.02.1931

Hamann considers God a part of nature & at the same time like nature.

And doesn't this express the religious paradox: "How can nature be a part of nature?" It is curious: Moses Mendelssohn appears already in his letters to Hamann like a journalist.

Dealing with authors like Hamann and Kierkegaard makes their editors presumptuous. The editor of the Cherubinic Wanderer[8] would never _feel_ this temptation, nor would the editor of Augustine's Confessions or of a work by Luther.

---

6 In English in the original.
7 Marguerite Respinger.
8 Angelus Silesius' (1624–77) renowned work. It exerted a strong influence on Wittgenstein in his first period.

It is probably that the <u>irony</u> of an author <u>inclines</u> the reader to become presumptuous.

It is then roughly like this: they say they know that they don't know anything but are enormously proud of this recognition.

I am not interested in a natural moral law; or at least no <u>more</u> than in any other law of nature & no more than in that which makes someone transgress the moral law. If the moral law is natural I am inclined to defend its transgressor.
MT

25.02.1931
The idea that nowadays someone would convert from Catholicism to Protestantism or from Protestantism to Catholicism is embarrassing to me (as to many others). (In each of those cases in a different way.) Something that can (now) make the sense only as a tradition is changed like a conviction. It is as if someone wanted to exchange the burial rites of our country for those of another. – Anyone converting from Protestantism to Catholicism appears like a mental monstrosity. No good Catholic priest would have done that, had he been born a non-Catholic. And the reverse conversion reveals abysmal stupidity.

Perhaps the former proves a deeper, the latter a more shallow stupidity.
MT

01.03.1931
Have reason to suppose now that Marguerite does not particularly care for me. And that is very strange for me. One voice in me says: Then it's over, & you must lose heart. – And another one says: That must not get you down, you had to anticipate it, & your life cannot be <u>founded</u> upon the occurrence of <u>some</u>, even if greatly desired case.

And the latter voice is right, but then this is the case of a human being who lives & is tormented by pain. He must struggle so that the pain does not spoil life for him. And then one is anxious about tines of weakness.

This anxiety is of course only a weakness itself, or cowardice. For one always likes to rest, not having to fight. God be with her!

[...]

Beethoven is a realist through & through; I mean his music is <u>totally true</u>, I want to say: he sees life <u>totally</u> as it is & then exalts it. It is totally religion & not at all religious poetry. That's why he can console in real pain while the others fail & make one say to oneself: but this is not how it is. He doesn't lull one into a beautiful dream but redeems the world by viewing it like a hero, as it is.

Luther was no Protestant.
MT

06.05.1931
To be an apostle is a <u>life</u>. In part it surely expresses itself in what he says, but not in that it is true but in that he says it. Suffering for the idea defines him but here, too, it holds that the meaning of the sentence "this one is an apostle" lies in the mode of its verification. To describe an apostle is to describe a life. What impression this description makes on others must be left to them. Believing in an apostle means to relate toward him in such & such a way – relate actively.

If one does not want to get angry any more, one's joy too must change, it must not be the correlate to anger any longer.

On Kierkegaard: I represent a life for you & now see how you relate to it, whether it tempts (urges) you to live that as well, or what other relation to it you attain. Through this representation I would like to as it were loosen up your life.

To what extent my thought takes flight is of no concern (that is I don't know & don't ponder it). It has a drive. –

"It is good because God commanded it" is the right expression for the lack of reason.

An ethical proposition states "You shall do this!" or "That is good!" but not "These people say that this is good". But an ethical proposition is a personal act. Not a statement of fact. Like an exclamation of admiration. Just consider that the justification of an "ethical proposition" merely attempts to refer the proposition back to others that make an impression on you. If in the end you don't have disgust for this & admiration for that, then there is no justification worthy of that name.

[...]

If one wants to understand as Dostoevsky did the miracles of Christ such as the Miracle at the wedding of Cana, one must consider then symbols. The transformation of water into wine is astounding at best & we would gaze in amazement at the one who could do it, but no more. It therefore cannot be what is magnificent. – What is magnificent is also not that Jesus provides wine for the people at the wedding & also not that he gives it to them in such an unheard of manner. It must be the marvellous that gives this action content & meaning. And by that I don't mean the extraordinary or the unprecedented but the spirit in which it is done and for which the transformation of water into wine is only a symbol (<u>as it were</u>) a gesture. A gesture which (<u>of course</u>) can only be made by the one who can do this extraordinary thing. The miracle must be understood as gesture, as expression if it is to speak to us. I could also say: It is a miracle only when <u>he</u> does it who does it in a marvelous spirit. Without this spirit it is only an extraordinary strange fact. I must, as it were, know the person already before I can say that it is a miracle. I must read the whole of it already in the <u>right</u> spirit in order to sense the miracle in it.

When I read in a fairy tale that the witch transforms a human being into a wild animal, it is also the spirit of this action, after all, that makes the impression upon me.

(One says of someone that, if he could, his looks would kill the <u>opponent</u>)

[...]

Fortunate is he who wants to be just not from cowardice but from a sense of justice, or from a regard for the other. – Most of the time my justness, when I am just, stems from cowardice.

By the way I don't condemn <u>that</u> justness in me which plays itself out on, say, a religious plane onto which I flee from the dirty basement of my pleasure and displeasure. This flight is right when it <u>happens</u> out of fear of the dirt.

That is, I am doing right when I proceed to a more spiritual plane <u>on which</u> I can be a human being – while others can be human also on a less spiritual one.

I just don't have the right to live on that floor as they do & on their plane feel my inferiority rightfully.

I must live in a more rarified atmosphere and belong here; & should resist the temptation of wanting to live in the thicker layer of air with the others, who are allowed to do so.

MT

1931

How should we feel if we had never heard of Christ?

Should we feel left alone in the dark?

Do we not feel like that only in the way a child doesn't when he knows there is someone in the room with him?

Religious madness is madness springing from irreligiousness.

CV

1931

I look at the photographs of Corsican brigands and reflect: these faces are too hard & mine too soft for Christianity to be able to write on them. The faces of the brigands are terrible to behold & yet they are certainly no more distant from a good life & are simply situated on a different side of it than am I.

CV

1931
A confession has to be part of one's new life.[9]
CV

19.08.1931
In Christianity it is as though God said to human beings: Don't act a tragedy, that is to say, don't enact heaven & hell on earth, heaven & hell are *my* affair.
CV

24.08.1931
We keep hearing the remark that philosophy really does not progress, that we are still occupied with the same philosophical problems as were the Greeks. Those who say this however don't understand why it is so. It is because our language has remained the same & keeps seducing us into asking the same questions. As long as there is still a verb 'to be' that looks as though it functions in the same way as 'to eat' and 'to drink', as long as we still have the adjectives 'identical', 'true', 'false', 'possible', as long as we continue to talk of a river of time & an expanse of space, etc., etc., people will keep stumbling over the same cryptic difficulties & staring at something that no explanation seems capable of clearing up.

---

9 The matter Wittgenstein is dealing with in such a statement is of particular relevance for his life. Fania Pascal, in her memories on Wittgenstein, recalls that at one point Wittgenstein wanted to make a personal confession before members of his family and some friends in order to repair dishonest behaviours of his past life. In some of his texts, Wittgenstein shows the importance of making a confession of past misdeeds and of repairing the mistakes made and the lies told. See (in this compilation) for instance: *Movements of Thought* 19.11.1936, 20.11.1936 and 24.03.1937; MS 183, 146 (25.11.1936); MS 119, 140r-140v (18.11.1937). Pascal's memories (in *Personal Recollections*) show two "sins" Wittgenstein told her about (he mentioned some others she did not remember by the time of her "memories"). One of them concerned his Jewish ancestry. Most of his friends thought he was 75% Aryan and 25% Jewish (because of his grandparents), but the truth was just the other way round. Another sin had to do with a problem when he was a schoolteacher in Lower Austria. On one occasion, he punished a pupil (a girl) hurting her. The girl complained to the school's headmaster and when he asked Wittgenstein about the issue, Wittgenstein lied saying that he had not done so. Rowland Hutt mentions other episodes also included in the confession. One of them is the pretended reaction before the news of an American friend's death: when Wittgenstein was told about that he reacted as if he did not know it, although he was aware of the death. Another one was in relation to his experiences during the First World War, as he allegedly behaved somehow cowardly on some occasion; another concerned the widespread idea that he was virgin although he had had sexual intercourse with a woman when he was young (cf. R. Monk, op. cit., p. 369).

And this satisfies besides a longing for the supernatural for in so far as people think they can see the "limit of human understanding", they believe of course that they can see beyond it.
CV

13.09.1931
It is often said that a new religion brands the gods of the old one as devils. But in reality they have <u>presumably by that time</u> already become devils.
CV

05.10.1931
The inexpressible (what I find enigmatic & cannot express) perhaps provides the background, against which whatever I was able to express acquires meaning.
CV

12.10.1931
Once I read in Claudius[10] a quote from Spinoza in which he writes about himself but I couldn't quite come to terms with <u>this reflection</u>. And now it occurs to me that I distrusted it in one regard without being able to say really in what. But now I believe that my feeling is that Spinoza did not <u>recognize himself</u>. Thus, just what I have to say about myself. don't blather!

<u>He did not seem to recognize that he was a poor sinner. Of course I can write now that I am one</u>. But I do not recognize it or else I would.

The word recognize is misleading, after all, for it is a deed which requires courage.

One could say of an autobiography: one of the damned is writing this from hell.
MT

13.10.1931
Something is serious only to the extent that it is really serious.

Perhaps, just as some like to hear themselves talk, I like to hear myself write?

That something occurs to you is a gift from heaven, but it depends on what you make of it.

Of course such good teachings, too, are rightly <u>a</u> deed through which you act according to them. (In the previous sentence I was thinking of Kraus).

---

10 The work of Matthias Claudius (1740–1815), popularized by Karl Kraus.

Know thyself[11] & you will see that you are in every way again and again a poor sinner. But I don't want to be a poor sinner & seek in all manner to slip away (use anything as a door to slip away from this judgment).

My sincerity always gets stuck at a certain point!

MT

31.10.1931

One could say: You despise the natural virtues because you don't have them! – But it is not much more marvellous – or just as marvellous– that a human being <u>without</u> these gifts can still be human!

"You make a virtue of necessity". Sure, but it is not <u>marvellous</u> that one <u>can</u> make a virtue of necessity.

One could put it like this: The marvellous is that what is dead cannot sin. And that what lives can sin but <u>also renounce sin</u>: I can be bad only to the extent that I can also be good.

I sometimes imagine human beings like balls: one out of genuine gold through & through, the other a layer of worthless material with gold underneath; the third a deceptive but false gilding and underneath – gold. Yet another where there is dirt under the gilding & one where in this dirt there is again a kernel of genuine gold. Etc. etc.

MT

07.11 or 12.1931

The idea that someone uses a trick to get me to do something is unpleasant. It is certain that it takes great courage (to us this trick) & that I would not – not remotely– have this courage; but it's a question whether if I had it, it would be right to use it. I <u>think</u> that aside from courage it would also take a lack of love of one's fellow human being. One could say: What you call love for the fellow human being is self-interest. Well, then I don't know any love without self-interest, for I cannot intervene in the eternal salvation of another. I can only say: I want to love him as I – who cares for my soul– wish that he would love me.

In a certain sense he cannot want what is eternally best for me; he can only be good to me in a <u>worldly</u> sense & show respect for all that seems to reveal in me a striving for what's highest.

---

11 Translation of Greek aphorism "gnothi seauton", motto inscribed on the temple of Apollo at Delphi.

When I am thinking of my confession, I understand the expression "... & had not love etc". For, even this confession would be of no use to me if it were <u>made</u> as it were like an artful ethical trick. But I don't want to say that I refrained from it because the mere trick was not enough for me: I am too cowardly for it.

(An artful ethical trick is something that I perform for others, or also only for me (<u>myself</u>, in order to show what I can do).
MT

15.11 or 12.1931
Christianity is really saying: let go of all intelligence.

When I say I would like to discard vanity, it is questionable whether my wanting this isn't yet again only a sort of vanity. I <u>am</u> vain & insofar as I am vain, my wishes for improvement are vain, too. I would then like to be like such & such person who was not vain & whom I like, & in my mind I already estimate the benefit which I would have from "discarding" vanity. As long as one is on stage, one is an actor after all, regardless of what one does.

[...]

Of religious offense one could also say: tu te faches, donc tu as tort.[12] For one thing is sure: You are wrong to be angry, your anger shall surely be overcome. And then there is only the question whether what the other one said is right in the end. When Paul says that the crucified Christ is an offense to the Jews[13] then this is certain & also that the offense is in the wrong. But the question is: What is the right solution of this offense?

God as a historical event in the world is so paradoxical, just as paradoxical as that a certain action in my life was sinful then & there. That is, that a moment of <u>my</u> history has eternal significance is no more or less paradoxical than that a moment or span of time in world history has eternal meaning. I may doubt Christ only insofar as I may also doubt my own birth – For Christ lived in the same time in which my sins occurred (only further back). And so one must say: If good & evil are historical at all then the divine order of the world & its temporal beginning & center are also conceivable.

But if I now think of my sins & it is only a hypothesis that I have performed these acts, why do I regret them as if any doubt about them was impossible? That I now remember them is my evidence & the basis of my remorse & of the reproach that I am too cowardly to confess them.

---

12 "You are angry, therefore you are wrong".
13 See the First Epistle to the Corinthians, 1:23.

Saw photographs of the faces of Corsican brigands & thought: these faces are too hard & mine too soft for Christianity to be able to write on them. The faces of the brigands are terrible to look at, heartless, in a certain way cold and hardened; & yet they are probably no further removed from the right life than I, they are standing only on another side away from the righteous (see **CV** 1931).

Weakness is a horrible vice.
MT

1931
I had now moved from my rooms in Trinity to the Theological College, Wescott House. Wittgenstein came to see me there. Noticing a crucifix over my bed, he looked at me very sternly.

> WITTGENSTEIN: "Drury, don't allow yourself to become too familiar with holy things."

We then went and sat for a while in the college chapel. There was no organ in the chapel but instead a piano in the loft. While we were sitting in silence, someone else came in and started to play the piano. Wittgenstein jumped up at once and hurried out; I followed.

> WITTGENSTEIN: "Blasphemy! A piano and the Cross. Only an organ should be allowed in a church".

He was obviously very disturbed. I felt that my life hitherto had been superficial and aesthetic. That something much more costly was required of me. I began for the first time to have serious doubts about continuing my plan to be ordained in the Anglican Church.
M. O'C. DRURY, PR, p. 136

01.01.1932 (?)
It's like when I say, the world could have ended 3 minutes ago and the ideas and memories of mine that would now be quite remarkable, would have remained. This is precisely where we have Descartes' devil but a deception which cannot be reached ex hypothesi is no deception. ("The one whom God deceives is well deceived".)
MS 156a 12r–12v

29.02.1932
Philosophers who say: "after death a timeless state will supervene", or "at death a timeless state supervenes" & do not notice that they have used in a temporal sense the words "after" & "at" & "supervenes" & that temporality is embedded in their grammar.
CV

1932-3[14] (Lectures Cambridge 1932-5)[15]
28. Let us look at the grammar of ethical terms, and such terms as "God", "soul", "mind", "concrete", "abstract". One of the chief troubles is that we take a substantive to correspond to a thing. Ordinary grammar does not forbid our using a substantive as though it stood for a physical body. The words "soul" and "mind" have been used as though they stood for a thing, a gaseous thing. "What *is* the soul?" is a misleading question, as are questions about the words "concrete" and "abstract", which suggest an analogy with solid and gaseous instead of with a chair and the permission to sit on a chair. Another muddle consists in using the phrase "another *kind*" after the analogy of "a different *kind* of chair", e.g., that transfinite numbers are another kind of numbers than rationals, or unconscious thoughts a different kind of thought from conscious ones. The difference in the case of the latter pair is not analogous to that between a chair we see and a chair we don't see. The word "thought" is used differently when prefaced by these adjectives. What happens with the words "God" and "soul" is what happens with the word "number". Even though we give up explaining these words ostensively, by pointing, we don't give up explaining them in substantival terms. The reason people say that a number is a scratch on the blackboard is the desire to point to something. No sort of process of pointing is connected with explaining "number", any more that it is with explaining "permission to sit in a seat at the theatre".

Luther said that theology is the grammar of the word "God" [see *Philosophical Investigations* *373]. I interpret this to mean that an investigation of the word would be a grammatical one. For example, people might dispute about how many arms God had, and someone might enter the dispute by denying that one could talk about arms of God. This would throw light on the use of the word. What is ridiculous or blasphemous also shows the grammar of the word.
LC 1932-5, pp. 31-2

29. Changing the meaning of a word, e.g., "Moses", when one is forced to give a different explanation, does not indicate that it had no meaning before.

---

14 These lectures are the result of notes taken by Alice Ambrose. In fact, Ambrose arrived in Cambridge in 1932. She would become one of the students to whom Wittgenstein would dictate his Blue and Brown Books, which clearly demonstrated Wittgenstein's philosophical change of heart. The relationship between him and Ambrose ended soon enough, in 1935. In 1938, she married the philosopher Morris Lazerowitz.

15 The published lectures include the so-called Yellow Book, also from the notes taken by Alice Ambrose relating to "Wittgenstein's Lectures and Informal Discussions", as well as the dictation of *The Blue Book*, or from between the lines in the dictation. The third part of these *Lectures* is the complete result of the notes taken by Alice Ambrose and Margaret MacDonald.

The similarity between new and old uses of a word is like between an exact and a blurred boundary. Our use of language is like playing a game according to the rules. Sometimes it is used automatically, sometimes one looks up the rules. Now we get into difficulties when we believe ourselves to be following a rule. We must examine to see whether we are. Do we use the word "game" to mean what all games have in common? It does not follow that we do, even though we were to find something they have in common. Nor is it true that there are discrete groups of things called "games". What is the reason for using the word "good"? Asking this is like asking why one calls a given proposition a solution to a problem. It can be the case that one trouble gives way to another trouble, and that the resolution of the second difficulty is only connected with the first. For example, a person who tries to trisect an angle is led to another difficulty, posed by the question "Can it be done?" Proof of the impossibility of a trisection takes the place of the first investigation; the investigation has changed. When there is an argument about whether a thing is good, the discussion shows what we are talking about. In the course of the argument the word may begin to get a new grammar. In view of the way we have learned the word "good" it would be astonishing if it had a general meaning covering all of its applications. I am not saying it has four or five different meanings. It is used in different contexts because there is a transition between similar things called "good", a transition which continues, it may be, to things which bear no similarity to earlier members of the series. We *cannot* say "If we want to find out the meaning of 'good' let's find what all cases of good have in common". They may not have anything in common. The reason for using the word "good" is that there is a continuous transition from one group of things called good to another.
LC 1932–5, pp. 32–3

---

30. There is one type of explanation which I wish to criticize, arising from the tendency to explain a phenomenon by *one* cause, and then to try to show the phenomenon to be "really" another. This tendency is enormously strong. It is what is responsible for people saying that punishment must be one of three things, revenge, a deterrent, or improvement. This way of looking at things comes out in such questions as, Why do people hunt?, Why do they build high buildings? Other examples of it are the explanation of striking a table in a rage as a remnant of a time when people struck to kill, or of the burning of an effigy because of its likeness to human beings, who were once burnt. Frazer[16] concludes that since people at one time were burnt, dressing up an effigy for burning is what remains of that

---

16 Sir James George Frazer (1854–1941). Anthropologist in the Positivist tradition. His most renowned work was *The Golden Bough*, strongly criticized by Wittgenstein.

practice. This may be so; but it need not be, for this reason. The idea which underlies this sort of method is that *every* time what is sought is *the* motive. People at one time thought it useful to kill a man, sacrifice him to the god of fertility, in order to produce good crops. But it is not true that something is always done because it is useful. At least this is not the sole reason. Destruction of an effigy may have its own complex of feelings without being connected with an ancient practice, or with usefulness. Similarly, striking an object may merely be a natural reaction in rage. A tendency which has come into vogue with the modern sciences is to explain certain things by evolution. Darwin seemed to think that an emotion got its importance from one thing only, utility. A baby bares its teeth when angry because its ancestors did so to bite. Your hair stands on end when you are frightened because hair standing on end served some purpose for animals. The charm of this outlook is that it reduces importance to utility.
LC 1932–5, pp. 33–4

---

31. Let us change the topic to a discussion of *good*. One of the ways of looking at questions in ethics about *good* is to think that all things said to be good have something in common, just as there is a tendency to think that all things we call games have something in common. Plato's talk of looking for the essence of things was very like talk of looking for the *ingredients* in a mixture, as though qualities were ingredients of things. But to speak of a mixture, say of red and green colors, is not like speaking of a mixture of a paint which has red and green paints as ingredients. Suppose you say "*Good* is a quality of human actions and events". This is apparently an intelligible sentence. If I ask "How does one know an action has this quality?", you might tell me to examine it and I would find out. Now am I to investigate the movements making up the action, or are they only symptoms of goodness? If they are a symptom, then there must be some independent verification, otherwise the word "symptom" is meaningless. Now there is an important question which arises about goodness: Can one know an action in all its details and yet not know whether it is good? A similar question arises about beauty. Consider the beauty of a face. If all its shapes and colors were determined, is its beauty determined also? Or are these merely symptoms of beauty, which is to be determined otherwise? You may say that beauty is an indefinable quality, and that to say a particular face is beautiful comes to saying it has the indefinable quality. Is our scrutiny intended to find out whether a face has this indefinable quality, or merely to find out what the face is like? If the former, then the indefinable quality can be attributed to a particular arrangement of colors. But it need not be, and we must have some independent verification. If not separate investigation is required, then we only mean by a beautiful face a certain arrangement of colors shapes.
LC 1932–5, p. 34

32. The word "stupid" as applied to hands is still another game. The same is the case with "beautiful". It is bound up with a particular game. And similarly in ethics: the meaning of the word "good" is bound up with the act it modifies.

How can we know whether an action or event has the quality of goodness? And can one know the action in all of its details and not know whether it is good? That is, is its being good something that is independently experienced? Or does its being good follow from the thing's properties? If I want to know whether a rod is elastic I can find out by looking through a microscope to see the arrangement of its particles, the nature of their arrangement being a symptom of its elasticity, or inelasticity. Or I can test the rod empirically, e.g., see how far it can be pulled out. The question in ethics, about the goodness of an action, and in aesthetics, about the beauty of a face, is whether the characteristics of the action, the lines and colors of the face, are like the arrangements of particles: a *symptom* of goodness, or of beauty. Or do they constitute them? *a* cannot be a symptom of *b* unless there is a possible independent investigation of *b*. If no separate investigation is possible, then we mean by "beauty of face" a certain arrangement of colors and spaces. Now no arrangement is beautiful in itself. The word "beauty" is used for a thousand different things. Beauty of face is different from that of flowers and animals. That one is playing utterly different games is evident from the difference that emerges in the discussion of each. We can only ascertain the meaning of the word "beauty" by seeing how we use it.

LC 1932–5, pp. 35–6

33. What has been said of "beautiful" will apply to "good" in only a slightly different way. Questions which arise about the latter are analogous to those raised about beauty: whether beauty is inherent in an arrangement of colors and shapes, i.e., such that on describing the arrangement one would know it is beautiful, or not; or whether this arrangement is a symptom of beauty from which the thing's being beautiful is *concluded*.

In an actual aesthetic controversy or inquiry several questions arise: (1) How do we use such words as "beautiful"? (2) Are these inquiries psychological? Why are they so different, and what is their relation to psychology? (3) What features make us say of a thing that it is the ideal, e.g., the ideal Greek profile?

Note that in an aesthetic controversy the word "beautiful" is scarcely ever used. A different sort of words crops up: "correct", "incorrect", "right", "wrong". We never say "This is beautiful enough". We only use it to say, "Look, how beautiful", that is, to call attention to something. The same thing holds for the word "good".

LC 1932–5, p. 36

1932-3[17] (Lectures Cambridge 1930-3)
By G.E. Moore
[E] He concluded (III) by a long discussion which he introduced by saying "I have always wanted to say something about the grammar of ethical expressions, or, *e.g.*, of the word 'God'". But in fact he said very little about the grammar of such words as "God", and very little also about that of ethical expressions. What he did deal at length was not Ethics but Aesthetics, saying, however, "Practically everything which I say about 'beautiful' applies in a slightly different way to 'good'". His discussion of Aesthetics, however, was mingled in a curious way with criticism of assumptions which he said were constantly made by Frazer in the "Golden Bough", and also with criticism of Freud.

About "God" his main point seemed to be that this word is used in many *grammatically* different senses. He said, for instance, that many controversies about God could be settled by saying "I am not using the word in such a sense that you can say ...", and that different religions "treat things as making sense which others treat as nonsense, and don't merely deny some proposition which another religion affirms"; and he illustrated this by saying that if people use "god" to mean something like a human being, then "God has four arms" and "God has two arms" will both have sense, but that others so use "God" that "God has arms" is nonsense – would say "God *can't* have arms". Similarly, he said of the expression "the soul", that sometimes people so use that expression that "the soul is a gaseous human being" has sense, but sometimes so that it has not. To explain what he meant by "grammatically" different senses, he said he wanted terms which are not "comparable" as *e.g.* "solid" and "gaseous" are comparable, but which differ as, *e.g.* "chair" differs from "permission to sit on a chair", or "railway" from "railway accident".

He introduced his whole discussion of Aesthetics by dealing with one problem about the meaning of words, with which he said he had not yet dealt. He illustrated this problem by the example of the word "game", with regard to which he said both (1) that, even if there is something common to all games, it doesn't follow that this is what we mean by calling a particular game a "game", and (2) that the reason why we call so many different activities "games" need not be that there is anything common to them all, but only that there is a "gradual transition" from one use to another, although there may be nothing in common between the two

---

17 Moore had attended the conferences and discussions during the school terms in 1930, and during the first two in 1931. In September 1931, he stopped attending the conferences – although not the discussions – but he returned to them in May 1932. He spent the time taking notes at the conferences, something that made Wittgenstein happy as he thought that if something happened to him, his thoughts would have been recorded. The extracts that appear here belong to the group of conferences Wittgenstein gave in the third term of 1932.

ends of the series. And he seemed to hold definitely that there is nothing in common in our different uses of the word "beautiful", saying that we use it "in a hundred different games" – that, *e.g.* the beauty of a face is something different from the beauty of a chair or a flower or the binding of a book. And of the word "good" he said similarly that each different way in which one person, A, can convince another, B, that so-and-so is "good" fixes the meaning in which "good" is used in that discussion – "fixes the grammar of that discussion"; but that there will be "gradual transitions", from one of the meanings to another, "which take the place of something in common". In the case of "beauty" he said that a difference of meaning is shown by the fact that "you can say more" in discussing whether the arrangement of flowers in a bed is "beautiful" than in discussing whether the smell of lilac is so.

[...]

As regards Frazer's "Golden Bough", the chief points on which he seemed to wish to insist were, I think, the three following. (1) That it was a mistake to suppose that there was *only one* "reason", in the sense of "motive", which led people to perform a particular action – to suppose that there was "one motive, which was *the* motive". He gave as an instance of this sort of mistake Frazer's statement, in speaking of Magic, than when primitive people stab an effigy of a particular person, they believe that they have hurt the person in question. He said that primitive people do not *always* entertain this "false scientific belief", though in some cases they may: that they may have quite different reasons for stabbing the effigy. But he said that the tendency to suppose that there is "one motive which is *the* motive" was "enormously strong", giving as an instance that there are theories of play each of which gives *only one* answer to the question "Why do children play?" (2) That it was a mistake to suppose that *the* motive is always "to get something useful". He gave as an instance of this mistake Frazer's supposition that "people at a certain stage thought it useful to kill a person, in order to get a good crop". (3) That it was a mistake to suppose that why, *e.g.* the account of the Beltane Festival "impresses us so much" is because it has "developed from a festival in which a real man was burnt". He accused Frazer of thinking that this was the reason. He said that our puzzlement as to why it impresses us is not diminished by giving the *causes* from which the festival arose, but is diminished by finding other similar festivals: to find these may make it seem "natural", whereas to give the causes from which it arose cannot do this. In this respect he said that the question "Why does this impress us?" is like the aesthetics question "Why is this beautiful?" or "Why will this bass not do?"

He said that Darwin, in his "expression of the Emotions", made a mistake similar to Frazer's, *e.g.* in thinking that "because our ancestors, when angry, wanted to bite" is a sufficient explanation of why we show our teeth when angry. He said you

might say that what is satisfactory in Darwin is not such hypotheses, but his "putting the facts in a system" – helping us to make a synopsis of them.
LC 1930-3, pp. 103, 104, 106, 107

01.01.1933 (?)
A person says "Oh God" and looks upwards to the heavens. That can teach us the meaning of the phrase "that God lives in the heavens".

One could say very casually that those people in whose nature it is to kneel down in certain situations and put their hands together, know a personal God.

Complete grammar of a word. Complete list of rules of a game. Let's just establish that this is the complete list of rules of our game!

In the question and answer game (as a type of language) I think of Plato where question and answer appear much more frequently than we would use them.

Keller (in *Green Henry*)[18] once writes about a man who says he doesn't believe in God and yet uses all the common expressions containing the word "God". ("Thanks be to God", "God willing", etc) And Keller thinks the man is contradicting himself by doing so. But there shouldn't be any contradiction in what he says, and one could say: I can gather what you mean by the word "God" from the sentences you use containing this word which are in fact meaningless to you. For I too use the word "sense of a sentence", "meaning of a word" in certain contexts and still don't know one thing, 'the meaning of the word' and a shadow of an event 'the sense of a sentence'.
MS 219, 6

01.01.1933 (?)
A says to B: "God be with you". – B: "Do you believe in God then?" A: "Yes; in the sense in which it makes sense for me to say, for example, 'God be with you'".

I believe we have to say that, in the same way that the word "wish" is used, it is fundamental that it makes no sense to give someone the order to wish for something. This is when we're talking about an articulated wish that must be accompanied by the expression of a specific experience.
MS 219, 9

01.01.1933 (?)
Words whose grammar consists, so to speak, of bits of grammar from an ordinary noun or an adjective: eg "good". All the ethics seems to be based on this illusion.

---

18 Published in 1855 (*Der grüne Heinrich*).

This person is said to be better than that one and immediately it seems we are dealing with a series of quantitative definitions like a series of weights. Someone says "I derive more pleasure from visiting the cinema than I do from this gathering" and then the person thinks a calculus of pleasure and displeasure should revealed itself upon closer scrutiny. Etc. etc.

MS 219, 11

1933

We were sitting and talking in my bedroom when he noticed a copy of Thomas à Kempis[19] by my bedside.

>   WITTGENSTEIN: "Are you reading this book?"
>   DRURY: "I find it a help when I feel in a despondent mood".
>   WITTGENSTEIN: "It wasn't written for that purpose. It was written to be remembered in all moods".

M. O'C. DRURY, PR, p. 138

1933–4 (*The Yellow Book*)[20]

Suppose someone said that since our space has three dimensions we can therefore describe the path of a particle by the increases and decreases of three coordinates but not of four. He will claim that this imposes a restriction on our grammar since it is of the nature of space to have three dimensions. I would reply, "Aren't four dimensions just as good? The fourth variable could be darkness and light. If the particle gets darker, the fourth variable has a lower value". Another example of a description given sense is the following: S says science and religion are coming to agree more and more, as the fourth dimension makes it easy to understand how Christ came into a room without passing through the door. He came by the fourth dimension. S thinks this explanation makes the statement easier to understand. And of course it *could* be described in these terms. Suppose we take time as our fourth dimension, measuring the point where Christ is by a watch. Where he is spatially could be described by three dimensions and where he is between vanishing and reappearing by the fourth. Now someone might object that he wants the new grammar to be analogous to the old. So let's have analogy so far as the formula is concerned, by giving the distance as [...]. This of course is not the only

---

19 Thomas à Kempis (1379–1471). Author of the *Imitation of Christ*, one of the most influential books in spirituality.
20 Notes taken by Alice Ambrose. In 1934, Wittgenstein dictated the *Brown Book* to Alice Ambrose and Francis Skinner.

thing that could be called analogous to distance with three dimensions. Usually there is one analogy that psychologically appeals to us most. We can do anything we please, but we'll see that certain conventions are too cumbrous to be used. Whether they are cumbrous or not depends upon our nature and the natural facts, e.g., that bodies do not vanish in one place and appear in another. If this appeared to happen we could say our vision failed us, but we *need not* say this.

LC 1932–5, pp. 66–7

1935 (?)[21]

Easter time at Woolacombe in North Devon. Wittgenstein had come to spend the holiday there with me and the other members of my family. On Easter morning we all presented each other with chocolate eggs and Wittgenstein of course was included in the ceremony. He showed real pleasure at this. Afterwards when we were out walking he told me how much he liked keeping up these old customs. We walked up the hill to Mortehoe and then out along the point. I said to him that in earlier years the ceremonies of Holy Week and Easter had meant a great deal to me; and now I felt a sense of emptiness when I no longer took part in them.

> WITTGENSTEIN: "But Drury, when I wanted to dissuade you from becoming a parson I didn't mean that you should at the same time cease to attend your church services. That wasn't the idea at all. Though it may be that you have to learn that these ceremonies haven't the importance you once attached to them – but that doesn't mean that they have no importance. Of course it does often happen that, as one develops, a man's expression of his religion becomes much drier. I had a protestant aunt, and the only religious observance she kept was to observe every Good Friday in complete silence and complete abstinence".

M. O'C. DRURY, PR, pp. 143–4

19.11.1936[22]

Skjolden

About 12 days ago I wrote to Hänsel a confession of my lie concerning my ancestry. Since that time I have been thinking again & again how I can & should

---

21 This is the year that Wittgenstein travels to the Soviet Union, where he is offered the chair of Philosophy at the University of Kazan, which he does not accept. In October, he starts teaching Philosophy of Psychology at Cambridge.

22 The fellowship Wittgenstein had received from Trinity in December 1930 ended in June 1936. In August, he left for Norway, where he continued to work on his projects over the following nine months. He would not return to Cambridge until January 1938.

make a full confession to everyone I know. I <u>hope</u> & <u>fear</u>! Today I feel a bit sick, chilled. I thought: "Does God want to put an end to me before I could do the difficult thing?" May it turn out well!
MT

20.11.1936

Weary & disinclined to work or really in<u>capable</u>. But that would not be a terrible ill. I could sit & rest, after all. But then my soul clouds over. How easily I forget the favors of heaven!

After having now made that <u>one</u> confession it is as if I couldn't support the whole edifice of lies anymore, as if I had to collapse entirely. If only it had entirely collapsed already! So that the sun could shine on the grass & the ruins.

The most difficult is the thought of a confession to Francis[23] because I fear for him & the horrible responsibility I then have to bear.[24] *Only love can bear this. May God help me.*
MT

21.11.1936

You can't call Christ the savior without calling him God. For a human being cannot save you.
MT

25.11.1936

Today[25] *God let it occur to me – for I can't say it any other way – that I should confess my misdeeds to the people in the village here. And I said, I couldn't do it! I don't want to, even though I should. I don't dare confess even to Anna Rebni & Arne Draegni.*[26] *Thus it was shown to me that I am a scoundrel. Not long before this occurred to me I had been telling myself that I was prepared to be crucified.*

I would like <u>so</u> much after all for everyone to have a good opinion of me! Even if it is a false one; & I know that it is false! –

It[27] *has been* <u>granted</u> *to me, – & I want praise for it! So instruct me –!*
MT

---

23 Francis Skinner (1912–41). A student of Mathematics at Cambridge and a close friend of Wittgenstein's. He died from polio.
24 In code.
25 In code.
26 Villagers from Skjolden.
27 In code.

1936
There was in our dining room a steel engraving of a portrait of Pope Pius IX.[28] A very striking face.

> WITTGENSTEIN: (after looking at the picture for some time) "The last of the *real* Popes, I would think. If it was declared that, whenever the Pope sat on a particular chair, what he then pronounced was to be believed and obeyed by all Catholics – then I would understand what the doctrine of infallibility meant. But as long as the words *ex cathedra* are not defined, the doctrine of infallibility decides nothing."

He told me he had been reading Newman's[29] *Apologia* and that he admired Newman's obvious sincerity. But when he came to read the last sermon Newman preached to his friends at Littlemore, he thought of himself, "I wouldn't wish to speak to my friends like that".

M. O'C. DRURY, PR, p. 145

1936
Sunday morning. Wittgenstein and I went for a walk.

> WITTGENSTEIN: "I saw you and your mother coming back through the garden before breakfast this morning. Had you been to church?
> DRURY: "Yes, we had been to Holy Communion together".
> WITTGENSTEIN: "I wish I could have been with you".

That same evening we were walking back through the cathedral close as people were going in to Evensong.

> WITTGENSTEIN: "Let's go in with them".

We sat at the back of the nave listening to the service. When it came to the sermon the preacher chose as his text: "It is expedient for you that I go away: for if I go not away, the Comforter will not come to you".[30] After a few minutes Wittgenstein leant over and whispered to me, "I am not listening to a word he is saying. But think about the text, that is wonderful, that is really wonderful".

M. O'C. DRURY, PR, p. 146

---

28 Giovanni Maria Mastai Ferreti (1792-1878). Pope of the Catholic Church (1846-78) with the name of Pius IX. Promoted the First Vatican Council (1869-1870), where the dogmas concerning papal infallibility and the demonstration of the existence of God by means of natural reason were proclaimed.
29 John Henry Newman (1801-1890). Catholic philosopher and theologian who became cardinal of the Catholic Church, though he was formerly Anglican.
30 The Gospel According to John, 16:7.

1936

On the way home we mentioned a student we had both known in Cambridge, who had been killed fighting with the International Brigade in Spain.[31] Some of his friends had said to Wittgenstein, "What a relief to know that this was the end of his sufferings and that we don't have to think of a 'future life'." Wittgenstein said he was shocked at their speaking in this way. I tried to explain to him that for me the only perfect moments in my life were when I had been so absorbed in the object – nature or music- that all self-consciousness was abolished. The 'I' had ceased to be.

> WITTGENSTEIN: "And so you think of death as the gateway to a permanent state of mind as such".
> DRURY: "Yes, that is how I think of a future life".

He seemed to be disinclined to continue with this conversation; but I had the feeling that he thought what I had said was superficial.
M. O'C. DRURY, PR, p. 147

1936

We called round at my brother's architectural office in Bedford Circus. My brother was out on a site, but Wittgenstein spent some time talking to the senior partner, Mr. Tonar. They seemed to be having a lively conversation. I was amused afterwards when Mr. Tonar said to me in private: "That's a very intelligent young man". One of the assistant draughtsmen was designing an altar cross. Wittgenstein became quite agitated: "I couldn't for the life of me design a cross in this age; I would rather go to Hell than try and design a cross". We hadn't left the office for long when he turned back, saying, "I shouldn't have said what I did about designing a cross; that can do no good. We must go back and tell the man not to take the slightest notice of what I said".
M. O'C. DRURY, PR, p. 149

1936

When we were out walking a few days later, Wittgenstein began to talk to me about Lessing. He quoted with great emphasis Lessing's remark:

> If God held closed in his right hand all truth, and in his left the single and untiring striving after truth, adding even that I always and forever make

---

31 The International Brigades were groups of volunteers from different countries recruited to fight for the Republican Army in the Spanish Civil War (1936-9). Such brigades were promoted by the communist Komintern. The first group of volunteers arrived at Albacete (Spain) on 14 October 1936. Accordingly, the text must belong to sometime after that date. It is possible that the student Drury refers to is John Cornford (1915-36), the English poet, member of the British Communist Party who studied at Cambridge and died in a village in Jaén (South Spain) on 28 December 1936. But if this were so, the date for Drury's text would be dubious at best.

mistakes, and said to me: "Choose!", I should fall humbly before his left hand and say: Father grant me! The pure truth is for you alone.

Then he said he would like to read to me something of Lessing's. So we turned back and hurried up to the public library to see if we could find anything either in German or in English. We found nothing; and I had to regret that I never heard him selecting what it was he wanted me to know.

On the way home through the Cathedral Close we passed the statue of Richard Hooker.[32] Wittgenstein asked me who he was.

> DRURY: "He was an Elizabethan Divine who wrote a famous apologia for the Anglican Reformation, a book called *Laws of Ecclesiastical Polity*. In it, he tried to steer a middle course between Catholicism and Calvinism".
>
> WITTGENSTEIN: "That sounds to me impossible. How could there by any compromise between two such completely divergent doctrines".

The next day he had obviously thought about this and said to me that he could now see that a thoroughly bourgeois culture might want such compromise.

M. O'C. DRURY, PR, pp. 149–50

1936

Another letter from Wittgenstein, in which he suggested that if he did qualify as a doctor he and I might practise together as psychiatrists. He felt that he might have a special talent for this branch of medicine. He sent me as a birthday present a copy of Freud's *Interpretation of Dreams*. This, he wrote, was the most important of Freud's writings. When he first read it he said to himself, "Here at last is a psychologist who has something to say".

When we talked about this later, he said he would not want to undergo what was known as a training analysis. He did not think it right to reveal all one's thoughts to a stranger. Psychoanalysis as presented by Freud was irreligious. "It is a very dangerous procedure; I know a case where it did infinite harm".

M. O'C. DRURY, PR, p. 151

1936

I told him I had been asked to be godfather at the christening of my nephew.

---

32 Richard Hooker (1554–1600). Drury mentions his masterpiece, a work in eight volumes.

DRURY: "The godparents have to promise in the child's name 'To renounce the devil and all his works, the pomps and vanities of this wicked world, and all the sinful lusts of the flesh'. I feel it would be hypocrisy for me to speak those words. It is something that I haven't done myself".
WITTGENSTEIN: "To renounce the pomps and vanities of this wicked world. Just think what that would really involve. Who of us today even thinks of doing such a thing? We all want to be admired. St. Paul said. 'I die daily'.[33] Just think what that must have meant!"

M. O'C. DRURY, PR, p. 153

27.01.1937
On[34] the return from Vienna & England, on the trip from Bergen to Skjolden. My conscience presents me as a miserable human being to myself; weak, that is unwilling to suffer, <u>cowardly</u>: in fear of making an unfavourable impression on others, for example on the doorman at the hotel, the servant, etc. Unchaste. Most heavily, though, I feel the charge of cowardice. But behind it stands indifference (& arrogance). But the <u>shame</u> I feel now is also no good insofar as I feel my outward defeat more strongly than the defeat of truth. My pride & my vanity are hurt.

With the Bible I have nothing but a book in front of me. But why do I say "nothing but a book"? I have a book in front of me, a <u>document</u> which, if it remains alone, cannot have greater value than any other document.

(This is what Lessing meant). In and of itself this document cannot 'attach' me to any belief in the doctrines which it contains, – just as little as <u>any other</u> document which could have fallen into my hands. If I am to believe these doctrines I should do so not because this & not something else was reported to me. Instead they must be <u>evident</u> to me: & with that I don't just mean doctrines of ethics but historical doctrines. Not the letter, only conscience can command me – to believe in resurrection, judgement, etc. To believe not as in something probable but in <u>a different</u> sense. And I can be reproached for my unbelief only insofar as either my conscience commands the belief – if there is such a thing –, or in that it accuses me of depravities, which in some manner, <u>that I am not aware of, however,</u> don't let me attain belief. This means, so it seems to me, that I should say: You cannot know anything about such a belief now, it must be a state of mind of which you know nothing at all and which is of no concern to you as long as your conscience does not reveal it to you; whereas you must not follow your conscience in what it

---

33 First Epistle of St. Paul to the Corinthians 15:31.
34 In code.

tells you. A dispute about religious belief cannot exist for you since you don't know what the dispute is about (aren't acquainted with it). The sermon can be the precondition of belief, but in virtue of what happens in it, it cannot aim to impel belief. (If these words could attach one to belief, other words could also attach one to belief). Believing begins with belief. One must begin with belief; from words no belief follows. Enough.
MT

28.01.1937
Still on the journey by boat. We were mooring at the landing dock & I watched the steel cable by which the boat was secured, and the though came to me: walk on the cable; of course you will fall into the water after a few steps – but the water wasn't deep & I would not have drowned but only gotten wet; & most of all I would have been laughed at of course or considered a little crazy. I immediately shrank back from the thought of doing this & had to tell myself right away that I am not a free man but a slave. Of course it would have been 'unreasonable' to follow the impulse; but what does that say?! I understood what it means that belief is bliss for a human being, that is, it frees him from the fear of others by placing him immediately under God. He becomes so to speak an imperial subject. It is a weakness not to be a hero, but it is by far a weaker weakness to play the hero, thus not even to have the strength too clearly & without ambiguity acknowledge the deficit on the balance sheet. And that means: to become modest: not in a few words which one says once but in life.

To have an ideal is alright. But how difficult not to want to playact one's ideal. Instead to see it at a distance from oneself at which it is! Yes, is this even possible – or would one either have to become good or go mad over it? Wouldn't this tension, if it were fully grasped either open the person to everything or destroy him.

Is it a way out here to cast oneself into the arms of grace?

Last night the following dream: I stood with Paul & Mining, it was as if on the front platform of a street car but it wasn't clear that it was that. Paul told Mining how enthusiastic my brother-in-law Jerome was about my unbelievable musical gift; the day before I had so wonderfully sung along in a work of Mendelssohn, it was called "The Bacchantae"[35] (or something like this); it was as if we had performed from this work among ourselves at home & I had sung along with extraordinary expressiveness & also with especially expressive gestures. Paul & Mining seemed to completely agree with Jerome's[36] praise. Jerome was to have said again and again. "What talent!"

---

35 None of Mendelssohn's works is entitled so.
36 Jerome (Steinberger) Stonborough (1873–1938). Margarethe Wittgenstein's husband.

(or something similar; I don't remember this for sure). I held a withered plant in my hand with blackish seeds in the little pods that had already opened & thought: if they were to tell me what a pity it is about my unused musical talent, I will show them the plant & say that nature isn't stingy with its seed either & that one shouldn't be afraid & just throw out a seed. All of this was carried on in a self-satisfied manner. – I woke up & was angry or ashamed because of my vanity. – This was not the sort of dream that I have been having very often during the last 2 months (roughly): namely where I act despicably in the dream, lie, for example, & wake up with the feeling: Thank God that this was a dream; & take this dream also as a sort of warning. *May[37] I not become completely base and also not mad! May God have mercy on me.*
MT

31.01.1937

Consider how the noun "time" can conjure a medium; how it can lead us astray so that we chase (back and forth) after a phantom.

Adam names the animals –
God[38] let me be pious but not eccentric!

I feel as if my intellect was in a very unstable equilibrium; so as if a comparatively slight push would make it flip. It is as when one sometimes feels close to crying, feels the approaching crying fit. One should then try to breathe quite calmly, regularly & deeply until the fit is eased. And if God wills I will succeed.
MT

04.02.1937

I may well reject the Christian solution of the problem of life (salvation, resurrection, judgement, heaven, hell) but this does not solve the problem of my life, for I am not good & not happy. I am not saved. And thus how can I know what I would envision as the only acceptable image of a world order if I lived differently, lived completely differently. I can't judge that. After all, another life shifts completely different images into the foreground, necessitates completely different images. Just like trouble teaches prayer. That does not mean that through the other life one will necessarily change one's opinions. But if one lives differently, one speaks differently. With a new life one learns new language games.

Think more of death, for example – & it would be strange if through that you wouldn't get to know new conceptions, new tracts of language.
MT

---

37 In code.
38 In code.

07.02.1937
My writing is lacking piety & devotion again. So I am concerned that what I produce now might appear worse to Bachtin[39] than what I have given him. *How can anything good come from such stupidity. –*
MT

09.02.1937
"I actually feel well now; I seem to have managed to deceive God."
MS 157a, 60v

15.02.1937
Like the insect around the light so I buzz around the New Testament.

Yesterday I had this thought: If I disregard entirely punishments in the hereafter: Do I find it right that a person suffers an entire life for the cause of justice, then dies perhaps a terrible death, – & now has no reward at all for this life? After all, I admire such a person & place him high above me & why don't I say, he was an ass that he used his life like that. Why is he not stupid? Or also: why is he not the "most miserable of human beings?" Isn't that what he should be, if now that is all: that he had a miserable life until the end? But consider now that I answer: "No he was not stupid since he is doing well now after his death". That is also not satisfying. He does not seem stupid to me, indeed, on the contrary, seems to be doing what's right. Further I seem to be able to say: he does what's right for he receives the just reward and yet I can't think of the reward as an award after his death. Of such a person I want to say "This human being must come home".

One images eternity (of reward or of punishment) normally as an endless duration. But one could equally well imagine it as an instant. For in an instant one can experience all terror & all bliss. If you want to imagine hell you don't need to think of unending torment. I would rather say: Do you know what unspeakable dread a human being is capable of? Think of that & you know what hell is even though this is not at all a matter of duration.

And furthermore, those who know what dread they are capable of, know that this is nothing yet in comparison to something even far more terrible which as it were remains covered up as long as we can be still distracted by externalities. (Mephisto's last speech in Lenau's Faust). The abyss of hopelessness cannot show itself in life. We can look into it only down to a certain depth, for "where there is life, there is hope". In Peer Gynt it goes: "An hour of this consuming strife is too dear a price to pay for life".[40] – When one is in pain one says something like: "These pains have already

---

39 Nicholas Bachtin (1896–1950). Russian philologist. Friend of Wittgenstein with whom he read the *Tractatus* at the time he was thinking of publishing the *Philosophical Investigations*.

40 These verses come from Michael Meyer's translation of the second act of Henrik Ibsen's (1828–1906) dramatic poem *Peer Gynt* of 1876.

lasted 3 hours now, when will they finally stop", but in hopelessness one does not think "it lasts so long already!" for in a certain sense time does not pass at all in it.

Now, can't one say to someone & I to myself: "You are doing right to be afraid of hopelessness! You must live in such a way that your life can't come to a head in hopelessness, in the feeling: Now it's too late". And it appears to me that it could come to a head in different ways.

But can you imagine that the life of the one who is truly just also comes to a head only like that? Mustn't he receive the "crown of life"? Don't I demand nothing but this for him? Don't I demand his glorification?! Yes! But how can I imagine his glorification? In accord with my feelings I could say: not only must he see the light, but get immediately to the light, become of one nature with it now, – and the like. It therefore seems that I could use all these expressions which religion really uses here.

These images thus impose themselves upon me. And yet I am reluctant to use these images & expressions. Above these there are not similes, of course. For what can be said by way of a simile, that can also be said without a simile. These images & expressions have a life rather only in a high sphere of life, they can be rightfully used only in this sphere. All I could really do is make a gesture which means something similar to "unsayable", & say nothing. – Or is this absolute version to using words here some sort of flight? A flight from a reality? I don't think so; but I don't know. *Let[41] me not shy away from any conclusion, but absolutely also not be superstitious!! I do not want to think uncleanly!*
MT

16.02.1937

God![42] Let me come into a relation to you in which I "can be cheerful in my work"! Believe that at any moment God can demand everything from you! Be truly aware of this! Then ask that he grant you the gift of life! For you can fall into madness at any time or become unhappy through & through if you don't do something that is demanded of you!

It is one think to talk to God & another to talk of God to others.

Sustain[43] my intellect pure & unblemished!

I would like to be deep; – & yet I shy away from the abyss in the human heart!! –

[...]

What I recognize is actually: how terribly unhappy a human being can become. The recognition of an abyss; & I want to say: God grant that this recognition does not become clearer.
MT

---

41 In code.
42 In code.
43 In code.

17.02.1937

The horrible instant in an unblessed death must be the thought: "Oh if I only had ... Now it's too late". Oh if only I had lived right! And the blessed instant must be: "Now it is accomplished" – But how must one have lived in order to tell oneself this! I think there must be degrees here too. *But[44] I myself, where am I? How far from the good & how close to the lower end!*
MT

18.02.1937

Few things are as difficult for me as modesty. Now I am noticing this again as I read in Kierkegaard. Nothing is as difficult for me as to feel inferior; even though it is only a matter of seeing reality as it is.

Would[45] I be able to sacrifice my writings for God?
I would much rather hear "If you don't do that, you will gamble away your life", than: "If you don't do that, you will be punished". The former really means: If you don't do that, your life will be an illusion, it does not have truth & depth.
MT

19.02.1937

What[46] helps in praying is not the kneeling, but one kneels.
  Call it a sickness! What have you said by that? Nothing.
  Don't explain! – Describe! *Submit[47] your heart & don't be angry that you must suffer so! This is the advice I should be giving myself. When you are sick, accommodate yourself to the sickness; don't be angry that you are sick.*
  This, however, is true, that just as soon as I can barely breathe a sigh of relief, vanity stirs in me.
  Let[48] me confess this: After a difficult day for me I kneeled during dinner today & prayed & suddenly said, kneeling & looking up above: "There is no one there". That made me feel at ease as if I had been enlightened in an important matter. But what it really means, I do not know yet. I feel relieved. But that does not mean, for example: I had previously been in error. For if it was an error, what protects me against falling back into it?! Thus there can be no talk of error here & the overcoming of this error. And if one calls it sickness once again there can be no talk of an overcoming, for any time the sickness can overcome me

---

44 In code.
45 In code.
46 In code.
47 In code.
48 In code.

again. *For*[49] *after all, I also didn't say this word just when I wanted to, but it came. And just as it came something else can come, too.* – *"Live in such a manner that you can die well!"*
MT

20.02.1937
You shall live so that you can hold your own in the face of madness when it comes. *And*[50] *you shall not flee madness.* It is good fortune when it isn't there, but *flee* if you shall not, or so I think I must tell myself. For madness is the most severe judge (the most severe court) of whether my life is right or wrong; it is horrible but nevertheless you shall not flee it. For you don't know anyway how you can elude it, & while you are fleeing from it, you behave disgracefully, after all.

I am reading[51] *in the N.T.*[52] *& don't understand many & essential things but much I do understand after all. I feel much better today than yesterday. Would that it stay.*

One could tell me: "You shouldn't get so involved with the N.T., it may yet drive you crazy" – But why 'shouldn't' I, -unless I felt myself that I should not. When I believe that through stepping into a room I can see – or find- what's important, what's true, then I can feel, after all, I should step in, no matter what happens to me inside & I shall not avoid stepping in out of fear. *Perhaps*[53] *it looks* ghastly *inside, and one wants to immediately run out again; but should I not try to remain steadfast? In such a case I want someone to pat me on the shoulder & say to me: "Fear not! For this is right".*

I thank God that I have come to Norway into the loneliness!

How is it that the psalms I read today (the penitential psalms) are nourishment for me & the N.T. up to now really not? Is it only too serious for me?

The one who is innocent must speak differently & must make different demands than the one who is guilty. It can't say in David:[54] "Be perfect"; it doesn't say that one should sacrifice one's life, & there is no promise of eternal bliss. And the acceptance of this teaching requires – so it seems to me – that one says: "This life with all sorts of pleasure & pain is nothing, after all! It can't be there for these! It must be something far more absolute, after all. It must strive toward the absolute. And the only absolute is, to battle through life toward death, like a fighting, a charging soldier. Everything else is wavering, cowardice, sloth, thus wretchedness". This is no Christianity, of course, since, for example, there is no mention of eternal life here & eternal punishment. But I would also understand if someone

---

49 In code.
50 In code.
51 In code.
52 New Testament.
53 In code.
54 King David. The second king of Israel. Author of the Book of Psalms.

said: Happiness <u>understood as eternal</u> can be achieved only <u>like this</u> & cannot be achieved by dwelling here among all sorts of small happiness. But there is still no mention yet of eternal damnation.

This striving for the absolute which makes all worldly happiness appear too petty, which turns our gaze upward & not level, toward the things, appears as something glorious, sublime to me; but I <u>myself</u> turn my gaze towards the worldly things; unless "God visits me" & that state comes over me in which this becomes impossible. I <u>believe:</u> I should do this & that, & not do this & that; & all of this I can <u>do in such a rather dim illumination from above</u>; this is not that state. Why should I burn my writings today?! No way! – But I <u>do</u> think of it when the darkness has descended upon me & threatens to remain there. Then it is as if I had my hand on an object & the object was getting hot & I had the choice between letting go & burning up. In this situation one wants to use the words of the penitential psalms.

(The actual <u>Christian faith</u> – as opposed to <u>faith –</u> I don't understand at all yet).

But[55] to <u>seek</u> it out that would be recklessness.

Consider someone in horrible pain, say when something particular is happening in his body, yelling "Away, away!", even though there is nothing that he wishes away, –could one say now: "<u>These words are wrongly applied</u>"?? One wouldn't say such a thing. Equally, if, for example, he makes a 'defensive' gesture or rather falls upon his knees & folds his hands, one couldn't reasonably declare these things to be <u>wrong</u> gestures. <u>This is just what he does</u> in such a situation. There can be no talk of 'wrong' here. Which application would be right if a <u>necessary</u> one is wrong? On the other hand couldn't one say, it was a right application of the gesture & <u>thus</u> there was someone here before whom he has knelt. Unless both of these statements are to have identical sense, & then the "thus" is wrong, too. Apply this to prayer. How could one say of him who <u>must</u> wring his hands & beseech, that he is mistaken or in an illusion.

MT

21.02.1937

To get rid of the torments of the mind, that is to get rid of religion.

Have[56] you not been somehow tormented in your whole life (just not in this way) & would you rather return to <u>those</u> torments now?!

I am good natured but an extraordinary coward & therefore bad. I want to help people where no great exertion but <u>most of all</u> where no courage is required. If this

---

55 In code.
56 In code.

gets me into the <u>slightest</u> danger, I shy away. And by danger I mean, for example, losing some of the high opinion people have of me.

The only way I could ever charge the enemy line is when I am shot at from behind.

If I must suffer it is better, after all, by way of a battle of the good against the bad in me, rather than by way of a battle within the evil.

What I believe now: I believe that I should not fear people and their opinions when I want to do what I consider right.

I believe that I should not lie; that I should be good to people; that I should see myself as I really am; that I should sacrifice my comfort when <u>something higher is at stake</u>; that I should be cheerful in a good way when it is granted to me and when not, that I should then endure the gloom with patience & <u>steadfastness</u>; that the condition which demands everything from me is not taken care of by the words "sickness" or "madness", that is: that in this condition I am just as responsible as out of it, that it belongs to my life like any other and that it <u>thus</u> deserves full attention. I don't have a belief in a salvation through the death of Christ; or at least not yet. I also don't feel that I am on the way to such a belief, but I consider it possible that one day I will understand something here of which I understand nothing now, which means nothing to me now & that I will then have a belief that I don't have now. – <u>I believe</u> that I should not be superstitious, that is, that I should not perform magic on myself with words I may be reading, that is, that I should and must not talk myself into a sort of faith, a sort of unreason. I shall not sully reason. (But madness does <u>not sully</u> reason. Even if it is not its guardian).

I believe that human beings can let their lives be guided <u>by inspirations entirely in all their actions</u> and I must now believe that this is the <u>highest</u> life. I know that I could live like that if I <u>wanted</u> to, if I had the courage for it. But I don't have it and must hope that this won't make me unhappy unto death, <u>that is</u>, eternally.

May gloom, the feeling of misery, somehow cleanse while I am writing all this!

I read again and again in the letters of the apostle Paul & I don't like reading in them. And I don't know whether the resistance & revulsion I feel stem at least in part from the <u>language</u>, namely from the German, Germanic, thus from the translation. But I don't know it. It appears to me as if it were not <u>merely</u> the teaching which repulses me through its gravity, greatness, through its seriousness, but (<u>somehow</u>) also the personality of the one who teaches it. It seems to me as if, aside from all that, there was something <u>alien</u> & <u>thereby</u> repulsive to me in the teaching. When, for example, he says "Far from it!" I find something unpleasant in the mere manner of the raisonnement. But isn't it possible that this would shed itself entirely if I were gripped more by the spirit of the letter. But I consider it possible that this is <u>not</u> unimportant.

I hope that the present sadness & agony will consume the <u>vanity</u> in me. But won't it come back very soon when the agony ends? And shall it therefore <u>never</u> end?? May God prevent this.

In my soul there is winter (<u>now</u>) like all around me. Everything is snowed in, nothing turns green & blossoms. But I should therefore patiently await whether I am destined to see a spring.
MT

22.02.1937
Have courage & patience even toward death, then perhaps you will be granted life! If only the snow around me would begin to regain beauty & not just have sadness!

[...]

Thank[57] *God that I feel a bit quieter & better today. But whenever I feel better, I am very close to vanity.*

Now I often tell myself in doubtful <u>times</u>: "There is no one here". and look around. Would that this not become something based in me!

I think I should tell myself: "Don't be servile in your religion!" Or try not to be! For that is in the direction of superstition.

A human being lives his ordinary life with the illumination of a light of which he is not aware until it is extinguished. Once it is extinguished, life is suddenly deprived of all value, meaning, or whatever one wants to say. One suddenly becomes aware that mere existence – as one would like to say – is in itself completely empty, <u>bleak</u>. It is as if the sheen was wiped away from all things,

In my stupid thoughts I compare myself to the highest human beings!

Really, the horrible that I wanted to describe is that one "doesn't have a right to anything anymore". "There is no blessing with anything". That is, this seems to me as if someone on whose friendly regard everything depends said: "Do as you wish but you don't have my consent!" Why does it say: "The Lord is wrathful". – He can <u>ruin</u> you. The one can say that one is descending to hell. But this is not really an 'image', for if I really had to descend into an abyss this wouldn't have to be frightful. An abyss is nothing terrible, after all & what is hell anyway: that one could compare something to it, that is, explain it through this image? One must rather call this condition "a presentiment of hell" – for in this condition one also wants to say: It can get more horrible still: for all hope is not yet <u>completely</u> extinguished. Can one say that one must therefore live in such a way that when one can hope no longer, one has something to <u>remember?</u>

Live[58] *so that you can prevail in the face of that condition: for <u>all your wit, all your intellect won't do you any good then</u>. You are lost <u>with</u> them as if you didn't have*

---

57 In code.
58 In code.

them at all. (You might as well try to use your good legs while falling through the air). Your <u>whole life</u> (<u>after all</u>) is undermined, and therefore you, with all you have. You hang tremblings, with all you have, above the abyss. It is horrible that such a thing can be. Perhaps I have these thoughts because I now see so little light here; but there <u>is</u> so little light here now and <u>I have them</u>. Wouldn't it be funny to tell someone: Don't mind that, you are only dying now because you can't breathe for a few minutes. With all conceit, with all your pride <u>in this & the other</u>, you are lost then, these don't hold you, for they are undermined <u>along with all you have</u>. But you should not <u>fear</u> this condition even though it is frightful. You shouldn't forget it frivolously & <u>yet</u> not fear it. It[59] will then give your life <u>seriousness</u> & not dread. (I believe so).
MT

23.02.1937
One kneels & looks up & folds one's hands & speaks, & says one is speaking with God, one says God sees everything I do; one says God speaks to me in my <u>heart</u>: one speaks of the eyes, the hand, the mouth of God, but not of the other parts of the body: Learn from this the grammar of the word "God"! [I read somewhere, Luther had written that theology is the "grammar of the word of God", of the holy scripture] [See **PI** *373].

Respect[60] for madness – that is really all I am saying.

Again and again I keep sitting through the comedy, instead of walking out into the street.

A <u>religious question</u> is either a question of life or it is (<u>empty</u>) chatter. This language game – one could say- gets played only with questions of life. Much like the word "ouch" does not have any meaning – except as a scream of pain.

I want to say: If eternal bliss means nothing for my life, <u>my</u> way of life, then I don't have to rack my brain about it; if I am to rightfully think about it, then what I think must stand in a <u>precise</u> relation to my life, otherwise what I think is rubbish or my life is in danger. – An authority which is not <u>effective</u>, which I don't <u>have</u> to need, is no authority. If I rightfully speak of an authority I must also be dependent upon it.
MT

24.02.1937
Only[61] if I am no (<u>base</u>) egoist can I <u>hope</u> for a peaceful death.

---

59 In code.
60 In code.
61 In code.

The one who is pure has a hardness which is tough to bear. That is why one accepts the admonitions of a Dostoevsky more easily than those of a Kierkegaard. One of them is still squeezing while the other is already <u>cutting</u>.

If you are not willing to sacrifice your work for something still higher, there is no blessing with it. For it attains its height only when you place it at its true altitude in relation to the ideal.

That is why vanity destroys the <u>value</u> of the work. <u>This</u> is how the work of Kraus, for example, has become a 'tinkling bell'. (Kraus was an <u>architect of sentences, extraordinarily</u> talented at that).

It appears I am gradually <u>regaining</u> energy to work again. For in the last 2–3 days I was able to think more & more about philosophy again, though still little, & write remarks. On the other hand I have in my breast a feeling as if perhaps I was nevertheless not permitted to work. That is, while working I feel only tolerably or only <u>half</u> happy & have a certain fear that it may yet be prohibited. That is, that a feeling of gloom might come over me which will render continued work meaningless & force me to give up work. But would that this not happen!! – But all of this is connected to the feeling that I am not <u>loving</u> enough, that is, too <u>egotistic</u>. That I care too little what feels good to <u>others</u>. And how can I live calmly if all the while I can't hope to die peacefully. *God,[62] make it better!!*

"There is no one here", – but I can go mad all by myself, too.

It is strange that one says God created the world & not: God is creating, continually, the world. For why should it be a greater miracle that it began to be, rather than that it continued to be. One is led astray by the simile of the craftsperson. That someone <u>makes</u> a shoe is an accomplishment, but once made (<u>out of what is existing</u>) it endures on its own for a while. But if one thinks of God as creator, must the conservation of the universe not be a miracle <u>just as great</u> as its creation, – yes, aren't the two <u>one and the same</u>? Why should I postulate a singular act of creation & not a continuous act of conservation – which began at some point, which had a temporal beginning, or what amounts to the same, a continuous creating?

MT

27.02.1937

Christianity[63] says: Here (in this world) – so to speak – you should not be <u>sitting</u> but <u>going</u>. You must away from here, & should not suddenly be torn away, but be dead when your body dies.

---

62 In code.
63 In code.

The question is: *How do you go through this life – (Or: Let this be your question!) – Since my work, for example, is only a sitting in the world, after all. But I am supposed to go & not just sit.*
MT

03.03.1937
Kneeling[64] *means that one is a slave. (Religion might consist in this).*
  Lord, if only I knew that I am slave!
MT

15.03.1937
To know oneself is horrible, because one simultaneously recognizes the living demand, &, that one does not satisfy it. But there is no better means to get to know oneself than seeing the perfect one. Thus the perfect one must arouse in people a storm of outrage; unless they want to humiliate themselves through and through. I think the words "Blessed is he who does not get angry at me"[65] mean: Blessed is he who can stand the view of the perfect one. For you must fall into dust before him, & you don't like doing that. What do you want to call the perfect one? Is he a human being? – Yes, in a certain sense he is of course a human being. But in another sense he is yet something completely different. What do you want to call him? don't you have to call him 'God'? For what would correspond to this idea, if not that? But formerly you saw God perhaps in the creation, that is, in the world; & now you seen him, in another sense, in a human being.

Now at one time you say: "God created the world" & at another: "This human being is – God". But you do not mean that this human being created the world, & yet there is a unity here.

We have two different conceptions of God: or, we have two different conceptions & use the word God for both.

But now if you believe in providence: that is, if you believe that nothing that happens, happens any other way than through the will of God, then you must also believe that this greatest thing happened through the will of God, namely that a human being was born who is God. Mustn't this fact then be of 'decisive significance' for you? I mean: mustn't it then have implications for your life, commit you to something? I mean: mustn't you enter into an ethical relation with him? For you have duties, for example, due to the fact that you have a father & a mother & weren't, for example, put into the world without them. Don't you therefore have duties also through & towards this fact?

---

64 In code.
65 Luther's translation of Matthew 11:6.

Do I feel such duties, however? My faith is too weak.

I mean, my belief in providence, my feeling: "everything happens through the will of God". And this is no opinion – also not a conviction, but an attitude toward the things & what is happening. *May[66] I not become frivolous!*
MT

16.03.1937

Yesterday I thought of the expression: "a pure heart"; why don't I have one? That means, after all: why are my thoughts so impure! In my thoughts there is again and again vanity, swindle, resentment. May God steer my life so that it becomes different.
MT

17.03.1937

Because[67] of the clouds it is impossible to see whether the sun is above the mountain already or not yet & I am almost sick from the longing to finally see it. (I want to quarrel with God).
MT

18.03.1937

The sun should be above the mountain now but is invisible because of the weather. If you want to quarrel with God, that means that you have a false concept of God. You are superstitious. You have an incorrect concept when you get angry with fate. You should rearrange our concepts. Contentment with your fate ought to be the first command of wisdom.

Today I saw the sun from my window at the moment when it started rising from behind the western mountain. Thank God. But to my shame I now believe that this word was not sufficiently heartfelt. For I was quite glad when I really saw the sun but my joy was not deep enough, too merry, not truly religious. Oh[68] if only I were deeper!
MT

20.03.1937

I believe: I understand that the state of mind of believing can make the human being blissful. For when people believe, wholeheartedly believe, that the perfect one has sacrificed himself for them, that he has therefore – from the beginning – reconciled them with God, so that from now on you shall simply live in a way that

---

66 In code.
67 In code.
68 In code.

is worthy of this sacrifice, – then this must refine the whole person, elevate him to nobility, so to speak. I understand – I want to say – that this <u>is</u> a movement of the soul toward bliss.

It is written – I believe – "Believe that you are now reconciled, & don't sin 'henceforth any more'!"[69] – But it is also clear that this belief is a blessing. And, I deep enough, too merry, not truly believe, the condition for it is that we do our utmost & see that it leads us nowhere, that, no matter how much we torment ourselves, we remain unreconciled. <u>Then</u> the reconciliation comes rightfully. But now, is that person lost who is not of this belief? I can't believe that; or rather can't believe it yet. For <u>perhaps</u> I will believe it. If one is speaking here of the 'secret' of that sacrifice: you would have to understand the grammar of the word <u>secret</u> here!

There is *no one* here: & yet I speak & thank & petition. But is this speaking & thanking & petitioning an <u>error</u>?!

I would rather say: "<u>This</u> is what is strange!"

In doubt what to do in the immediate future. An inner voice tells me that I should now get away from here, & to Dublin. But then again I hope that I won't have to do this now. I would like to say: Would that I am granted that I can work here some more time! – But I have, so to speak, arrived at the end of a section of my work.

God, what a blessing it is to be able to live without horrible problems! Would that it stays with me!

MT

23.03.1937

I am like a beggar who sometimes reluctantly admits that he is no king.

Today the sun showed itself above the mountain from roughly 11:45 until 1:15, then a moment at 3:45 & before it sets it shines again.

Help[70] *& Illuminate!* But if I believe something tomorrow that I don't believe today, I was not therefore in an error today. For this 'believing' is not <u>holding an opinion</u>, after all. But my belief tomorrow can be <u>lighter</u> (or darker) than my belief today. *Help & Illuminate* & would that no darkness descend upon me!

MT

24.03.1937

I am petitioning & *I*[71] *already have it as I want to have it: namely half heaven, half hell!*

---

69 See the Gospel According to John 8:11.
70 In code.
71 In code.

[...]

I had this thought today: At the time when I had written down my confession I thought a few times also of my mom & thought that I could in some sense retroactively redeem her through my confession; for I thought she, too, was carrying such a confession in her heart & hadn't unburdened it in her life for she remained withdrawn. And my confession, so it seemed to me, was finally speaking in her name, too; & she could now somehow identify with it retroactively. (It would be as if I paid the debt that had already burdened her & as if her spirit could tell me: "Thank God that you paid it off now"). – Now, I was thinking outside today about the meaning of the doctrine of the redemptive death & I thought: Might the re-

---

25.03.1937
demption through the sacrifice consist in the fact that <u>he did</u> what all of us want to, but can't do. But in believing one identifies with <u>him</u>, that is, one pays the debt now in the form of humble recognition; one shall therefore become quite <u>abject</u> because one can't become good.

The thought occurred to me that I should fast tomorrow (on Good Friday) & I thought: I will do that. But immediately afterwards it appeared to me like a commandment, as if I <u>had</u> to do it & I resisted that. I said: "I want to do it if it comes from my heart & not because I was <u>commanded</u> to". But this then is no obedience! There is no <u>mortification</u> in doing what comes from the heart (even if it is friendly or in some sense pious). You don't <u>die</u> in this, after all. Whereas you <u>die</u> precisely in obedience to a command, from mere obedience. This is agony but can be, is supposed to be, a pious agony. That's at least how I understand it. But I myself! – I confess that I do not want to die off, even though I understand that it is the higher. *This[72] is horrible; & may this horribleness become illuminated by the light shining in!*

Have been sleeping quite badly for a few nights & feel dead, can't work; my thoughts are dim & I am depressed but in a glowering way. (That is, I am afraid of certain religious thoughts).
MT

26.03.1937
I am as illuminated as I am; I mean: my religion is as illuminated as it is. <u>I</u> haven't illuminated myself less yesterday & not more today. For had I been <u>able</u> to view it that yesterday, I would have definitely viewed it like that.

---

72 In code.

One shouldn't be puzzled that one age doesn't believe in witches & a later one does believe in witches & that this & similar things go away & come back, etc; but in order to no longer be puzzled you only need to look at what happens to yourself. – One day you can pray but another perhaps not, & one day you <u>must</u> pray, & on another not.

Through[73] *mercy I am doing much better today than yesterday.*
MT

06.04.1937

An exegesis of the Christian teaching: Wake up completely! When you do that you recognize that you are no good & thus the joy you take in this world comes to an end. And it can't come back either if you <u>stay</u> awake. But now you need <u>salvation</u>, – otherwise you are lost. But you must stay alive (and this world is dead to you) so you need a new light from elsewhere. In this light there can be no cleverness, wisdom; for to this world you are dead. (Since this world is the paradise in which, because of your sinfulness, you can't go about anything, however). You must acknowledge yourself as dead & receive <u>another</u> life (for without that it is impossible to acknowledge yourself as dead without despair). This life must uphold you as if in suspension above this earth; that is, when you are walking on the earth, you nevertheless no longer <u>rest</u> on the earth, but <u>hang</u> in the sky; you are held from <u>above</u>, not supported from below. – But this life is love, human love, of the perfect one. And <u>this love</u> is faith.

'Everything else works itself out'.

God[74] *be praised that I am clearer today & feeling better.*
MT

09.04.1937

"You must love the perfect one more than anything, then you are blessed". This seems to me the sum of the Christian doctrine.
MT

11.04.1937

To[75] *God alone be praise!*
MT

---

73 In code.
74 In code.
75 In code.

17.04.1937

Is being alone with oneself – or with God, not like being alone with a wild animal? It can attack you any moment. – But isn't that precisely why you shouldn't run away?! Isn't that, so to speak, what's glorious?! Doesn't it mean: grow fond of this wild animal! – And yet one must ask: Lead us not into temptation![76]
MT

19.04.1937

I believe: the word "believing" has wrought horrible havoc in religion. All the knotty thoughts about the 'paradox' of the <u>eternal</u> meaning of a <u>historical</u> fact and the like. But if instead of "belief in Christ" you would say: "love of Christ", the paradox vanishes, that is, the irritation of the intellect. What does religion have to do with such a tickling of the intellect. (For someone or another this too may belong to their religion).

It is not that now one could say: Yes, finally everything is simple – or intelligible. Nothing at all is <u>intelligible</u>, it is just not <u>unintelligible</u>. –
MT

1937

In one day you can experience the horrors of hell; that is plenty of time.
CV

1937

If you offer a sacrifice & then are conceited about it, you will be cursed along with your sacrifice.
CV

19.08.1937

<u>I can't bear the thought of staying here until Christmas</u> (as I did last year) for there is no prospect of being able to fill this time with working and thinking. – I feel quite different now. – I can and should, however, use my being here now and think and work but not for an indefinite period of time! I'm dreading it and justifiably so, I believe. I can remain for about 6 weeks however my work goes. If I have no clear reasons for assuming at the end of that time that I can work better here than anywhere else then it will be time to move on. May God grant that I use well the time that I have left here!
MS 118 6r–6v

---

[76] Statement belonging to the Our Father.

25.08.1937
I was feeling terribly tired this morning, moved over my hut and wondered what it would be like? When I finally arrived with all my belongings, I suddenly felt fresher – both physically and spiritually! I am tired now but don't feel so gloomy. Once again I am able to look at my surroundings with joy. Thanks be to God. – I feel more relaxed and although I am now closer to everything of which I should be afraid, I feel more alive. God knows what is to become of me. May I be granted rest! – Temperature normal, although I have been moving around and eating quite a lot. Grant that I may act sensibly for I'm feeling somewhat unbalanced. This is partly due to a longing that I have at the back of my mind to see Francis which is troubling me. "God, into your hands I commend my spirit!"[77] is what I should have said.
MS 118 10r–10v

26.08.1937
I feel much better than I did yesterday and am only in slight pain now. I once again take pleasure in looking at nature and am overwhelmed with gifts. And yet I behave badly and have <u>shabby</u> and vulgar pleasures and thoughts. Two letters from Drury and Francis.[78] Both of which were <u>moving</u> and kind. How little I deserve them. Wretched individual that I am. Invite Francis to come. May it be good! And grant that I may be reasonably decent. I am forever wanting to be unfaithful to God.
MS 118 115v–116r

27.08.1937
The solution of the problem you see in life is a way of living which makes what is problematic disappear (cf. **TLP** 6.521).

The fact that life is problematic means that your life does not fit life's shape. So you must change your life, & once it fits the shape, what is problematic will disappear.

But don't we have the feeling that someone who doesn't see a problem there is blind to something important, indeed to what is most important of all?

Wouldn't I like to say he is living aimlessly – just blindly like a mole as it were; & if he could only see, he would see the problem?

---

77 Wittgenstein is referring here to the final words of Christ before giving up the ghost, as they appear in the Gospel of Luke 23:46. It must be noted, though, that Wittgenstein introduces a slight change at the start of the phrase. The Gospel says "Father" and Wittgenstein writes "God".
78 Skinner.

Or shouldn't I say: someone who lives rightly does not experience the problem as *sorrow*, hence not after all as a problem, but rather as joy, that is so to speak as a bright halo round his life, not a murky background.
CV

29.08.1937
I detest all that is sentimental and ingenuous about the religion of the ancient Germans, or Westerners which means it provides no access to religion for me. This is, of course, not a criticism of another's religion. It means <u>theirs</u> is not my way – and I have nothing to do with everything that looks like this. It's like a national costume – but it's not mine.

When someone says: "Only the innocent go to heaven", I can say: No, that is not my religion. – That's why I appear to be at a disadvantage if I wish to learn religion from an innocent person but I'm not really at any disadvantage at all. So I am then inclined to say: "If only I had the right teacher of religion …!" Having to swim against the current is no disadvantage if swimming is the objective.
MS 118, 30v

04.09.1937
Christianity is not a doctrine, not, I mean, a theory about what has happened & will happen to the human soul, but a description of something that actually takes place in human life. For 'recognition of sin' is an actual occurrence & so is despair & so is redemption through faith. Those who speak of it (like Bunyan), are simply describing what has happened to them; whatever gloss someone may want to put on it!
CV

07.09.1937
I'm not well. I'm irreligious but also fearful as a consequence.
MS 118, 62v

07.09.1937
When it's stormy outside, it's not comfortable here in the way that the worse the weather is outside, the more comfortable you feel indoors. The raging storm makes me feel agitated inside and stops me from working. It's as if the walls were too thin providing no sense of protection or security. It's as if the protective wall was so thin that it could collapse at any moment. Does solitude have the same effect? These feelings of mine are certainly provoked by the light draught going through the hut and by the shaking walls which are in fact strong enough.

I was tempted to curse God in the thunderstorms and bad weather which is just evil and superstitious. Afterwards I had the grace to think: stamp this storm firmly into your memory so that you learn something from it and then I felt better. (I can never get rid of my vanity.)
MS 118, 63r–63v

11.09.1937

If certain graphic propositions for instance are laid down <u>for human beings</u> as dogmas governing thinking, namely in such a way that opinions are not thereby determined, but the *expression* of opinions is completely controlled, this will have a very strange effect. People will live under an absolute, palpable tyranny, yet without being able to say that they are not free. I think the Catholic Church does something like this. For dogma is expressed in the form of an assertion & is unshakable, & at the same time any practical opinion can be made to accord with it; admittedly this is easier in some cases, more difficult in others. It is not a *wall* setting limits to belief, but like a *brake* which in practice however serves the same purpose; almost as though someone attached a weight to your foot to limit your freedom of movement. This is how dogma becomes irrefutable & beyond the reach of attack.
CV

11.09.1937

In civil life as in religious life there is an honour to which various people are sensitive to varying degrees. One person may consider verbal abuse to be a negation of his moral personality and only blood can cleanse him of it, whilst another person soon forgets the abuse. One person says: "how can I live when I have been verbally abused?" and the other is able to carry on living all the same.
MS 118, 88v

24.09.1937

Religious similes can be said to move on the edge of the abyss. B<unyan>'s allegory for instance. For what if we simply add: "and all these traps, swamps, wrong turnings, were planted by the Lord of the Road, the monsters, thieves, robbers were created by him?"

Without doubt, that is not the sense of the simile! But this sequel is too obvious! For many & for me it robs the simile of its power.

But more especially if this is – as it were – suppressed. It would be different if it were said openly at every turn: 'I am using this as a simile, but look: it doesn't fit here'. Then you wouldn't feel you were being cheated, that someone were trying to convince you by trickery. You can say to someone for instance: "Thank God for the good you receive but don't complain about the evil, as you would of course do if a human being were to do you good and evil by turns". Rules of life are dressed up in pictures. And these pictures can only serve to *describe* what we are supposed to do, but not to *justify* it. Because to be a justification they would have to hold good in others respects too. I can say: "Thank these bees for their honey as though they were good people who have prepared it for you"; that is *intelligible* & describes how I wish you to behave. But not: <">. Thank them, for look how good they are!" – since the next moment they may sting you.

Religion says: *Do this!* – *Think like that!* But it cannot justify this and it only need try to do so to become repugnant; since for every reason it gives, there is a cogent counter-reason.

It is more convincing to say: "Think like this! – however strange it may seem –." Or: "Won't you do this? – repugnant as it is –."

Election by grace: It is only permissible to write like this out of the most frightful suffering – & then it means something quite different. But for this reason it is not permissible for anyone to cite it as truth, unless he himself says it in torment. – It simply isn't a theory –. Or as one might also say: if this is truth, it is not the truth it appears at first glance to express. It's less a theory than a sigh, or a cry.
CV

04.10.1937

The spring that flows quietly & clearly in the Gospels seems to foam in Paul's Epistles. Or that is how it seems to *me*. Perhaps it is just my own impurity that reads muddiness into it; for why shouldn't this impurity be able to pollute what is clear? But for *me* it's as though I saw human passion, something like pride or anger, which does not square with the humility of the *Gospels*. It is as though he really is insisting here on his own person, & *doing so moreover as a religious act*, something which is foreign to the Gospel. I want to ask – & may this be no blasphemy-: "What would Christ perhaps have said to Paul?"

But a far rejoinder to that would be: What business is that of yours? Look after making *yourself* more decent! In your present state, you are quite incapable of understanding what may be the truth here.

In the Gospels – as it seems to me – everything is *less pretentious*, humbler, simpler. There you find huts; – with Paul a church. There all human beings are equal & God himself is a human being; with Paul there is already something like a hierarchy; honours, and official positions. – That is, as it were, what my NOSE tells me.
CV

16.10.1937
I haven't heard from Francis for about 12 days and am somewhat concerned because he hasn't written from England yet. Oh God, how much wretchedness and misery there is in this world.
MS 119, 123–4

17.10.1937
Received a letter from Francis. Am relieved and delighted! May God help us.
MS 119, 137

21.10.1937
If you saw the Perfect One, how would you want to address him if not as "God"?! –

First a firm, hard stone needs to be in place to build upon before the blocks can be laid <u>unhewn</u> one on top of the other. <u>Then</u>, of course, it is important that the stone can actually be built upon (that it is) not all too hard.
MS 119, 147 (74)

22.10.1937
Kierkegaard writes: If Christianity were so easy and cosy, why would God have moved Heaven & Earth in his Scripture, threatened *eternal* punishments – . – Question: But why is this Scripture so unclear then? If we want to warn someone of a terrible danger, do we do it by giving him a riddle to solve, whose solution is perhaps the warning? – But who is to say that the Scripture really is unclear: isn't it possible that it was essential in this case to tell a riddle? That a more direct warning, on the other hand, would necessarily have had the *wrong* effect? God has *four* people recounting the life of the incarnate God, each one differently, & contradicting each other – but can't we say: It is important that this narrative should not have more than quite middling historical plausibility, *just so* that this should not be taken as the essential, decisive thing. So that the *letter* should not be believed more strongly than is proper & the *spirit* should receive its due. I.e.: What you are supposed to see cannot be communicated even by the best, more accurate, historian; *therefore* a mediocre account suffices, is even to be preferred. For that too can tell you what you are supposed to be told. (Roughly in the way a mediocre stage set can be better than a sophisticated one, painted trees better than real ones, – which distract attention from what matters.)

The Spirit puts what is essential, essential for your life, into these words. The point is precisely that you are SUPPOSED to see clearly only what even *this* representation clearly shows. (I am not sure how far all this is exactly in the spirit of Kierkegaard.)
CV

26.10.1937
I'm not writing any more now but read my typescript all day long and make notes on every paragraph. There is much thought given to these remarks. But for various reasons only a few of the remarks can be used for a book without the need for revision. I have now looked through almost a quarter of the book. If all goes smoothly, I could have it ready in approx 6 days. But then what? Now try to gather together what might be useful – which is of course very difficult! I often thought today that it might mean that I would have to go away from here, to Drury or Maurice, if God wills, for I don't know if I can do this work in this loneliness. All will be revealed however. –

I often pray during the day and yet I have to say that I really can't pray properly, for I lack seriousness. I am praying for enlightenment; may it be granted to me even though I cannot even ask for it properly. Vanity and meanness creep into everything I write or think without exception.

Meanness is always **next door**[79] at least.
MS 119, 80r–81r

29.10.1937
I would have much to write about myself, my bad thoughts, feelings, anxieties and malevolencies but I'll omit them. I would also have much to write about religion, half-heartedness, frivolousness, but I am living superficially. Grant that things will be different! And yet I do not wish suffering and loss upon myself.
MS 119, 81v

18.11.1937
Last year, with God's help, I managed to pull myself together and went to confession. This brought me into purer waters, gave me a better relationship with people and made me more serious. All this has now come to an end, so to speak, and I now feel I am back to where I started. More than anything else I am such a coward. If I don't do anything good, I'll end up in stormy waters again.

I'm afraid of everything. I am just about as far as I could be from hating my life for God. I don't even want to leave my friend for Him. May God help me.
MS 119, 140r–140v

19.11.1937
Feeling very irritable today. I long to be gone from here and amongst people with whom I can converse. God grant that I may live and do something good with my life!
MS 120, 1r

---

79 In English in the original.

20.11.1937
In religion it must be the case that corresponding to every level of devoutness there is a form of expression that has no sense at a lower level. For those still at the lower level this doctrine, which means something at the higher level, is null & void; it *can* only be understood *wrongly*, & so these words are *not* valid for such a person.

Paul's doctrine of election by grace for instance is at my level irreligiousness, ugly non-sense. So it is not meant for me since I can only apply wrongly the picture offered me. If it is a holy & good picture, then it is so for a quite different level, where it must be applied in life quite differently than I could apply it.
CV

22.11.1937[80]
I am now counting the days until I leave. A little less than 3 weeks. Will I survive? – I'm afraid of everything; of staying here, of my trip to Germany; I'm even a little afraid of Vienna and the future. Yes, I am now so-to-speak screwed up. I feel lost. May God turn things around!

To discover yourself in the world – that's what counts. Not to demand anything of the world, but to find oneself in the world as it is. This means not making a novel out of it and then being surprised and offended by the lack of harmony in the world. But this is precisely what I do. I feel quite wretched.
MS 120, 7v–8r

26.11.1937
I am counting the days until I leave but it's not good to count them! Not only are they good and important days for me but they are no different from all the days that have preceded them when something could have happened to me just as easily then as it could in the next 14 days!

I just feel tired now and worn out. I'm pulling the vehicle hard but I feel afraid I won't be able to pull it as far as home.

Only repose in God can help me.
MS 120, 16r–16v

27.11.1937
Thanks to God I was able to work better today. Went to fetch milk from Anna Rebni. In spite of our conversation she is unfriendly and strange.
MS 120, 17r

---

80 He was living in Norway by that time. Wittgenstein was full of anxieties and fears concerning his life and work. He was working on the foundations of mathematics.

28.11.1937
May I be illuminated by religious spirits because of the rheumatism in my soul. By Claudius again. I believe it is right that I should do this even though there is no improvement to be seen. There is no doubt no improvement to be expected either.

I always seem to feel what a devout person would never feel, namely that God is responsible for what I am. It's the opposite of piousness. I keep wanting to say:

"God what can I do if you don't help me!" And although I agree with a lot of what is written in the bible, I don't agree with the attitude of pious people but I can't fight this part of my thoughts – at least not directly. All I can do is endeavour to act decently as opposed to acting in a vulgar, cowardly or unpleasant way (with God coming and going as it were). If I manage to succeed then maybe there will also be a change in my way of thinking – in my use of the word "God".

You have to strive for it – **never mind God**.[81] How this links with rewards and punishments is another matter over which you have no influence anyway.
MS 120, 17r–17v

08–09.12.1937
Christianity is not based on a historical truth, but presents us with a (historical) narrative & says: now believe! But not believe this report with the belief that is appropriate to a historical report, – but rather: believe, through thick & thin you can do this only as the outcome of a life. *Here you have a message! – don't treat it as you would another historical message!* Make a *quite different* place for it in your life. – There is no *paradox* about that!

[...]

Queer as it sounds: the historical accounts of the Gospels might, in the historical sense, be demonstrably false, & yet belief would lose nothing through this: but *not* because it has to do with 'universal truths of reason'! rather, because historical proof (the historical proof-game) is irrelevant to belief. This message (the Gospels) is seized on by a human being believingly (i.e. lovingly): *That* is the certainty of this "taking-for-true", nothing *else*.

The believer's relation to these messages is *neither* a relation to historical truth (probability) *nor yet* that to a doctrine consisting of 'truths of reason'. There is such a thing. –(We have quite different attitudes even to different species of what we call fiction!)
CV

---

81 In English in the original.

12.12.1937
A great blessing for me to be able to work *today*. But I so easily forget all my blessings!

I am reading: "& no man can say that Jesus is the Lord, but by the Holy Ghost."[82] And it is true: I cannot call him *Lord*; because that says absolutely nothing to me. I could call him "the paragon", "God" even or rather: I can understand it when he is so called; but I cannot utter the word "Lord" meaningfully. *Because I do not believe* that he will come to judge me; because *that* says nothing to me. And it could only say something to me if I were to live *quite* differently.

What inclines even me to believe in Christ's resurrection? I play as it were with the thought. – If he did not rise from the dead, then decomposed in the grave like every human being. *He is dead & decomposed*. In that case he is a teacher, like any other & can no longer *help*; & we are once more orphaned & alone. And have to make do with wisdom & speculation. It is as though we are in hell, where we can only dream & are shut out from heaven, roofed in as it were. But if I am to be REALLY redeemed, – I need *certainty* – not wisdom, dreams, speculation – and this certainty is faith. And faith is faith in what my *heart*, my *soul*, needs, not my speculative intellect. For my soul, with its passions, as it were with its flesh & blood, must be redeemed, not my abstract mind. Perhaps one may say: Only *love* can believe the Resurrection. Or: it is *love* that believes the Resurrection. One might say: redeeming love believes even in the Resurrection; holds fast even to the Resurrection. What fights doubt is *as it were redemption*. Holding fast to *it* must be holding fast to this belief. So this means: first be redeemed & hold on tightly to your redemption (keep hold of your redemption) – then you will see that what you are holding on to is this belief. So this can only come about if you no longer support yourself on this earth but suspend yourself from heaven. Then *everything* is different and it is 'no wonder' if you can then do what now you cannot do. (It is true that someone who is suspended looks like someone who is standing but the interplay of forces within him is nevertheless a quite different one & hence he is able to do quite different things than can one who stands.)
CV

Letter from Wittgenstein to Ludwig Hänsel
Dear Hänsel!
[Skjolden, after October 12, 1937]

Thank you for your dear letter. The money of which you write I will surely receive soon. But please, for God's sake, don't send any more! First of all the whole thing

---

82 1 Corinthians, 3.

isn't worth mentioning, second, I have <u>no</u> use <u>at all</u> now for what you are sending me. If it must be I will allow you to repay me every cent – <u>when I can use it</u>.

I really haven't given Hermann any <u>advice</u>, except the <u>one</u> to take his conscience & everything having to do with religion <u>seriously</u>. (I hope, & believe, he will hold up better than I would have under the same circumstances).

<u>Think much of God & the right thing will also come out between the two of you</u>. But I don't have the right to give good advice, for I am a swine myself.

And that brings me to Drobil: have you seen him recently? Is he doing sensible work? Greet everyone <u>most sincerely</u>.

Your old friend
Ludwig Wittgenstein

LH

Letter to M. O'C. Drury
February 1938

Dear Drury,

I have thought a fair amount about our conversation on Sunday and I would like to say, or rather not to say but write, a few things about these conversations. Mainly I think this: Don't think about yourself, but think about others, e.g. your patients. You said in the Park yesterday that possibly you had made a mistake in having taken up medicine: you immediately added that probably it was wrong to think such a thing at all. I am sure it is. But not because being a doctor you may not go the wrong way, or go to the dogs, but because if you do, this has nothing to do with your choice of a profession being a mistake. For what human being can say what would have been the right thing if this is the wrong one? You didn't make a mistake because there was nothing at the time you knew or ought to have known that you overlooked. Only this one could have called making a mistake; and even if you had made a mistake in this sense, this would not have regarded as a datum as all the other circumstances inside and outside which you can't alter (control). The thing now is to live in the world in which you are, not to think or dream about the world you would like to be in. Look at people's sufferings, physical and mental, you have them close at hand, and this ought to be a good remedy for your troubles. Another way is to take a rest whenever you ought to take one and collect yourself. (Not with me because I wouldn't rest you.) As to religious thoughts I do not think the craving for placidity is religious; I think a religious person regards placidity or peace as a gift from heaven, not as something one ought to hunt after. Look at your patients more closely as human beings in trouble and enjoy more the opportunity you have to say 'good night' to so many people. This alone is a gift from heaven which many

people would envy you. And this sort of thing ought to heal your frayed soul, I believe. It won't rest it; but when you are healthily tired you can just take a rest. I think in some sense you don't look at people's faces closely enough.
WCB

Circa Summer 1938
LECTURES ON RELIGIOUS BELIEF[83]

I
An Austrian general said to someone: "I shall think of you after my death, if that should be possible." We can imagine one group who would find this ludicrous, another who wouldn't.

(During the war, Wittgenstein saw consecrated bread being carried in chromium steel. This struck him as ludicrous.)

Suppose that someone believed in the Last Judgement, and I don't, does this mean that I believe the opposite to him, just that there won't be such a thing? I would say: "not at all, or not always."

Suppose I say that the body will rot, and another says "No. Particles will rejoin in a thousand years, and there will be a Resurrection of you."

If some said: "Wittgenstein, do you believe in this?" I'd say: "No." "Do you contradict the man?" I'd say: "No."

If you say this, the contradiction already lies in this.

Would you say: "I believe the opposite", or "There is no reason to suppose such a thing"? I'd say neither.

Suppose someone were a believer and said: "I believe in a Last Judgement," and I said: "Well, I'm not so sure. Possibly." You would say that there is an enormous gulf between us. If he said "There is a German aeroplane overhead," and I said "Possibly. I'm not so sure," you'd say we were fairly near.

It isn't a question of my being anywhere near him, but on an entirely different plane, which you could express by saying: "You mean something altogether different, Wittgenstein."

The difference might not show up at all in any explanation of the meaning.

Why is it that in this case I seem to be missing the entire point?

Suppose somebody made this guidance for this life: believing in the Last Judgement. Whenever he does anything, this is before his mind. In a way, how are we to know whether to say he believes this will happen or not?

Asking him is not enough. He will probably say he has proof.

---

[83] The notes that make up these lectures were taken by Yorick Smythies, a pupil of Wittgenstein's who would later convert to Roman Catholicism.

But he has what you might call an unshakeable belief. It will show, not by reasoning or by appeal to ordinary grounds for belief, but rather by regulating for all in his life.

This is a very much stronger fact – foregoing pleasures, always appealing to this picture. This is one sense must be called the firmest of all beliefs, because the man risks things on account of it which he would not do on things which are by far better established for him. Although he distinguishes between things well-established and not well-established.

Lewy: Surely, he would say it is extremely well-established.

First, he may use "well-established" or not use it at all. He will treat this belief as extremely well-established, and in another way as not well-established at all.

If we have a belief, in certain cases we appeal again and again to certain grounds, and at the same time we risk pretty little – if it came to risking our lives on the ground of this belief.

There are instances where you have a faith – where you say "I believe" – and on the other hand this belief does not rest on the fact on which our ordinary everyday beliefs normally do rest.

How should we compare beliefs with each other? What would it mean to compare them?

You might say: 'We compare the states of mind."

How do we compare states of mind? This obviously won't do for all occasions. First, what you say won't be taken as the measure for the firmness of a belief? But, for instance, what risks you would take?

The strength of a belief is not comparable with the intensity of a pain.

An entirely different way of comparing beliefs is seeing what sorts of grounds he will give.

A belief isn't like a momentary state of mind. "At 5 o'clock he had very bad toothache."

Suppose you had two people, and one of them, when he had to decide which course to take, thought of retribution, and the other did not. One person might, for instance, be inclined to take everything that happened to him as a reward or punishment, and another person doesn't think of this at all.

If he is ill, he may think: "What have I done to deserve this?" This is one way of thinking of retribution. Another way is, he thinks in a general way whenever he is ashamed of himself: "This will be punished."

Take two people, one of whom talks of his behaviour and of what happens to him in terms of retribution, the other one does not. These people think entirely differently. Yet, so far, you can't say they believe different things.

Suppose someone is ill and he says: "This is a punishment," and I say: "If I'm ill, I don't think of punishment at all." If you say: "Do you believe the opposite?" – you can call it believing the opposite, but it is entirely different from what we would normally call believing the opposite.

I think differently, in a different way. I say different things to myself. I have different pictures.

It is this way: if someone said: "Wittgenstein, you don't take illness as punishment, so what do you believe?" – I'd say: "I don't have any thoughts of punishment."

There are, for instance, these entirely different ways of thinking first of all – which needn't be expressed by one person saying one thing, another person another thing.

What we call believing in a Judgement Day or not believing in a Judgement Day – The expression of belief may play an absolutely minor role.

If you ask me whether or not I believe in a Judgement Day, in the sense in which religious people have belief in it, I wouldn't say: "No. I don't believe there will be such a thing." It would seem to me utterly crazy to say this.

And then I give an explanation: "I don't believe in ...", but then the religious person never believes what I describe.

I can't say. I can't contradict that person.

In one sense, I understand all he says – the English words "God", "separate", etc. I understand. I could say: "I don't believe in this," and this would be true, meaning I haven't got these thoughts or anything that hangs together with them. But not that I could contradict the thing.

You might say: "Well, if you can't contradict him, that means you don't understand him. If you did understand him, then you might." That again is Greek to me. My normal technique of language leaves me. I don't know whether to say they understand one another or not.

These controversies look quite different from any normal controversies. Reasons look entirely different from normal reasons.

They are, in a way, quite inconclusive.

The point is that if there were evidence, this would in fact destroy the whole business.

Anything that I normally call evidence wouldn't in the slightest influence me.

Suppose, for instance, we knew people who foresaw the future; make forecasts for years and years ahead; and they described some sort of a Judgement Day. Queerly enough, even if there were such a thing, and even if it were more convincing than I have described, belief in this happening wouldn't be at all a religious belief.

Suppose that I would have to forego all pleasures because of such a forecast. If I do so and so, someone will put me in fires in a thousand years, etc. I wouldn't budge. The best scientific evidence is just nothing.

A religious belief might in fact fly in the face of such a forecast, and say "No. There it will break down."

As it were, the belief as formulated on the evidence can only be the last result – in which a number of ways of thinking and acting crystallize and come together.

A man would fight for his life not to be dragged into the fire. No induction. Terror. That is, as it were, part of the substance of the belief.

That is partly why you don't get in religious controversies, the form of controversy where one person is *sure* of the thing, and the other says: 'Well, possibly.'

You might be surprised that there hasn't been opposed to those who believe in Resurrection those who say "Well, possibly."

Here believing obviously plays much more this role: suppose we said that a certain picture might play the role of constantly admonishing me, or I always think of it. Here, an enormous difference would be between those people for whom the picture is constantly in the foreground, and the others who just didn't use it at all.

Those who said: "Well, possibly it may happen and possibly not" would be on an entirely different plane.

This is partly why one would be reluctant to say: "These people rigorously hold the opinion (or view) that there is a Last Judgement". "Opinion" sounds queer.

It is for this reason that different words are used: 'dogma', 'faith'.

We don't talk about hypothesis, or about high probability. Nor about knowing.

In a religious discourse we use such expressions as: "I believe that so and so will happen," and use them differently to the way in which we use them in science.

Although, there is a great temptation to think we do. Because we do talk of evidence, and do talk of evidence by experience.

We could even talk of historic events.

It has been said that Christianity rests on an historic basis.

It has been said a thousand times by intelligent people that indubitability is not enough in this case. Even if there is as much evidence as for Napoleon. Because the indubitability wouldn't be enough to make me change my whole life.

It doesn't rest on an historic basis in the sense that the ordinary belief in historic facts could serve as a foundation.

Here we have a belief in historic facts different from a belief in ordinary historic facts. Even, they are not treated as historical, empirical, propositions.

Those people who had faith didn't apply the doubt which would ordinarily apply to *any* historical propositions. Especially propositions of a time long past, etc.

What is the criterion of reliability, dependability? Suppose you give a general description as to when you say a proposition has a reasonable weight of probability. When you call it reasonable, is this *only* to say that for it you have such and such evidence, and for others you haven't?

For instance, we don't trust the account given of an event by a drunk man.

Father O'Hara is one of those people who make it a question of science.

Here we have people who treat this evidence in a different way. They base things on evidence which taken in one way would seem exceedingly flimsy. They base enormous things on this evidence. Am I to say they are unreasonable? I wouldn't call them unreasonable.

I would say, they are certainly not *reasonable*, that's obvious.

'Unreasonable' implies, with everyone, rebuke.

I want to say: they don't treat this as a matter of reasonability.

Anyone who reads the Epistles will find it said: not only that it is not reasonable, but that it is folly.

Not only is it not reasonable, but it doesn't pretend to be.

What seems to me ludicrous about O'Hara is his making it appear to be *reasonable*.

Why shouldn't one form of life culminate in an utterance of belief in a Last Judgement? But I couldn't either say "Yes" or "No" to the statement that there will be such a thing. Nor "Perhaps," nor "I'm not sure."

It is a statement which may not allow of any such answer.

If Mr. Lewy is religious and says he believes in a Judgement Day, I won't even know whether to say I understand him or not. I've read the same things as he's read. In a most important sense, I know what he means.

If an atheist says: "There won't be a Judgement Day, and another person says there will," do they mean the same? – Not clear what criterion of meaning the same is. They might describe the same things. You might say, this already shows that they mean the same.

We come to an island and we find beliefs there, and certain beliefs we are inclined to call religious. What I'm driving at is, that religious beliefs will not ... They have sentences, and there are also religious statements.

These statements would not just differ in respect to what they are about. Entirely different connections would make them into religious beliefs, and there can easily be imagined transitions where we wouldn't know for our life whether to call them religious beliefs or scientific beliefs.

You may say they reason wrongly.

In certain cases you would say they reason wrongly, meaning they contradict us. In other cases you would say they don't reason at all, or "It is an entirely different kind of reasoning." The first, you would say in the case in which they reason in a similar way to us, and make something corresponding to our blunders.

Whether a thing is a blunder or not – it is a blunder in a particular system. Just as something is a blunder in a particular game and not in another.

You could also say that where we are reasonable, they are not reasonable – meaning they don't use *reason* here.

If they do something very like one of our blunders, I would say, I don't know. It depends on further surroundings of it.

It is difficult to see, in cases in which it has all the appearances of trying to be reasonable.

I would definitely call O'Hara unreasonable. I would say, if this is religious belief, then it's all superstition.

But I would ridicule it, not by saying it is based on insufficient evidence. I would say: here is a man who is cheating himself. You can say: this man is ridiculous because he believes, and bases it on weak reasons.

II

The word 'God' is amongst the earliest learnt – pictures and catechisms, etc. But not the same consequences as with pictures of aunts. I wasn't shown [that which the picture pictured].

The word is used like a word representing a person. God sees, rewards, etc.

"Being shown all these things, did you understand what this word meant?" I'd say: "Yes and no. I did learn what it didn't mean. I made myself understand. I could answer questions, understand questions when they were put in different ways – and in that sense could be said to understand."

If the question arises as to the existence of a god or God, it plays an entirely different role to that of the existence of any person or object I ever heard of. One said, had to say, that one *believed* in the existence, and if one did not believe, this was regarded as something bad. Normally if I did not believe in the existence of something no one would think there was anything wrong in this.

Also, there is this extraordinary use of the word 'believe'. One talks of believing and at the same time one doesn't use 'believe' as one does ordinarily. You might say (in the normal use): "You only believe – oh well ...." Here it is used entirely differently; on the other hand it is not used as we generally use the word 'know'.

If I even vaguely remember what I was taught about God, I might say: "Whatever believing in God may be, it can't be believing in something we can test, or find means of testing." You might say: "This is nonsense, because people say they believe on *evidence* or say they believe on religious experiences." I would say: "The mere fact that someone says they believe on evidence doesn't tell me enough for me to be able to say now whether I can say of a sentence 'God exists' that your evidence is unsatisfactory or insufficient."

Suppose I know someone, Smith. I've heard that he has been killed in a battle in this war. One day you come to me and say: "Smith is in Cambridge." I inquire, and find you stood at Guildhall and saw at the other end a man and said: "That was Smith." I'd say: "Listen. This isn't sufficient evidence." If we had a fair amount of evidence he was killed I would try to make you say that you're being credulous. Suppose he was never heard of again. Needless to say, it is quite impossible to make inquiries: "Who at 12.05 passed Market Place into Rose Crescent?" Suppose you say: "He was there". I would be extremely puzzled.

Suppose there is a feast on Mid-Summer Common. A lot of people stand in a ring. Suppose this is done every year and then everyone says he has seen one of his dead relatives on the other side of the ring. In this case, we could ask everyone in the ring. "Who did you hold by the hand?" Nevertheless, we'd all say that on that day we see our dead relatives. You could in this case say: "I had an extraordinary experience. I had the experience I can express by saying: 'I saw my dead cousin'." Would we say you are saying this on insufficient evidence? Under certain circumstances I would say this, under other circumstances I wouldn't. Where what is said sounds a bit absurd I would say: "Yes, in this case insufficient evidence." If altogether absurd, then I wouldn't.

Suppose I went to somewhere like Lourdes in France. Suppose I went with a very credulous person. There we see blood coming out of something. He says: "There you are, Wittgenstein, how can you doubt?" I'd say: "Can it only be explained one way? Can't it be this or that?" I'd try to convince him that he'd seen nothing of any consequence. I wonder whether I would do that under all circumstances. I certainly know that I would under normal circumstances.

"Oughtn't one after all to consider this?" I'd say: "Come on. Come on." I would treat the phenomenon in this case just as I would treat an experiment in a laboratory which I thought badly executed.

"The balance moves when I will it to move." I point out it is not covered up, a draught can move it, etc.

I could imagine that someone showed an extremely passionate belief in such a phenomenon, and I couldn't approach his belief at all by saying: "This could just as well have been brought about by so and so" because he could think this blasphemy on my side. Or he might say: "It is possible that these priests cheat, but nevertheless in a different sense a miraculous phenomenon takes place there."

I have a statue which bleeds on such and such a day in the year. I have red ink, etc. "You are a cheat, but nevertheless the Deity uses you. Red ink in a sense, but not red ink in a sense."

Cf. Flowers at seance with label. People said: "Yes, flowers are materialized with label." What kind of circumstances must there be to make this kind of story not ridiculous?

I have a moderate education, as all of you have, and therefore know what is meant by insufficient evidence for a forecast. Suppose someone dreamt of the Last Judgement, and said he now knew what it would be like. Suppose someone said: "This is poor evidence." I would say: "If you want to compare it with the evidence for it's raining to-morrow it is no evidence at all." He may make it sound as if by stretching the point you may call it evidence. But it may be more than ridiculous as evidence. But now, would I be prepared to say: "You are basing your belief on extremely slender evidence, to put it mildly." Why should I regard this dream as evidence – measuring its validity as though I were measuring the validity of the evidence for meteorological events?

If you compare it with anything in Science which we call evidence, you can't credit that anyone could soberly argue: "Well, I had this dream ... therefore ... Last Judgement". You might say: "For a blunder, that's too big." If you suddenly wrote numbers down on the blackboard, and then said: "Now, I'm going to add," and then said: "2 and 21 is 13," etc. I'd say: "This is no blunder."

There are cases where I'd say he's mad, or he's making fun. Then there might be cases where I look for an entirely different interpretation altogether. In order to see what the explanation is I should have to see the sum, to see in what way it is done, what he makes follow from it, what are the different circumstances under which he does it, etc.

I mean, if a man said to me after a dream that he believed in the Last Judgement, I'd try to find what sort of impression it gave him. One attitude: "It will be in about 2,000 years. It will be bad for so and so and so, etc." Or it may be one of terror. In the case where there is hope, terror, etc., would I say there is insufficient evidence if he says: "I believe ..."? I can't treat these words as I normally treat "I believe so and so". It would be entirely beside the point, and also if he said his friend so and so and his grandfather had had the dream and believed, it would be entirely beside the point.

I would not say: "If a man said he dreamt it would happen to-morrow, would he take his coat?", etc.

Case where Lewy has visions of his dead friend. Cases where you don't try to locate him. And case where you try to locate him in a business-like way. Another case where I'd say: "We can presuppose we have a broad basis on which we agree."

In general, if you say: "He is dead" and I say: "He is not dead" no one would say: "Do they mean the same thing by 'dead'?" In the case where a man has visions I wouldn't offhand say: "He means something different."

Cf. A person having persecution mania.

What is the criterion for meaning something different? Not only what he takes as evidence for it, but also how he reacts, that he is in terror, etc.

How am I to find out whether this proposition is to be regarded as an empirical proposition – 'You'll see your dead friend again?' Would I say: "He is a bit superstitious?" Not a bit.

He might have been apologetic. (The man who stated it categorically was more intelligent than the man who was apologetic about it).

"Seeing a dead friend," again means nothing much to me at all. I don't think in these terms. I don't say to myself: "I shall see so and so again" ever.

He always says it, but he doesn't make any search. He puts on a queer smile. "His story had that dreamlike quality." My answer would be in this case "Yes," and a particular explanation.

Take "God created man". Pictures of Michelangelo showing the creation of the world. In general, there is nothing which explains the meanings of words as well as a picture, and I take it that Michelangelo was as good as anyone can be and did his best, and here is the picture of the Deity creating Adam.

If we ever saw this, we certainly wouldn't think this the Deity. The picture has to be used in an entirely different way if we are to call the man in that queer blanket "God", and so on. You could imagine that religion was taught by means of these pictures. "Of course, we can only express ourselves by means of picture." This is rather queer ... I could show Moore the pictures of a tropical plant. There is a technique of comparison between picture and plant. If I showed him the picture of Michelangelo and said: "Of course, I can't show you the real thing, only the picture" .... The absurdity is, I've never taught him the technique of using this picture.

It is quite clear that the role of pictures of Biblical subjects and role of the picture of God creating Adam are totally different ones. You might ask this question: "Did Michelangelo think that Noah in the ark looked like this, and that God creating Adam looked like this?" He wouldn't have said that God or Adam looked as they look in this picture.

It might seem as though, if we asked such a question as: "Does Lewy *really* mean what so and so means when he says so and so is alive?" – it might seem as though there were two sharply divided cases, one in which he would say he didn't mean it literally. I want to say this is not so. There will be cases where we will differ, and where it won't be a question at all of more or less knowledge, so that we can come together. Sometimes it will be a question of experience, so you can say: "Wait another 10 years." And I would say: "I would disencourage this kind of reasoning" and Moore would say: "I wouldn't disencourage it." That is, one would *do* something. We would take sides, and that goes so far that there would really be great differences between us, which might come out in Mr. Lewy saying: "Wittgenstein is trying to undermine reason", and this wouldn't be false. This is actually where such questions rise.

III

Today I saw a poster saying: "'Dead' Undergraduate speaks."

The inverted commas mean: "He isn't really dead." "He isn't what people call dead. They call it 'dead' not quite correctly."

We don't speak of "door" in quotes.

It suddenly struck me: "If someone said 'He isn't really dead, although by the ordinary criteria he is dead' – couldn't I say "He is not only dead by the ordinary criteria; he is what we all call 'dead'."

If you now call him 'alive', you're using language in a queer way, because you're almost deliberately preparing misunderstandings. Why don't you use some other word, and let "dead" have the meaning it already has?

Suppose someone said: "It didn't always have this meaning. He's not dead according to the old meaning" or "He's not dead according to the old idea".

What is it, to have different ideas of death? Suppose you say: "I have the idea of myself being a chair after death" or "I have the idea of myself being a chair in half-an-hour" – you all know under what circumstances we say of something that it has become a chair.

Cf. (1) "This shadow will cease to exist."

(2) "This chair will cease to exist." You say that you know what this chair ceasing to exist is like. But you have to think. You may find that there isn't a use for this sentence. You think of the use.

I imagine myself on the death-bed. I imagine you all looking at the air above me. You say "You have an idea".

Are you clear when you'd say you had ceased to exist?

You have six different ideas [of 'ceasing to exist'] at different times.

If you say: "I can imagine myself being a disembodied spirit. Wittgenstein, can you imagine yourself as a disembodied spirit?" – I'd say: "I'm sorry. I [so far] connect nothing with these words."

I connect all sorts of complicated things with these words. I think of what people have said of sufferings after death, etc.

"I have two different ideas, one of ceasing to exist after death, the other of being a disembodied spirit."

What's it like to have two different ideas? What is the criterion for one man having one idea, another man having another idea?

You gave me two phrases, "ceasing to exist", "being a disembodied spirit". "When I say this, I think of myself having a certain set of experiences." What is it like to think of this?

If you think of your brother in America, how do you know that what you think is, that the thought inside you is, of your brother being in America? Is this an experiential business?

Cf. How do you know that what you want is an apple? [Russell].

How do you know that you believe that your brother is in America?

A pear might be what satisfied you. But you wouldn't say: "What I wanted was an apple."

Suppose we say that the thought is some sort of process in his mind, or his saying something, etc. – then I could say: "All right, you call this a thought of your brother in America, well, what is the connection between this and your brother in America?"

Lewy: You might say that this is a question of convention.

Why is it that you don't doubt that it is a thought of your brother in America?

One process [the thought] seems to be a shadow or a picture of something else.

How do I know that a picture is a picture of Lewy? – Normally by its likeness to Lewy, or, under certain circumstances, a picture of Lewy may not be like him, but like Smith. If I give up the business of being like [as a criterion], I get into an awful mess, because anything may be his portrait, given a certain method of projection.

If you said that the thought was in some way a picture of his brother in America – Yes, but by what method of projection is it a picture of this? How queer it is that there should be no doubt what it's a picture of.

If you're asked: "How do you know it is a thought of such and such?" the thought that immediately comes to your mind is one of a shadow, a picture. You don't think of a causal relation. The kind of relation you think of is best expressed by "picture", "shadow," etc.

The word "picture" is even quite all right – in many cases it is even in the most ordinary sense, a picture. You might translate my very words into a picture.

But the point is this, suppose you drew this, how do I know it is my brother in America? Who says it is him – unless it is here ordinary similarity?

What is the connection between these words, or anything substitutable for them, with my brother in America?

The first idea [you have] is that you are looking at your own thought, and are absolutely sure that it is a thought that so and so. You are looking at some mental phenomenon, and you say to yourself "obviously this is a thought of my brother being in America". It seems to be a super-picture. It seems, with thought, that there is no doubt whatever. With a picture, it still depends on the method of projection, whereas here it seems that you get rid of the projecting relation, and are absolutely certain that this is thought of that.

Smythies's muddle is based on the idea of a super-picture.

We once talked about how the idea of certain superlatives came about in Logic. The idea of a super-necessity, etc.

"How do I know that this is the thought of my brother in America?" – that *what* is the thought?

Suppose my thought consists of my *saying* "My brother is in America" – how do I know that I *say* my brother is in America?

How is the connection made? – We imagine at first a connection like strings.

Lewy: The connection is a convention. The word designates.

You must explain "designates" by examples. We have learnt a rule, a practice, etc.

Is thinking of something like painting or shooting at something?

It seems like a projection connection, which seems to make it indubitable, although there is not a projection relation at all.

If I said "My brother is in America" – I could imagine there being rays projecting from my words to my brother in America. But what if my brother isn't in America? – then the rays don't hit anything.

[If you say that the words refer to my brother by expressing the proposition that my brother is in America – the proposition being a middle link between the words and what they refer to] – What has the proposition, the mediate link, got to do with America?

The most important point is this – if you talk of painting, etc. your idea is that the connection exists *now*, so that it seems as though as long as I do this thinking, this connection exists.

Whereas, if we said it is a connection of convention, there would be no point in saying it exists while we think. There is a connection by convention – What do we mean? – This connection refers to events happening at various times. Most of all, it refers to a technique.

["Is thinking something going on at a particular time, or is it spread over the words?" "It comes in a flash." "Always? – it sometimes does come in a flash, although this may be all sorts of different things."]

If it does refer to a technique, then it can't be enough, in certain cases, to explain what you mean in a few words; because there is something which might be thought to be in conflict with the idea going on from 7 to 7.5, namely the practice of using it [the phrase.]

When we talked of: "So and so is an automaton", the strong hold of that view was [due to the idea] that you could say: "Well, I know what I mean" ..., as though you were looking at something happening while you said the thing, entirely independent of what came before and after, the application [of the phrase]. It looked as though you could talk of understanding a word, without any reference to the technique of its usage. It looked as though Smythies said he could understand the sentence, and that we then had nothing to say.

What was it like to have different ideas of death? – What I meant was – Is having an idea of death something like having a certain picture, so that you can say "I have an idea of death from 5 to 5.1 etc."? "In whatever way anyone will use this word, I have now a certain idea" – if you call this "having an idea", then it is not what is commonly called "having an idea", because what is commonly called "having an idea", has a reference to the technique of the word, etc.

We are all here using the word "death", which is a public instrument, which has a whole technique [of usage]. Then someone says he has an idea of death. Something queer; because you might say "You are using the word 'death', which is an instrument functioning in a certain way."

If you treat this [your idea] as something private, with what right are you calling it an idea of death? – I say this, because we, also, have a right to say what is an idea of death.

He might say "I have my own private idea of death" – why call this an 'idea of death' unless it is something you connect with death. Although this [your 'idea'] might not interest us at all. [In this case,] it does not belong on the game played with 'death', which we all know and understand.

If what he calls his "idea of death" is to become relevant, it must become part of our game.

'My idea of death is the separation of the soul from the body' – if we know what to do with these words. He can also say: "I connect with the word 'death' a certain picture – a woman lying in her bed" – that may or may not be of some interest.

If he connects

with death, and this was his idea, this might be interesting psychologically.

"The separation of soul from body" [only had a public interest.] This may act like black curtains or it may not act like black curtains. I'd have to find out what the consequences [of your saying it] are. I am not, at least, at present at all clear. [You say this] – "So what?" – I know these words, I have certain pictures. All sorts of things go along with these words.

If he says this, I won't know yet what consequences he will draw. I don't know what he opposes this to.

Lewy: You oppose it to being extinguished.

If you say to me – "Do you cease to exist?" I should be bewildered and would not know what exactly this is to mean.

"If you don't cease to exist, you will suffer after death", there I begin to attach ideas, perhaps ethical ideas of responsibility. The point is, that although these are well-known words, and although I can go from one sentence to another sentence, or to pictures [I don't know what consequences you draw from this statement].

Suppose someone said: "What do you believe, Wittgenstein? Are you a sceptic? Do you know whether you will survive death?" I would really, this is a fact, say "I can't say. I don't know", because I haven't any clear idea what I'm saying when I'm saying "I don't cease to exist," etc.

Spiritualists make one kind of connection.

A Spiritualist says "Apparition" etc. Although he gives me a picture I don't like, I do get a clear idea. I know that much, that some people connect this phrase with a particular kind of verification. I know that some people don't – religious people e.g. – they don't refer to a verification, but have entirely different ideas.

A great writer said that, when he was a boy, his father set him a task, and he suddenly felt that nothing, not even death, could take away the responsibility [in doing this task]; this was his duty to do, and that even death couldn't stop it being his duty. He said that this was, in a way, a proof of the immortality of the soul – because if this lives on [the responsibility won't die.] The idea is given by what we call the proof. Well, if this is the idea, [all right].

If a Spiritualist wishes to give *me* an idea of what he means or doesn't mean by 'survival', he can say all sorts of things –

[If I ask what idea he has, I may be given what the Spiritualists say or I may be given what the man I quoted said, etc., etc.]

I would at least [in the case of the Spiritualist] have an idea of what this sentence is connected up with, and get more and more of an idea as I see what he does with it.

As it is, I hardly connect anything with it at all.

Suppose someone, before going to China, when he might never see me again, said to me: "We might see one another after death" – would I necessarily say that I don't understand him? I might say [want to say] simply, "Yes. I *understand* him entirely."

Lewy: In this case, you might only mean that he expressed a certain attitude.

I would say "No, it isn't the same as saying 'I'm very fond of you'" – and it may not be the same as saying anything else. It says what it says. Why should you be able to substitute anything else?

Suppose I say: "The man used a picture."

"Perhaps now he sees he was wrong." What sort of remark is this?

"God's eye sees everything" – I want to say of this that it uses a picture.

I don't want to belittle him [the person who says it.]

Suppose I said to him "You've been using a picture", and he said "No, this is not all" – mightn't he have misunderstood me? What do I want to do [by saying this]? What would be the real sign of disagreement? What might be the real criterion of his disagreeing with me?

Lewy: If he said: 'I've been making preparations [for death].'

Yes, this might be a disagreement – if he himself were to use the word in a way in which I did not expect, or were to draw conclusions I did not expect him to draw. I wanted only to draw attention to a particular technique of usage. We should disagree, if he was using a technique I didn't expect.

We associate a particular use with a picture.

Smythies: This isn't all he does – associate a use with a picture.

Wittgenstein: Rubbish. I meant: what conclusions are you going to draw? etc. Are eyebrows going to be talked of, in connection with the Eye of God?

He could just as well have said so and so" – this [remark] is foreshadowed by the word "attitude". He couldn't just as well have said something else.

If I say he used a picture, I don't want to say anything he himself wouldn't say. I want to say that he draws these conclusions.

Isn't it as important as anything else, what picture he does use?

Of certain pictures we say that they might just as well be replaced by another – e.g. we could, under certain circumstances, have one projection of an ellipse drawn instead of another.

[He *may* say]: "I would have been prepared to use another picture, it would have had the same effect...."

The whole *weight* may be in the picture.

We can say in chess that the exact shape of the chess-men plays no role. Suppose that the main pleasure was, to see people ride; then, playing it in writing wouldn't be playing the same game. Someone might say: "All he's done is change the shape of the head" – what more could he do?

When I say he's using a picture I'm merely making a *grammatical* remark: [What I say] can only be verified by the consequences he does or does not draw.

If Smythies disagrees, I don't take notice of this disagreement.

All I wished to characterize was the conventions he wished to draw. If I wished to say anything more I was merely being philosophically arrogant.

Normally, if you say "He is an automaton" you draw consequences, if you stab him, [he'll not feel pain]. On the other hand, you may not wish to draw any such consequences, and this is all there is to it – except further muddles.

1939[84]

I should say that if it was a mathematical proof, God didn't know more than any one of us what the result of the calculation was.

"For us human beings, the best thing we can arrive at, the nearest we can get, is that we always get it, or someone who had a lot of experience always got it". As if only God really knew. – Turing[85] suggested this, and that is just where he and I differ. Actually there is nothing to stop us postulating that your result is right – so that in future all your children will have to copy what is written on that blackboard. And then it is right. – There is nothing there for a higher intelligence to know – except what future generations will do. We know as much as God does in mathematics.
LFM, pp. 103–4

---

84 This year, Wittgenstein was awarded the chair of Philosophy following Moore's retirement. John Wisdom applied for the same post but the award was quite clear. C.D. Broad would even say later that denying Wittgenstein the chair would have been like denying Einstein the Physics chair. As can be seen by some of the chosen texts, Wittgenstein was immersed in work on the philosophical foundations of mathematics. That same year, on 2 June, he was awarded British citizenship because of the dangers that being an Austrian Jew posed following the Anschluss.

85 Alan Mathison Turing (1912–54), British mathematician. Elected member of King's College (Cambridge) in 1935. From 1936 to 1938, he worked with A. Church at the University of Princeton. In 1948 he began to lecture at Manchester University. In 1937, he proposed the concept of a universal calculating machine, known as the Turing machine. Turing can be considered as the father of *Artificial Intelligence*.

"They all reasoned wrongly".

This may mean all sorts of things. – If you don't know the special case, you don't know at all what they did – you don't know what 'reasoning wrongly' means.

We might mean, for example, "If only we had said to them so-and-so they'd have seen it". – But often this isn't so. Think of disputes about transubstantiation. It is not true that if someone had said to Luther and Zwingli that the meaning of the word 'wine' is the method of its verification, they would have said, "oh, now I see" and stopped arguing. On the contrary they might have killed you – and perhaps rightly. That is, I am not saying that they would be behaving stupidly.

LFM, p. 110

Let's go back a little. Does the fact that one cannot mate with two pawns "rest on a mathematical fact" or "... on a mathematical reality? One might say, "God when he created things made it *possible* to mate with so-and-so. He created the world with certain mathematical properties, through which this is *impossible*".

"God made it impossible in such a game as chess to mate with two pawns": if that can be said, then it can also be said that this is the mathematical world he did create.

LFM, p. 147

1939

I decided that I would return to Exeter for a few days before receiving my calling up papers. Wittgenstein and Francis decided to come with me. During the few days we had together Wittgenstein was concerned about what he should do, now that war was declared. He did not want to remain at Cambridge but thought that possibly he and Francis might be able to join an ambulance brigade.

The day before he was due to leave we had a final walk together, Francis remaining behind.

> WITTGENSTEIN: "I have been reading Luther recently. Luther is like an old gnarled oak, as strong as that. That isn't just a metaphor".
> DRURY: "The little I have read of Luther made a deep impression on me".
> WITTGENSTEIN: "But don't mistake me: Luther was no saint. No, indeed, he was no saint".
> DRURY: "Certainly not in the sense that Francis of Assisi was a saint".
> WITTGENSTEIN: "Francis of Assisi, so far as we can tell, seems to have been pure spirit and nothing else. On the whole I prefer the English Authorised Version of the Bible to Luther's translation into German. The English translators had such reverence for the text that when they

couldn't make sense of it they were content to leave it unintelligible. But Luther sometimes twists the sense to suit his own ideas. For instance, when Luther comes to translate the salutation of the Angel to Mary, *Ave gratia plena*,[86] he uses a popular phrase from the marketplace which reads something like 'Mary you little dear'".

DRURY: "Luther didn't hesitate to make his own selection from the cannons of scripture. He considered the Epistle of James, the Epistle to the Hebrews, and the Book of Revelation, as of little authority".

WITTGENSTEIN: "Isn't it strange that such a book as 'Ecclesiastes' was included in the canon. Speaking for myself, I don't care for the second epistle of St. Peter. Peter there speaks about 'our beloved brother Paul',[87] whereas it is clear that they were constantly in conflict".

DRURY: "It is generally agreed that the Second Epistle of St. Peter is a late document, and certainly not written by the apostle. Even Calvin, in spite of his great reverence for the Scriptures, agreed about that".

WITTGENSTEIN: "Oh, I am glad to hear that".

M. O'C. DRURY, PR, pp. 157–8

1939–1940

The Old Testament seen as the body without its head; the New T.: the head; the Epistles of the Apostles: the crown on the head.

If I think of the Jewish Bible, the Old Testament on its own, I should like to say: the head is (still) missing from this body. The solution to these problems is missing The fulfilment of these hopes is missing. But I do not necessarily think of a head as having a *crown*.

CV

1939–40

The comparisons of the N.T.[88] leave room for as much depth of interpretation as you like. They are bottomless.

They have less style than the first speech of a child. Even a work of supreme art has something that can be called 'style', yes even something that can be called 'fashion'. **CV**

---

86 See the Gospel According to Luke, 1:28.
87 Second Epistle of St. Peter, 3:15.
88 New Testament.

Letter to Norman Malcolm[89]
22.06.1940
Trinity College
Cambridge

My dear Malcolm,

Thanks for your letter da[ted] May 31st and for the 1½d. They'll come in very handy. Congratulations to your Ph.D.! And now: may you make good use of it! By that I mean: may you not cheat either yourself or your students. Because, unless I'm very much mistaken, *that's* what will be expected from you. And it will be *very* difficult not to do it, and perhaps impossible; and in this case: may you have the strength *to quit*.

This ends today's sermon. – I've had a good deal of worry lately as Skinner, about a month ago, fell ill with something called "glandular fever" of which he's only now recovering slowly. – I saw Moore the other day and his healt[h] is all right and he is in quite good spirits. – I have found it almost impossible to work for many weeks, and I have therefore arranged with Lewy that I'ld give him every day an hour or two of talk on the foundations of maths and similar subjects. It doesn't do him any harm and it helps me and seems to be the only way just now to get my brain moving a little. It's a shame – but there it is. – Smythies has gone down and I don't know exactly where he is but I hope to hear from him soon.

May I not prove too much of a skunk when I shall be tried.[90]

I wish you good not necessarily clever thoughts, and decency that won't come out in the wash.

Affectionately
Ludwig Wittgenstein

WCB

Letter to Raymond Townsend
19.07.1940

Dear Townsend,

I wonder how you are. I don't dare to leave Cambridge now as, if things should start happening while I was away, I might not be able to come back, & I don't want

---

89 Norman Malcolm (1911–90), attended Wittgenstein's lectures in 1939, becoming a close friend of him. In 1949, Wittgenstein went to the USA, lodging at Malcolm's house.
90 Wittgenstein is here referring to the Last Judgement.

to leave Skinner in any serious trouble – though God knows whether I'll be able to help him in the least. Are you going to be anywhere near here before long? I should like to hear from you soon.

I've been reading a good deal lately in a book called "Prayers & Meditations" by Dr Johnson. I like it very much.

I wish you good luck, outside & inside!

Affectionately yours
Ludwig Wittgenstein

WTB

JOHN KING
(Early 30s)
Our other main topic of conversation was literature. Early on I must have told him that I had read *The Brothers Karamazov*, though apart from the murder, the trial scene and the hostility within the family, I could remember little. He questioned me searching about this, no doubt to see whether I had been impressed by Father Zossima, the legend of the Grand Inquisitor etc; but of this, after five years, I had remembered little or nothing. I gathered that I missed much, and immediately after my Tripos[91] bought a copy of it and later of other of Dostoievsky's works, which I have read with great profit a number of times since. He went on the recommend Tolstoy, and encouraged me to read the *Twenty Three Tales*; and when I had bought a copy he marked those which he thought most important. These were *What Men Live By*; *The Two Old Men*; *The Three Hermits*, and *How Much Land Does A Man Need?* "There you have the essence of Christianity!" he said. I am not surprised to learn more than forty years later that he liked *The Three Hermits* best.
PR, p. 87
What I learned from him was some faint understanding that philosophy would not answer my questions. I learned also what I see to be the essence of Christianity, an appreciation of its symbolism and its profundity. And I learned something of the ethical and the mystical, things which I find difficult to express and of which indeed according to his philosophy "one cannot speak".[92]
PR, p. 90

---

91 System of courses offered by the University of Cambridge to undergraduate students.
92 The background reference here once again is the *Tractatus* and its theory of the "unsayable".

4

1941–1951

At the end of the 1930s humanity entered the Second World War, which was much more globalized and horrendous than the First. This historical circumstance spurred Wittgenstein's conscience; his academic schedule at Cambridge was by no means full and he again started to think of something beneficial he could do for others. In September 1941 he took "a 28-shilling-a-week job"[1] as a dispensary porter at London's Guy's Hospital delivering "medicines from the dispensary to the wards".[2] Wittgenstein experienced first-hand the sufferings caused by the worldwide conflict while finding his academic life quite frustrating and arduous.

In 1942 he went to Swansea where he stayed with Rush Rhees while remaining linked with the hospital. During this time he was finalizing his new philosophical view. Much of his reflection was dedicated to the foundations of mathematics and the philosophy of psychology – a matter he would be dealing with until his death. Between 1945 and 1946 he finished Part 1 of *Philosophical Investigations*, which was fully completed by 1949 (including Part 2). In 1944 he had returned to Cambridge to pursue his academic career. There, a famous incident with Karl Popper took place on 25 October 1946. The encounter between Wittgenstein and Popper is attractively described by David Edmonds and John Eidinow.[3] Although the accounts of the meeting do not match entirely, the core issue seems clear enough. According to the minutes taken by Wasfi Hijab, Secretary of the Moral Science Club, the discussion began after a brief speech by Popper. This was officially entitled *Methods in Philosophy*, though what he actually read was a

---

1 A. Waugh: *The House of Wittgenstein. A Family at War*. Bloombsbury, London, 2008, p. 280.
2 R. Monk: op. cit., p. 432.
3 *Wittgenstein's Poker: The Story of a Ten-Minute Argument between Two Great Philosophers*. London, Faber & Faber Ltd., 2001.

Ludwig Wittgenstein: The Meaning of Life, First Edition. Edited by Joaquín Jareño-Alarcón.
© 2023 John Wiley & Sons Ltd. Published 2023 by John Wiley & Sons Ltd.

conference on the existence or non-existence of philosophical problems. In an ensuing discussion, Wittgenstein possessively took the word in an attempt to demonstrate that there were no genuine problems in philosophy. While Popper argued to the contrary, Wittgenstein was nervously playing with a chimney poker. On Popper's mentioning the existence of philosophical problems on morality, Wittgenstein demanded an example of moral norm, and was deeply exasperated by Popper's famous answer: "You should not treat visiting lecturers with pokers". Wittgenstein reacted as expected: he immediately left the room. Although a mere anecdote, the story perfectly illustrates just how iconic Wittgenstein's position was in the Cambridge philosophical arena. He exerted an almost devotional influence on his students, generating a sort of personality cult among his followers, who also looked upon him with certain awe. The incident with Popper also reflects the controversial side of Wittgenstein, who, in a letter to Rhees three days later, wrote:

> On Friday I lectured (as usual) from 5 to 7 and attended a Moral Sc. Club meeting from 8.30 to 11, a lousy meeting, by the way, in which an ass, Dr Popper from London, talked more mushy rubbish than I've heard for a long time.

Wittgenstein's return to Cambridge was not as demanding as expected. In March 1944 he moved to Swansea, where he remained until October that year. Although, at the time of the poker incident, the end of Wittgenstein's professorship at Cambridge was only one year away, he continued to exert huge influence. His thinking was still very strong and he was really hoping to publish his *Philosophical Investigations*. The final version of the book's preface is dated January 1945, and he intended to publish it together with the *Tractatus* in order to make the drastic change in his philosophy clearly manifest.

Although Wittgenstein's health had weakened over the years, he continued to travel. During the summer of 1949, he spent some time in Norman Malcolm's house in the United States. He remained negative about academic life of Cambridge, finding the ambience intolerably superficial and self-sufficient. In a letter to G.H. von Wright (23 February 1948) he made the following comments on the latter's application for the professorship Wittgenstein had vacated after his resignation at the end of 1947:

> Miss Anscombe wrote to me a few weeks ago that you had put in for the professorship. I shall write the recommendation in a few days and send it to the Registrary as you suggest. May your decision be the right one! I have no doubt that you will be a better professor than any of the other candidates for the chair. But Cambridge is a dangerous place. Will you become

superficial? smooth? If you don't, you will have to suffer terribly. – The passage in your letter which makes me feel particularly uneasy is the one about your feeling enthusiasm at the thought of teaching in Cambridge. It seems to me: if you go to Cambridge you must go as a *sober* man. – May my fears have no foundation, and may you not be tempted beyond your powers!

Between December 1947 and June 1949 Wittgenstein was in Ireland where he continued writing, mainly on the philosophy of psychology. In September 1948 he travelled to Vienna to visit his seriously ill sister Hermine to whom he was very close. Her death on 11 February 1950 was a great blow to him; however, the philosopher himself did not have long to live. In May 1949 he was diagnosed with anaemia and, soon after, with prostate cancer. Between April and October 1950, Wittgenstein lived in Oxford, lodging in Elizabeth Anscombe's house, where he probably began to realise that his end was near. It was then that something particularly relevant for the core idea of this compilation happened. Wittgenstein asked Anscombe to help him get into contact with a Catholic priest, in order to talk about God in non-philosophical terms. The priest turned out to be Father Conrad Pepler, a Dominican who had instructed Smythies in his conversion to Catholicism. Monk, who contacted the priest in 1986, claims that Father Conrad told him the following about the meeting with Wittgenstein:

> He knew he was very ill and wanted to talk about God, I think with a view to coming fully to his religion, but in fact we only had, I think, two conversations on God and the soul in rather general terms.

In spite of the appearances, Anscombe was doubtful about the possibility of Wittgenstein fully embracing his childhood religion, while Kanterian's reflection on this matter seems quite plausible:

> The possibility that Wittgenstein wanted to embrace the Catholic faith, in which he had been baptized, might be doubted given his avowed inability to believe that its doctrines were literally true. It is not, however, an impossibility. The episode shows that in the last months of his life Wittgenstein was perhaps driven by a will to believe, in accordance with his lifelong concern with religious matters. It also shows that he took such matters to be strongly distinguished from philosophy.[4]

Wittgenstein spent his final days in Dr Edward Bevan's house in Cambridge, still writing in his moments of lucidity. His last texts were written only two days before

---

4 op. cit., p. 196.

his death (*On Certainty* **670–676). On the night of the 28 April 1951, Mrs Bevan stayed by the side of an exhausted Wittgenstein. When told that his friends would arrive the following morning and shortly before losing consciousness, Wittgenstein told Mrs Bevan: "Tell them I've had a wonderful life".[5]

Wittgenstein died peacefully on 29 April 1951, three days after his sixty-second birthday. Funeral arrangements proved a slight problem for his friends. M. O'C. Drury remembered that Wittgenstein had once told him he wanted his friends converted to Catholicism to pray for him. Hence, prayers were carried out according to the Catholic rite. Some doubts were also raised concerning the funeral itself, but it was finally conducted according to the Catholic rite, which G.E. Moore found astonishing. None of Wittgenstein's relatives attended.

---

[5] Joan Bevan: "Wittgenstein's Last Years"; in: F.A. Flowers III (ed.): *Portraits of Wittgenstein*, vol. 4. Thoemmes Press, Bristol 1999, p. 137.

1941 (January)
In another letter he told me that he had been reading a Swiss theologian, Karl Barth. "This writing must have come from a remarkable religious experience". In reply I reminded him that years ago at Cambridge I had tried to read something of Barth's to him, and he had dismissed it as 'very arrogant'. He did not refer to this again.
M. O'C. DRURY, PR, p. 160

Letter to Rowland Hutt
20.08.1941
Trinity College
Cambridge

Dear Roland,

I just had your letter dated [...]. I wrote to you a few days ago explaining why I hadn't written sooner. – I never had any particular book in mind when I wrote to you: would you like me to send you a book; & as in your reply you didn't mention any particular book. I took it that you didn't want me to send you one. I expected you to suggest a book if you wanted one.

About the 'Imitation'[6] you're wrong. I've never read the book nor did I take it to Russia. I believe you're mixing it up with Tolstoy's 'Short explanation of the gospels'.

I hope I shall see you when you're on leave & I hope it'll be good for both of us! I wonder what the surprise is you mention in your letter. Is it by any chance a mustache or beard that you've been growing? I hope it isn't. For I don't like people to change their faces; par[t]icularly when they are liable to change their souls! – To return to the book question: I don't know What book might be 'good for you'. You once mentioned that you had read in the 'Pilgrim's Progress'[7] & enjoyed it. If you like I could send you that. Let me know. – Francis' leg is steadily improving & so is mine.

As to your letters I should like to say this: one word that comes from your heart would mean more to me than 3 pages out of your head!

Good wishes as always!

Ludwig

WTB

---

6 *The Imitation of Christ*, by Thomas à Kempis.
7 A Christian allegory written by John Bunyan (1628–88), English preacher of Puritan belief.

01.01.1943

Go on, believe! It does no harm.

'Believing' means, submitting to an authority. Having once submitted to it, you cannot then, without rebelling against it, first call it in question & then once again find it convincing.

A cry of distress cannot be greater than that of *one* human being.

Or again *no* distress can be greater than what a single person can suffer.

Hence one human being can be in infinite distress & so need infinite help.

The Christian religion is only for the one who needs infinite help, that is only for the one who suffers infinite distress.

The whole Earth cannot be in greater distress than *one* soul.

Christian faith – so I believe – is refuge in this *ultimate* distress.

Someone to whom it is given in such distress to open his heart instead of contracting it, absorbs the remedy into his heart.

Someone who in this way opens his heart to God in remorseful confession opens it for others too. He thereby loses his dignity as someone special & so becomes like a child. That means without office, dignity & aloofness from others. You can open yourself to others only out of a particular kind of love. Which acknowledges as it were that we are all wicked children.

It might also be said: hate between human beings comes from our cutting ourselves off from each other. Because we don't want anyone else to see inside us, since it's not a pretty sight in there.

Of course you must continue to feel ashamed of what's within you, but not ashamed of yourself before fellow human beings.

There is not greater distress to be felt than that of One human being. For if someone feels himself lost, that is the ultimate distress.

CV

1943

As we walked by the river at Durham I began to tell him some of my experiences in Egypt. How on one occasion, when I had a period of leave, I had travelled down to see the temples at Luxor. A wonderful experience.

> DRURY: "One thing did surprise me and rather shocked me. On going into one of the temples there was on the wall a bas-relief of the god Horus with an erect phallus in the act of ejaculation and collecting the semen in a bowl!"
>
> WITTGENSTEIN: "Why in the world shouldn't they have regarded with awe and reverence that act by which the human race is perpetuated. Not every religion has to have St. Augustine's attitude to sex. Why even in our culture marriages are celebrated in a church, everyone present knows

what is going to happen that night, but that doesn't prevent it being a religious ceremony".

M. O'C. DRURY, PR, p. 162

23.03.1944
Assuming that people are continuously calculating the development of π, the omnipotent God knows whether they will have arrived at a figure of 777 by the end of the world. But can his omnipotence decide whether people would have arrived at that figure after the end of the world? It can't. I mean: God too could only decide mathematical things through mathematics. The rule of elaborating ideas on its own cannot decide anything for him that it cannot decide for us.

It could be expressed in another way: if we have been given the rule of development then a calculation can teach us that the figure "2" is in the fifth position.

Would God have known this, without this calculation, from the development rule alone? I would want to say no.
MS 124, 175–6

Letter to Y. Smythies
07.04.1944[8]

c/o Mrs. Mann
10 Langland Rd
Mumbles Swansea

Dear Smythies,

Thanks for your letter, dated Thursday. The news of your joining the roman catholic church was indeed unexpected.[9] But whether it's good, or bad news – how should I know? The following seems clear to me. Deciding to become a christian is like deciding to give up walking on the ground and do tight-rope walking instead [see **CV** 05.07.1948], where nothing is more easy than to slip and every slip can be fatal. Now if a friend of mine were to take up tight-rope walking and told me that in order to do it he thinks he has to wear a particular kind of garment I should say to him: If you're serious about that tight-rope walking I'm certainly not the man to tell you what outfit to wear, or not to wear, as I've never tried to walk anywhere

---

8 Wittgenstein found accommodation at this time in the house of the Methodist pastor Wynford Morgan, with whom he had many conversations about religious belief.
9 Wittgenstein thought he might have influenced in the conversion by suggesting Smythies read Kierkegaard.

else than on the ground. Further: your decision to wear than kind of garment is, in a way, terrible, however I look at it. For if it means that you're serious about the thing it's terrible, even though it may be the best and greatest thing you can do. And if you're dressing up and then don't do the tight-rope act its terrible in a different way. There's one thing, however, I want to warn you against. There are certain devices (weights attached in a particular way to the body) which steady you on the rope and make your act easy, and in fact no more dangerous than walking on the ground. This sort of device should not be part of your outfit. – All this comes to saying: I cannot applaud your decision to go in for rope walking, because, having always stayed on the ground myself, I have no right to encourage another man in such an enterprise. If, however, I am asked whether I'd rather you went in for rope walking, or for sham[m]ing, I'll certainly say: rather anything than the latter. – I *hope* you'll never despair, and I also hope that you'll always remain capable of despairing.

I sent you a letter yesterday saying why I'd rather not see you at the present moment. I should like to see you when my work here is done, or almost done.

I'm really interested in what sort of a *man* you are and will be. *This* will, for me, be the eating of the pudding.

So long! Good wishes!

Affectionately
Ludwig Wittgenstein

WCB

17.08.1944
How a word is understood is not conveyed by the words on their own. (Theology.)
MS 129, 189

Letter to Rush Rhees[10]
28.11.1944[11]

Trinity Coll.
Cambridge
Tuesday

---

10 Rush Rhees (1905–89). A former student of Wittgenstein's, Rhees became one of his closest friends and a member of the board of Wittgenstein's literary executors. Rhees was a renowned philosopher in the analytic tradition.

11 During his stay in Swansea in the spring and summer of that year, Wittgenstein proposed his thought on the private language argument as a preliminary step to the discussions on the philosophy of psychology. That argument had previously been considered for inclusion as the introduction of his work on the Philosophy of Mathematics.

Dear Rhees,

Thanks for your letter, dated Nov. 25th. I'm sorry to hear about the depressing circumstances under which you are working. Please don't give in, or despair! I know how immensely depressing things can look; &, of course, I'm the first man to think of running away, but I hope you'll pull yourself together. I wonder what lines for a logic course I recommended. Anyhow, there's nothing more difficult than to teach logic with any success when your students are all half asleep. (I've heard Braithwaite[12] snore in my lectures.) Please go the bloody rough way! – I wish you one moderately intelligent & awake pupil to sweeten your labour! Please look after your health. You can't expect good work when your health isn't really good, & colds are nasty things. I've so far been in good health, & consequently my classes haven't gone too bad. (Or should I say "badly"?) Thouless is coming to them, & a woman, Mrs so & so who calls herself Miss Anscombe, who certainly is intelligent, though not of Kreisel's caliber.

I heard from Malcolm recently who is executive Officer of a ship (whatever that means) & was, when he wrote me, in England, but only for a few hours. – Drury is in France & I get news from him regularly.

I have recently been reading a fair amount: a history of the Mormons[13] & two books of Newman's.[14] The chief effect of this reading is to make me feel a little more my worthlessness. Though I'm aware of it only as a slumbering man is aware of certain noises going on around him which, however, don't wake him up.

I repeat: Please go the bloody, rough way! Complain, swear, but go on. The students are stupid but they get something out of it.

Please give my good wishes to Mrs Rhees. Remember me to any of your people who remember me.

Smythies is coming up on Saturday to read a paper at the M. Sc. Cl.[15] (subject unknown). So long! Luck!

Ludwig Wittgenstein

WTB

---

12 Richard B. Braithwaite (1900–90). British philosopher. Lectured in Moral Philosophy at the University of Cambridge from 1928 to 1967. He was also deeply interested in Philosophy of Science.

13 Religious group whose name is "The Church of Jesus Christ of Latter-day Saints". It was founded in 1830 by Joseph Smith (1805–44). The Mormon doctrine is in an ongoing evolution as the Revelation is supposed not to have ended yet. Such doctrine is based not only in the Bible, but in the so-called *Book of the Mormon* as well (a book that Joseph Smith claimed to have found), and also in the *Thirteen Articles of Faiths* – written by Smith – and the *Book of Doctrine and Covenants*. Mormons' basic view is theocratic.

14 Cardinal John Henry Newman.

15 Moral Science Club.

Ca. 1944

People are religious to the extent that they believe themselves to be not so much *imperfect* as *sick*.

Anyone who is half-way decent will think himself utterly imperfect, but the religious person thinks himself *wretched*.

What's ragged should be left ragged.

A miracle is, as it were, a *gesture* which God makes. As a man sits quietly & then makes an impressive gesture, God lets the world run on smoothly & then accompanies the words of a Saint by a symbolic occurrence, a gesture of nature. It would be an instance if, when a saint has spoken, the trees around him bowed, as if in reverence. – Now, do I believe that this happens? I don't.

The only way for me to believe in a miracle in this sense would be to be *impressed* by an occurrence in this particular way. So that I should say e.g.: "It was *impossible* to see these trees & not to feel that they were responding to the words". Just as I might say "It is impossible to see the face of this dog & not to see that he is alert & full of attention to what his master is doing". And I can imagine that the mere report of the *words* & life of a saint can make someone believe the reports that the trees bowed. But I am not so impressed.

When I came home I expected a surprise & there was no surprise for me, so, of course, I was surprised.

CV

1944

The military hospital to which I was now attached was stationed at Llandeilo in South Wales. Wittgenstein was once again staying at Swansea, and I was able to see him from time to time. On one of these visits he told me that one of his pupils had written to him to say he had become a Roman Catholic ...

> WITTGENSTEIN: "I seem to be surrounded now by Roman Catholic converts! I don't know whether they pray for me. I hope they do".[16]

M. O'C. DRURY, PR, p. 162

01.05.1945 (?)

When Someone says he believes in God, he is making a very unclear statement."But surely 'believing' simply means 'holding something to be true'!" – Yes, it means

---

16 This would be one of the reasons why the Catholic prayer rite would be followed at his burial.

holding something to be true but this kind of definition doesn't explain anything that might be of interest to us.
MS 116, 345

01.06.1945 (?)
"You can't hear God speaking to another person unless you are the one being addressed." This is a grammatical comment.
MS 228, 158 *568

Letter to N. Malcolm
08.09.1945

c/o Rhees
96 Bryn Rd.
Swansea

[...]
The other day I read Johnson's "Life of Pope" and liked it very much. As soon as I get to Cambridge I'm going to send you a little book "Prayers and Meditations" by Johnson. You may not like it at all, – on the other hand you may. I do.
WCB

Letter to N. Malcolm
20.09.1945

c/o Rhees
96 Bryn Rd
Swansea

[...]
My landlord has a modern American translation of the Bible. I dislike the translation of the N.T.[17] (by a man E.J. Goodspeed) but the translation of the O.T.[18] (by a group of people) makes a lot of things clearer to me and seems to me *well* worth reading. Perhaps you'll see it one day.
So long! Look after yourself!

Affectionately
Ludwig

WCB

---

17 New Testament.
18 Old Testament.

Letter to N. Malcolm
06.10.1945

Trinity College
Cambridge

Dear Norman

This is the little book I promised to send to you. It seems to be out of print so I'm sending you my own copy. I wish to say that normally I can't read any printed prayers but that Johnson's impressed me by being *human*. Perhaps you'll see what I mean if you read them. As likely as not you won't like them *at all*. Because you will probably not look at them from the *angle* from which I see them. (But you might). If you don't like the book throw it away. Only first cut out the leaf with my dedication. For when I shall become *very* famous it'll become very valuable as an autograph, and your grandchildren may be able to sell it for a lot of "dough".
WCB

Ca. 1945
It isn't reasonable to be furious even at Hitler; let alone at God.
CV

HERMINE WITTGENSTEIN[19]
(1945?)

Already at that time,[20] a profound transformation was taking place in Ludwig, the results of which were not to be apparent until after the war, and which finally culminated in his decision not to possess any more wealth. By the soldiers he was called "the one with the bible", because he always carried Tolstoy's edition of the New Testament with him. Towards the end of the war he fought on the Italian front, was taken prisoner by the Italians during that strange truce, and, when he at last returned home, the first thing he did was to rid himself of his wealth. He gave it to us, his brothers and sisters, with the exception of our sister, Gretl[21] [Margarethe Stonborough-Wittgenstein], who at that time was still very wealthy, while we had forfeited much of our wealth.
PR, p. 4

---

19 Hermine was, for Wittgenstein, an especially beloved sister. She died on 11 February 1950.
20 See the remarks in relation with Wittgenstein's texts during the First World War.
21 Margarethe 'Gretl' Stonborough-Wittgenstein (1882–1958). Wittgenstein's youngest sister.

26.05.1946 (?)[22]
To say "God is the giver, God is the giving and God is the gift" really means that God doesn't give in the same way as a person gives and the gift is not a gift in the usual sense of the word (and neither is the giver, of course). We are only tempted or we are ordered to use the word give, etc in this case.

You can't hear God speaking to another person unless you are the one being addressed. This is a grammatical comment (cf. **MS 228, 158 *568**).

It isn't absurd to say from the outset that a person of lowly origins isn't driven over and over again to form sentences that make no sense. That is an ethical opinion. It could be said that to discuss this kind of nonsense is a passion and the person who doesn't have this passion is just small-minded. That's not my opinion, but I can understand it. In the same way as can be said: whoever makes no mistakes here is a poor devil.
MS 130, 6–8

26.05.1946 (?)
The feeling of confidence. How is it expressed in the way one behaves?
   Is the confidence justified?
   What people accept as being justified shows – in the way they think and live.

Question: to what extent can dogmatics be discussed in a hypothetical way? – Can it say for example: "If Christ had been born of a man, would he be a sinner like other people."? (Barth.)

As far as I can see the concept of causality plays a devastating role in theology. If one speaks, for example, of the supernatural effects of prayer or of the sacraments, what does "effect" mean in this context – or what does it mean when we don't understand God's intentions? What does "intention" mean in this context? And yet: – if this is stupidity why have intelligent people spoken in this way? And were they any worse because they spoke in this way? Would they have been better if they hadn't spoken in this way? I am certainly no better because I don't speak as they do!
MS 130, 9–10

26.05.1946 (?)
If we assume that others have the wrong way of thinking and that I think in the right way – why should I convert them to my way of thinking? Would they actually be better off in a certain sense if they think in a better way?

---

22 In the summer of that year, Wittgenstein was beginning to think of the possibility of renouncing his chair, something that he would indeed to at the end of 1947. The Michaelmas Term of 1947 was his last term as a professor. His successor in the post would be the Finnish philosopher Georg Henrik Von Wright, who would himself be succeeded by John Wisdom and Elizabeth Anscombe.

Can a religious person not become irreligious if he is made aware of an error in his way of thinking and if he is then not able to accept this error in a religious way?
MS 130, 11

26.05.1946 (?)
Indeed he can but what is the problem then? Is it <u>what</u> is actually expressed by the comment? – Is it that we don't understand it? – Or is it perhaps that we don't really understand it if we don't know how such a comment is used in communication?

"When I expressed the word in thoughts I meant ..." How was it preceded? <u>What</u> preceded it? – "Nothing", would be the answer. – And yet precisely <u>that</u>.

Oh! God grant that I may be satisfied with my fate! It's the same in life as in philosophy:

When a problem is hopeless the way a question is formulated is wrong. Or also: When you want to repeat a question to yourself hopelessly you would do well to prefer what is given.[Gain from the proud heart!]
MS 130, 154–5

11.08.1946
Religion would give me a certain degree of modesty which I lack for I am fairly conceited about anything half human in me and about any characteristic that <u>distinguishes</u> me.
MS 131, 15

12.08.1946
The remark by Jucundus in 'The Lost Laugh', that his religion consisted in: his knowing, if things are going well for him now, that his fate could take a turn for the worse – this is actually an expression of the same religion as the saying "The Lord hath given, the Lord hath taken away".[23]
CV

13.08.1946
This is a similar situation to when someone doesn't understand his position in a community. Should he try to dress like them, should it matter to him how he dresses, should he be proud of the fact that he doesn't dress like the others; should

---

23 The Book of Job, ch. 1, v. 21.

he intrude on their discussion, and what role should he play therein? It will be difficult if he becomes 'self-conscious'. What is the scientist? Is he a seeker of truth or a benefactor of humanity, or an artist, or is he a craftsman? If he had religion his difficulties would disappear.
MS 131, 33

14.08.1946
It is hard to understand yourself properly since something that you *might* be doing out of generosity & goodness is the same as you may be doing out of cowardice or indifference. To be sure, one may act in such & such a way from true love, but also from deceitfulness & from a cold heart too. Similarly not all moderation is goodness. And only if I could be submerged in religion might these doubts be silenced. For only religion could destroy vanity & penetrate every nook & cranny.
CV

19.08.1946
But how, when religion teaches us that the soul can still exist when the flesh has decayed? Do I understand what it teaches? Of course I understand: – I can imagine a lot about it. (Pictures of these things have even been painted. And why should such a picture be considered as the incomplete rendition of an expressed thought? Why should it not provide the same service as that which we say?) It's the service that matters.
MS 131, 69–70

20.08.1946
In former times people entered monasteries. Were they perhaps simpleminded, or obtuse people? – Well, if people like that took such measures so as to be able to go on living, the problem cannot be an easy one!
CV

03.09.1946
It is very *remarkable*, that we should be inclined to think of civilization – houses, streets, cars, etc – as separating man from his origin, from the lofty, eternal, etc. Our civilized environment, even its trees & plants, seems to us then cheap, wrapped in cellophane & isolated from everything great & from God as it were. It is a remarkable picture that forces itself on us here.
CV

08.09.1946
The purely corporeal can be uncanny. Compare the way angels and devils are portrayed. A so-called "miracle" must be connected with this. It must be as it were a *sacred gesture*.
CV

11.09.1946
The way you use the word "God" does not show *whom* you mean, but what you mean.
CV

05.10.1946[24]
Does this lie in the essence of the concept "to believe"? Certainly.

Might there be a language in which only the language game of making assumptions and not the game of assertions existed, in which people said "Assuming I believed ...", but never "I believe ..."?

Imagine, someone said "I wish, – but don't want my wish to be fulfilled". – (Lessing "If God in his laws ...") Can God be asked to give the wish, but <u>not</u> to fulfil it?

Here it would seem as if the assertion "I believe ..." was not the assertion of what the assumption "I believe" assumes!
MS 132, 122-3

11.10.1946
Amongst other things Christianity says, I believe, that sound doctrines are all useless. That you have to change your *life*. (Or the *direction* of your life.)

That all wisdom is cold; & that you can no more use it for setting your life to rights, than you can forge iron when it is *cold*.

For a sound doctrine need not *seize* you; you can follow it, like a doctor's prescription. – But here you have to be seized & turned around by something. –(I.e. this is how I understand it.) Once turned around, you must *stay* turned around.

Wisdom is passionless. By contrast Kierkegaard calls faith a *passion*.
CV

---

24 The year 1946–7 year was really his last full academic year as a professor. Wittgenstein has specialized in Philosophy of Psychology. The notes taken by his pupils P.T. Geach, K.J. Shah and A.C. Jackson appeared later, edited as a book.

Letter to Rush Rhees
15.10.1946
Trinity College
Cambridge

Dear Rhees,

I'm sorry I haven't written sooner & thanked you for your letter. Laziness was one cause but another was that I'm not feeling well. I get queer states of mental exhaustion which are very terrifying. I've had two lectures so far. There's a crowd coming to them as always at the beginning of the year when they don't know what to expect. Still my lectures went quite well, except for the fact that during my second lecture I sometimes got so exhausted that I could hardly speak. But my brain, oddly enough, was very active. What's to become of it all I don't know. I plan to see a doctor (not a psychologist) about it, hoping, completely against hope, that he can advise me something. I dislike this place intensely, & the worst part of it is that I haven't got a real friend here, i.e., someone who'ld go out of his way to do something for me.

I saw Moore a week ago for a short time. He had recently been ill (heart trouble) & looked aged, but his interest in philosophy was as lively & agreable as ever. I gave him your good wishes & he is returning them (or rather, not the identical ones but exactly similar ones).

Drury is in Dublin, studying for his M.D.: I wish he were nearer here. I believe he'll return to England about Christmas.

Malcolm is here & very seriously studying. He is having a discussion with me once a week. He is a decent & serious man.

May God help me, & may I be able to come to Swansea at Christmas as usual.

Let me hear from you before long!

As always,

WTB

16.10.1946
Religion is as it were the calm sea bottom at its deepest, remaining calm, however high the waves rise on the surface. –
CV

18.10.1946
"I never before believed in God" – that I understand. But not: "I never before really believed in Him."
CV

20.10.1946
Lenau's[25] Faust is remarkable in that here man has dealings only with the Devil. God does not stir himself.
CV

26.10.1946
Love is happiness. Happiness with pain maybe but happiness nevertheless. If happiness is missing or if it reduces to a short flare up, then love is lacking. – I must be able to rest in love. – But can you reject a warm heart? Is it a heart that beats warmly for me? – 'I'll rather do anything than to hurt the soul of friendship.' – I must know he won't hurt our friendship. The person cannot escape from his skin. I cannot give up a demand that lies deep with me and which is anchored by my whole life, for love is linked to nature; and were I to become unnatural then love would cease. – Can I say: "I will be sensible and not demand it anymore."? This works in many situations. It works for most people for a time but only as the means to another end not as the end. I can say: Let him do what he likes – things will be different some day. – Love is the pearl of great price that is kept close to one's heart and that one doesn't want to exchange for anything, that one considers to be the thing of most value. When you have it – you understand what something of great value is. You learn what it means to recognise the value. You learn what it means to pick out a precious stone from amongst all the others. The immense fondness one has for it teaches us the concept of unique value. Immense fondness leads us to see that it is our duty to protect it. Fondness leads us to seriousness. Passion leads us to seriousness. – If there is no fondness it is not love.

The terrible thing is uncertainty and in the uncertainty my mind is always preoccupied with picturing possibilities and always negative possibilities. It is sometimes good but usually evil. "Trust in God", but I am far from trusting in God. It's a long way from where I am now to trusting God.

Joyful hope and fear are related to each another. I cannot have one without it bordering on the other.
MS 133, 8r–8v–9r

10.11.1946
Ask yourself this question – who will grieve for you when you die; and <u>how deep</u> will the grief be? Who is grieving for Francis;[26] how deeply do I grieve for him who

---
25 Nikolaus Lenau (1802–50), Austrian poet born in Hungary. He wrote his epic poem *Faust* in 1836.
26 Francis Skinner had died in 1941.

has more reason for being grieved over than anyone else? Does he not deserve someone grieving over him for the whole of his life? If anyone does, he does. Here one could say: God will lift him up and <u>give</u> him what a bad man would deny him.
MS 133, 32v

24.11.1946
I cannot kneel to pray, because it's as though my knees were stiff. I am afraid of dissolution (of my own dissolution) should I become soft.
CV

01.01.1947 (?)
Imagine someone looking at a pendulum and thinking – that's how God lets it move.
   Doesn't God have the right to act in agreement with a calculation for once?
   And shouldn't every expression of behaviour be vague if it is to be useful?
   A vastly talented writer such as myself would still only be relatively untalented.
MS 167, 22r

01.01.1947 (?)
But consider: "I often take words from another, – so I should sometimes at least also take from my word the fact that I am of this or that conviction. When I report my observation half automatically, the report has nothing at all to do with my conviction. I could trust myself, or my observing I as equally as another does. I could therefore say: "I say 'it is raining' and probably is". Or: "the observer in me says 'it's raining' and I am inclined to believe him." – Isn't that how it is – or similar to how it is – when someone says God has spoken to him or through his mouth?
MS 245, 273 *1484

03.03.1947
Wisdom is something cold, & to that extent foolish. (Faith, on the other hand, a passion.) We might also say: wisdom merely *conceals* life from you. (Wisdom is like cold, grey ash covering the glowing embers.)
CV

04.03.1947
"I know whether I'm speaking for or against my convictions." Conviction is the most important thing. It's the background to my discussions and yet this image reveals so little!

There is the confession of a lie, just as there is the confession of an intention.

"But an intention must surely be an action – why else would you be ashamed of the intention? How could one believe that God would punish the intention?" If you name an 'action' of which you may be ashamed, then you have to take into account the intention to carry out the actions.
MS 134, 10–11

13–14.04.1947

The use of the word "fate". Our attitude to the future & the past. To what extent do we hold ourselves responsible for the future? How much do we speculate about the future? How do we think about past & future? If something unwelcome happens: – do we ask "Who's to blame?", do we say "Someone must be to blame for it"?, – or do we say "It was God's will", "It was fate"?

In the way in which asking a question, insisting on an answer, or not asking it, expresses a different attitude, a different way of living, *so* too, in this sense, an utterance like "It is God's will" or "We are not masters of our fate". What this sentence does, or at least something similar, a commandment too could do. Including one that you give to yourself. And conversely a commandment, e.g. "Do not grumble!" can be uttered like the affirmation of a truth.
CV

11.05.1947 (?)

Love isn't a feeling. Love is tested, pain isn't. Every joy is paid for and the soul is like a ploughed field. Nothing grows in it but it is receptive to seeds. If the seeds don't grow then that is God's will.
MS 134, 163

27.06.1947

"Wisdom is grey". Life on the other hand & religion are full of colour.
CV

27.07.1947

God grant the philosopher insight into what lies in front of everyone's eyes.
CV

28.07.1947

I don't feel well but don't really know why. I am tired and feel like a stranger. If there is no bond that links you with people or with God you <u>are</u> a stranger.
MS 135, 110

09.10.1947
Letter to Arvid Sjögren[27]

[...]

I would still like to write to you about something that Gretl mentioned during a discussion with me. She told me about Kügelgen's comment regarding the "poor sinner", which you quoted to your wife. When Gretl told me about it I wanted to speak to you about the matter, and now I want to write to you something about it which might be completely superfluous. – Strange as it may seem, there is something that could be called religious knowledge or understanding, and which one may possess a lot of, without having much religion, which is really a way of living. Many people who start becoming religious up to a certain point start with this kind of understanding and religious terms and expressions gradually begin to say something to that person. – Someone else however approaches religion from a different angle. For example, he starts to become more and more helpful and selfless, etc, and then religious words also start to mean something to him in the end. – What I mean is one person approaches religion through a kind of philosophy and another person journeys along a path that doesn't lead him anywhere near a philosophy. When Gretl told me about you I thought to myself: your wife is (by all accounts) not intellectually-minded; and so it is only normal when she doesn't understand words that would lead her on a quite different path (assuming she is even capable of reaching this point.) – I am, like you, a thinker. The natural way for me to approach religion and which, moreover, has taken me relatively far, is by thinking. But that is not to say it is the best way! One could call it "approaching religion from around the outside". Your wife will find it through ever-increasing earnestness if this exists. And to help her – if Someone can – seems to make more sense to me than showing her the end of a path that she cannot take and which she doesn't even need to take.

If this is all nonsense or irrelevant, as I am inclined to think, then please forget it!!

Greetings to your wife and mother.
WTB

21.12.1947

It appears to me as though a religious belief could only be (something like) passionately committing oneself to a system of coordinates. Hence although it's belief, it is really a way of living, or a way of judging life. Passionately taking up *this* interpretation. And so instructing in a religious belief would have to be

---

27 A Norwegian friend of Wittgenstein.

portraying, describing that system of reference & at the same time appealing to the conscience. And these together would have to result finally in the one under instruction himself, of his own accord, passionately taking up that system of reference. It would be as though someone were on the one hand to let me see my hopeless situation, on the other depict the <u>rescue-anchor</u>, until of my own accord, or at any rate not led by the hand by the *instructor*, I were to rush up & seize it.
CV

04.01.1948[28]
In just the same way as when you have no difficulty recognising a person's face in the grey and white of photography. – And what does that mean? We watch a film, for example, and follow all the details with great interest as if we were watching real people. God preserve me from madness!
MS 136, 60a

30.05.1948
"The cussedness of things"! – An unnecessary anthropomorphism. We might speak of a malice of the *world*; easily imagine the devil created the world, or part of it. And we need not imagine the demon intervening in particular situations; everything may happen 'in accordance with the laws of nature': it is just that the whole plan is directed at evil from the start. But a human being exists in this world in which things break, slide about, cause every possible mischief. And of course he is one of the things. – The 'malice' of the object is a stupid anthropomorphism. For the truth is much graver than this fiction.
CV

04.06.1948
Religious faith & superstition are quite different. The one springs from *fear* & is a sort of false science. The other is a trusting.
CV

26.06.1948
If God really does *choose* those who are to be saved, there is no reason why he should not choose them according to their nationalities, races, or temperaments.

---

[28] This would be the year Wittgenstein wrote his first will. He would not write the second until 1951.

Why the choice should not be expressed in the laws of nature. (He was of course *able* so to choose, that the choice follows a law.)

I have been reading extracts from the writings of St. John of the Cross, in which it is written that people have gone to their ruin, because they did not have the good fortune to find a wise spiritual director at the right moment.

And how can you say then that God does not try people beyond their strengths?

I am inclined to say here, it is true, that crooked concepts have done a lot of mischief, but the truth is, that I *do not know* at all, what does good & what does mischief.

CV

30.06.1948

Only God sees our most secret thoughts but why should these be so important? And should they be considered important by everyone?

Imagine people who only think out loud. It isn't obvious anyway that creatures think from the physical nature of the person; so they should think out loud, ie do nothing other than what we would also call thinking. (Your secret thoughts are monologues.)

MS 137, 59b

03.07.1948

If someone can believe in God with complete certainty, why not in Other Minds?

CV

05.07.1948

The honest religious thinker is like a tightrope walker. It almost looks as though he were walking on nothing but air. His support is the slenderest imaginable. And yet it really is possible to walk on it.

CV

25.07.1948

The problems of life are insoluble on the surface, & can only be solved in depth. In surface dimensions they are insoluble.

CV

1948 (Autumn)
I noticed in the paper that there was to be a discussion on the Third Programme between Ayer and Fr. Copleston[29] on 'The existence of God'. I mentioned this to Wittgenstein.

> WITTGENSTEIN: (laughing) "Oh, we mustn't miss that – Ayer discussing with a Jesuit, that would be too much to miss".

So on the evening concerned he came up to my room, and we listened to the talk. Wittgenstein said nothing while the broadcast was continuing, but the changing expression on his face was itself a commentary on what was being said. When it was over:

> WITTGENSTEIN: "Ayer has something to say, but he is incredibly shallow. Fr. Copleston contributed nothing at all to the discussion".

M. O'C. DRURY, PR, p. 172

04.11.1948
If God had taken a glimpse into our souls he wouldn't have been able to see of whom we were speaking.
MS 137, 88a

21.11.1948
Imagine someone watching a pendulum & thinking: God makes it move like that. Well, doesn't God have the right even to act in accordance with a calculation? (...)
CV

22.12.1948
"God has commanded it, therefore we must be able to do it." That means nothing. There is no "*therefore*" about it. The two expressions might at most mean the *same*.

"He has commanded it" means here roughly: He will punish anyone who does not do it. And nothing follows from that about being able. And *that* is the sense of 'election by grace'.

But that does not mean that it is right to say: "He punishes, although we *cannot* act otherwise." – Perhaps, though, one might say: here there is punishment, where punishment by human beings would be impermissible. And the whole concept of 'punishment' changes here. For the old illustrations can no longer be applied, or

---

29 Frederick Copleston SJ (1907–94), British priest and philosopher. In 1948 he debated the existence of God with Bertrand Russell. Both debates were broadcast by the BBC.

now have to be applied quite differently. Just look at an allegory like "The Pilgrim's Progress" & see how nothing – in human terms – is right. – But isn't it right all the same? i.e. can it not be applied? Indeed, it has been applied. (At railway stations there are dials with two hands, they indicate when the next train leaves. They look like clocks & aren't; but they have a use.) (There should be a better comparison here.)

To someone who is upset by this allegory it might be said: Apply it differently or don't bother with it! (But *some* will be far more confused than helped by it.)
CV

1949

If Christianity is the truth, then all the philosophy about it is false.
CV

02.02.1949

Could the concept of punishments of hell be explained in some other way than by way of the concept of punishment? Or the concept of God's goodness in some other way than by way of the concept of goodness?

If you want to achieve the right *effect* with your words, doubtless not.

Suppose someone were taught: There is a being who, if you do this & that, live in such & such a way, will take you after your death to a place of eternal torment; most people end up there, a few get to a place of eternal joy. – This being has picked out in advance those who are to get to the good place; &, since only those who have lived a certain sort of life get to the place of torment, he has also picked out in advance those who are to lead that sort of life.

What might be the effect of such a doctrine?

Well, there is no mention of punishment here, but rather a kind of natural law. And anyone to whom it is presented in such a light, could derive only despair or incredulity from it.

Teaching this could not be an ethical training. And if you wanted to train anyone ethically & yet teach him like this, you would have to teach the doctrine *after* the ethical training, and represent it as a sort of incomprehensible mystery.
CV

17.03.1949

God's essence is said to guarantee his existence[30] – what this really means is that here what is at issue is not the existence of something.

---

30 Wittgenstein is mentioning the ontological argument to probe the existence of God.

For could one not equally say that the essence of colour guarantees its existence? As opposed, say, to the white elephant. For it really only means: I cannot explain what 'colour' is, what the word "colour" means, without the help of a colour sample. So in this case there is no such thing as explaining 'what it *would be like* if the colours *were* to exist'.

And now we might say: There can be a description of what it would be like if there were gods on Olympus – but not: 'what it would be like if there were God'. And this determines the concept 'God' more precisely.

How are we taught the word "God" (its use, that is?) I cannot give an exhaustive systematic description. But I can as it were make contributions towards the description; I can say something about it & perhaps in time assemble a sort of collection of examples.

Reflect in this connection that in a dictionary one would perhaps like to give such descriptions of use, but in reality one gives only a few examples & explanations. But also that no more than this is necessary. What use could we make of an enormously long description? – Well, it would be no use to us if it dealt with the use of words in languages already familiar to us. But what if we came across such a description of the use of an Assyrian word? And in what language? Let's say in another language already known to us. – In this description the word "sometimes" will frequently occur, or "often", or "usually", or "nearly always" or "almost never".

It is difficult to form a good picture of a description of this sort.

And what I basically am after all is a painter, & often a very bad painter.

CV

20.05.1949

A picture that is firmly rooted in us may indeed be compared to superstition, but it may be said too that we *always* have to reach some sort of firm ground, be it a picture, or not, so that a picture at the root of all our thinking is to be respected & not treated as a superstition.

CV

July 1949[31]

From this point we went on from a suggestion of Norman's: Suppose Cesare Borgia said, "This is my ethical principle: I trample on other men's toes all I can".

---

31 Wittgenstein met Oets Kolk Bouwsma (1898–1978) for the first time in 1949, in a journey to the USA invited by his disciple Norman Malcolm, of whom Bouwsma had been tutor in Nebraska. Wittgenstein lodged in Malcolm's house and took the opportunity to discuss philosophy at Cornell University, sometimes having Bouwsma as his counterpart. They met in Oxford again in 1950. The last entry of the conversations between Wittgenstein and Bouwsma – as Bouwsma himself writes – is from 16 January 1951.

Norman was fascinated by his having stuck pins (Cleopatra) into people. At that W. frowned. Ethical principle! Not everything is an ethical principle. How is an ethical principle identified? This took us into de use of the expression "ethical". Nothing precise of course. A principle is ethical by virtue of its surroundings. What surroundings? You could imagine "surroundings" where one was justified and enjoined upon to enjoy sufferings, the sufferings of the wicked, for instance. At any rate there are limits surely to what is an "ethical" principle. It reminds me now of Herbert Feigl's[32] "choosing principles".

CB, pp. 5–6

06.08.1949

By the time we left our bench, it was dark, and we groped our way back along the path – got off once, going down into the gorge, to the road above the gorge. As we approached the car, he asked me whether I had ever had any acquaintance with the Mormons. They fascinated him. They are a fine illustration of what faith will do. Something in the heart takes hold. And yet to understand them! To understand a certain obtuseness is required. One must be obtuse to understand. He likened it to needing big shoes to cross a bridge with cracks in it. One mustn't ask questions.

CB, pp. 10–11

06.08.1949

ROMANS 9:21

"one vessel unto honor; another unto dishonor"

"vessels of wrath"

"vessels of mercy"

ISAIAH 45:9

"For as the heavens are higher than the earth, so are my ways higher than your ways, and my thoughts than your thoughts".

Both of these texts arose in W.'s discussions last evening.

CB, p. 12

08.08.1949

I am not very sure or very clear about this discussion. This seems to be it. Holding oneself responsible, holding another responsible – these are attitudes. So the attitude one takes towards a drunk – praising-blaming – is different from that we take toward a sober man who may do what the drunk does. In such cases we might say that it's a difference in chemistry, and one does not blame alcohol. It may be, of

---

32 Herbert Feigl (1902–88), Austrian philosopher. Member of the Vienna Circle.

course, that in the case of the sober man it's also a matter of chemistry. But when we hold him responsible we suppose that there is a difference. One of the lessons drawn from this is that we should perhaps never judge another. The man may be like the drunkard. But yourself you must judge. Conscience involves this. Calvin, Saint Paul, Romans 9. If you think of man as a pot and of God as the potter, then holding man, the pot, responsible, is what? The God is responsible? "The sins of the fathers are visited upon the children".[33] W. would not judge.

CB, pp. 15–16

20.08.1949

Again he stood up. Imagine this as a game. He went to his chair and said: "Here is a chair" (turning) "Here is a vase", "Here is a lamp" – then he turned about to go into the dining room, "And now I advance into the next room and go on drawing my map of this room. This also shows how these expressions fit into a situation". A way which is forbidden to man himself. Surely God instructs man, but as a man can be instructed.

What is the difference between the feeling and attitude towards the world as between that of the atheist and the believer? Here I am echoing something of John Wisdom's.[34] Atmosphere! Hope! Promise! More! Glory! And now, it's all given, you see what there is, that's all, nothing wonderful, nothing terrible! Just so-so.

CB, p. 33

22.08.1949

On the way as we passed the Jewish synagogue, he remarked that he did not understand modern Judaism. He did not see what could be left of it since sacrifice was no longer practiced. And now? What was left was too abstract. Prayers and some singing. Later I suggested that in Zionism there was perhaps some intention to restore the temple and the old rites. He thought very few. Jews had no such interest.

Later on our walk I suggested that from what he had said it must be that with the destruction of the temple the head of Judaism was gone. Now nothing is left but the body. But he checked me. The spirit may have gone out long before this. And even after this sects, very strict sects, most likely contrived. The passing of

---

33 It is a biblical principle.
34 John Wisdom (1904–93). Wittgenstein's disciple. He was strongly influenced by Wittgenstein's *second philosophy*. Professor of Philosophy in Cambridge since 1952. Wisdom is buried in the same cemetery as Wittgenstein, Moore, Ramsey and Anscombe (Ascension Parish Burial Ground, Cambridge).

Greek religion illustrates the same point. I was reminded of the allegorizing of Greek myth. But W. protested he was perhaps talking rubbish. In any case a religion is bound up with a culture, with certain externals in a way of life, and when these change, well, what remains?

Then he went on to cite the Oxford Movement[35] as a symptom of the same hollowness, lifelessness, in the Anglican church. I didn't understand all these things. I suppose that the point is that once the sacrifices, whatever there was in Greek religion, and the ceremonies and ritual in Anglicanism, were entered into with earnestness and serious intent, with spirit. At a later time, they were done listlessly, mechanically, and as unessential. Once this happens it is finished. But religion without ceremony, without ritual – this is impossible. W. stresses here, I think, the precise forms and practices, the very words to be spoken – creeds, sacraments, etc.

Later he asked me, had I read Newman? He was much impressed by Newman. Kingsley[36] accused him of insincerity. But Newman was sincere. He, W., had read *Grammar of Assent* too. That was puzzling. How a man of such learning and culture could believe such things! Newman had a queer mind.

Later I pressed him for an explanation. Did he mean by "queer" that a man like Newman should have become a Roman Catholic? Oh, no. My best friends and the best students I had are converts. What is queer about Newman is the kind of reason he gives for becoming a Roman Catholic. On miracles, Newman cites the case of Christians, who taken by savages had their tongues cut out, and yet they could speak. He gives a natural explanation for this – if the tongue is only half cut off a man cannot speak, but if wholly cut off a man still can – but Newman then goes on to say that it may nevertheless have been a miracle. Again: The pope excommunicated Napoleon. Napoleon said he didn't care so long as his soldiers' weapons did not fall out of their hands. Some years later in Moscow, in Russia, this is literally what happened.

What was Newman doing? He argued that miracles occur still? How? What God has done once he contrives to do – usually. This is the sort of thing that is so queer in Newman.

---

35 Movement arisinh within the Anglican Church during the years 1833–45. It attempted to stress the continuity between the Anglican Church and the Ancient Church in relation to dogmas, rites and the apostolic succession. The most prominent promoter of the Movement was John Henry Newman, who later converted to Catholicism and became cardinal of the Catholic Church. The Movement stressed the connections with Catholic tradition. Other relevant members of the Movement were John Keble (1792–1865), Richard Hurrell Froude (1803–36), Charles Marriot (1811–58), Robert Isaac Wilberforce (1802–57) and Edward Pusey (1800–82). The Movement derived into Anglo-Catholicism.

36 Charles Kingsley (1819–75). English writer and parish priest (Church of England), famous for his controversy with Cardinal Newman. Such controversy had Newman's *Apologia pro Vita Sua* as a result of the debate.

Later when we were sitting he remarked that twenty years ago he would have regarded Newman's action as incomprehensible, as insincere perhaps. But no more. When I prodded him about this, what changed him, he pondered, and then he said that he came gradually to see that life is not what it seems. He was quiet for several minutes. Then he said: It's like this: In the city, streets are nicely laid out. And you drive on the right and you have traffic lights, etc. There are rules. When you leave the city, there are still roads, but no traffic lights. And when you get far off there are no roads, no lights, no rules, nothing to guide you. It's all woods. And when you return to the city you may feel that the rules are wrong, that there should be no rules, etc.
CB, pp. 33–5

22.08.1949

J.M.E. McTaggart[37] he saw once at a squash [i.e., a reception] at McTaggart's. Came with Russell. Russell badgered McTaggart about his argument for immortality of the soul. McTaggart answered, but W. understood not a word of it.

"Of course, a man need not argue his religious beliefs. Newman did. Once he does this he must argue clearly – soundly. But one may believe without argument".
CB, p. 37

28.08.1949

ON THURSDAY AFTERNOON W. and I went for a walk exploring the falls at Taughannock. He loved it. "This is the finest walk you've taken me on".

On the way he asked me what we had discussed the evening before, and I told him: "I ought" implies "I can". As his manner is, he started out immediately. He said he thought that the Christian orthodox position was that this was not so. "Be ye perfect".[38] Still someone in deep earnest had said to him: But it is commanded. So it must be possible. Now "possible" or "can" has two different contexts: It is not possible to grow pears on an apple tree. This only means that there is a law, and the law says simply that apples grow on apple trees and pears grow on pear trees. And if someone makes a chemical analysis of the apple tree and of the pear, and now says: "So it is impossible", this is really no different. There is simply another law. On the other hand, "I can", "It is possible", means something like "I'll try" or "I'm still trying", just as "I can't" means: "I give up". One tugs at something to lift

---

37 J.M.E. McTaggart (1866–1925). Idealist metaphysician. Follower of Hegel, he taught at Trinity College in Cambridge. Mainly known as the author of a paradox on the unreality of time.
38 Matthew, ch. 5, v. 48.

it and finally says: "I can't", and this means I give up. Now when it comes to: "Be humble", there is no law. And one may try. That man cannot is more like a prophecy and the prophecy is that man cannot be humble, not that one cannot try. So the command in such cases may imply, not: "I can" but "I can try". So one can try to be humble.

Later when I pointed out that trying to be humble may not be clear at all in the way in which trying to lift a weight is, he said: You are completely right – then he went on with an analogy: It may be something like the doctor who does not pretend he can cure you, but he tells you to rest and not to eat certain foods, and sit in the sun – and as for the rest nature must do the work. So too, though he did not develop this, a priest might say: "Read the scriptures, say your prayers down on your knees, watch yourself – and God must do the rest".
CB, pp. 37–8

30.08.1949 (?)
On Saturday afternoon – after the morning and picnic at Taughannock – I met with Malcolm and W. It was my privilege to suggest a subject. I suggested that we discuss the difficulties involved in attempts to define "good".

W. sat back and considered. Then he began. Suppose that a certain people (the Jews, perhaps) have a prophet and he lays down the law to them: "Thou shalt not ..." etc. Now the people either obey such laws or when they do not they feel guilty. No one questions the authority of such laws. Here no one asks: "What is meant by good?" or "What kinds of things are good?" They all say: "So and so is a good man. He keeps the law. Such another is a bad man. He disobeys". But now imagine another reformer-prophet arises and he lays down another law: He wins a following. And now comes another and another. In this process the authority of all law is shaken. Now some men may be bewildered and shaken, and may quite sincerely ask: "What is good? What must I do?" But W. hesitated. Would someone in such a case ask for a definition? If he asked for a definition, to what end would he do this? Guidance? How could it guide him? W. pointed out – he worried over this for some time – that in order for it to serve him, it would have to do so as a resolution by which he would come to alter attitudes. (Good is whatever is conducive to the general welfare).

Definition of good? What would one do with this? Law courts have a use for definitions. Physics has a use for definition. It is hard to see what a definition here could be like. What one can do is describe certain aspects of the uses of the word "good". If you start out with "X is good" means "I approve of X" – well this is a common part of most uses of the word. But the use is infinitely complex. The use of a word in such cases is like the use of a piece in a game, and you cannot understand the use unless you understand the uses of other pieces. What you do with one sort of piece is intelligible only in terms of what you do with it in relation to what is done with the other pieces. So the word "good" is used in a terribly complex game, in which there are such other pieces as "ought to do", "conscience", "shame", "guilt", "bad", etc. And there are now no strict rules for the use of any and yet the uses are interdependent. Even such phrases as: "I approve" or "Someone approves" might not always apply. *I* approve but the law says so and so – a good Jew might say this.

Consider the use of the word "good" in the nursery and in the school, when we use it to encourage, as a part of moral training. Contrast this use with that in the New Testament or in the Old. Here we find: "Why callest me good?" At one point W, was asking whether it made any sense to speak of "good in the Christian sense". He finally decided that it did not unless it meant "good by Christian standards", which is something else.

Towards the end of our discussion which had lasted several hours, W. spoke of A.C. Ewing's[39] definition – in a Moral Science lecture, "Good is what it is right to admire". Then he shook his head over it. The definition throws no light. There are three concepts, all of them vague. Imagine three solid pieces of stone. You pick them up, fit them together and you get now a ball. What you've now got tells you something about the three shapes. Now consider you have three balls of or lumps of soft mud or putty – formless. Now you put the three together and mold out of them a ball. Ewing makes a soft ball out of three pieces of mud.

Here is another formulation of the issue. Imagine a tribe who when they viewed things that were horrible, loathsome to us, clapped their hands, their faces bright, and now they always uttered the word "doog". And now you are to translate the word "doog". How will you translate it? Will you hesitate about this? W. was trying here to bring out the unsatisfactory character of "I approve". The tribe apparently approves. Will "good" do? I suppose that this involves that the use of the word "good" is affected in some such way as this: That in reference to "good" the use of the word "good" comes to serve also in naming the things that are good. One might be horrified not simply at people's regarding such things good but also at their calling them good. Simply perhaps this. If we were to translate "doog" into "good", we should be suggesting not simply that they approve of certain things but also that these things are justified by our law, etc.

Plato's *Euthydemus, Protagoras, Philebus, Republic*.

The use of the word "good" is too complicated. Definition is out of the question.

CB, pp. 40–2

---

39 Alfred Cyril Ewing (1899–1973). Fellow of Jesus College (Cambridge). Advocate of a Neo-Realist school of thought. A critic of Wittgenstein's philosophy.

11.10.1949
Yesterday about noon we went for a ride to Mount Tom reservation. On the way up he began talking about teaching ethics. Impossible! He regards ethics as telling someone what he should do. But how can anyone counsel another? Imagine someone advising another who was in love and about to marry, and pointing out to him all the things he cannot do if he marries. The idiot! How can one know how these things are in another man's life?

I suggested: No man is wise from another man's woe, nor scarcely from his own. But he said: "Oh, no, not quite that. I can only imagine a teacher who is in some way higher than those he teaches and who suffers with those in respect to whose sufferings he is to give counsel". (Who was this teacher, but Jesus Christ?) And the taught must confess to him the innermost secrets of his life, holding nothing back. This would be teaching in ethics.

Later as we stopped on the hill looking down over the city, he asked me: Had I read any Kierkegaard? I had. He had read some. Kierkegaard is very serious. But he could not read him much. He got hints. He did not want another man's thought all chewed. A word or two was sometimes enough. But Kierkegaard struck him almost like a snob, too high, for him, not touching the details of common life. Take his prayers. They left him unmoved. But he once read the prayers and meditations of Samuel Johnson. They were his meat. "The violent incursions of evil thoughts". (I'm not sure about his judgment here of Kierkegaard).
CB, pp. 45–6

11.10.1949
He also talked about having spent two weeks as a nurse at the bedside of a nephew injured in a motorcycle accident. He and an old German woman servant took turns. This was in Roermond, Holland. There were the finest nurses he had ever met. Catholic nurses, sleepless for days, yet diligent and cheerful. This again struck him, I could tell, like the Mormons, people who are moved by faith. They've got something.
CB, p. 48

24.10.1949
IT HAD JUST OCCURRED TO ME this evening what it is about teaching ethics that made him shake his head so. The serious problem in ethics is asked by a man who has some terribly important decision to make: What shall I do? Perhaps the matter becomes ethical just at the point when the question or the decision is felt to be serious or important. What is serious or important in this way?
CB, pp. 50–1

1948–1949
108. If God looked into our minds he would not have been able to see who we were speaking of [**PI** II, xi, p. 217f.].
LWPPI

c.1949
But what is the difference between an attitude and an opinion?
 I would like to say: the attitude comes *before* the opinion.
 (*Isn't* belief in God an attitude?)
LWPPII, p. 38

1949
I told Wittgenstein I was reading some of the early Church Fathers, at the moment Tertullian.[40]

> WITTGENSTEIN: "I am glad you are doing that. You should continue to do so".
> DRURY: "I had been reading Origen before. Origen[41] taught that at the end of time there would be a final restitution of all things. That even Satan and the fallen angels would be restored to their former glory. This was a conception that appealed to me – but it was at once condemned as heretical".
> WITTGENSTEIN: "Of course it was rejected. It would make nonsense of everything else. If what we do now is to make no difference in the end, then all the seriousness of life is done away with. Your religious ideas have always seemed to me more Greek than Biblical. Whereas my thoughts are one hundred percent Hebraic".
> DRURY: "Yes I do feel that when, say, Plato talks about the gods, it lacks the sense of awe which you feel throughout the Bible – from Genesis to Revelation. 'But who may abide the day of his coming, and who shall stand when he appeareth?'".[42]
> WITTGENSTEIN: (standing still and looking at me very intently) "I think you have just said something very important. Much more important than you realize".

M. O'C. DRURY, PR, pp. 174–5

---

40 Tertullian (c.160–c.220).
41 Origen (c.185–c.254).
42 Malachi, ch. 3, v. 2. King James Bible.

1949
Walking in Phoenix Park.

> WITTGENSTEIN: "Drury, what is your favourite Gospel?"
> DRURY: "I don't think I have ever asked myself that question".
> WITTGENSTEIN: "Mine is St. Matthew's. Matthew seems to me to contain everything. Now, I can't understand the Fourth Gospel. When I read those long discourses, it seems to me as if a different person is speaking than in the synoptic Gospels. The only incident that reminds me of the others is the story of the woman taken in adultery".[43]
> DRURY: "That passage is not found in any of the best manuscripts, and most scholars consider it a latter addition. In some manuscripts it is found in St. Luke's Gospel".
> WITTGENSTEIN: "When I spoke to S— about my difficulty in understanding the Fourth Gospel, he looked at me with such a strange smile. I couldn't describe it to you. S— is the most religious man I have ever met. I would see nothing wrong in it if he became a Roman Catholic Priest – of course I know he can't now because he is married".

We continued to talk for some time about the New Testament.

> WITTGENSTEIN: "If you can accept the miracle that God became man, then all these difficulties are as nothing. For then it is impossible for me to say what form the record of such an event should take".
> DRURY: "One of the early Church Fathers, Lactantius[44] I think, said something like that. Novels and plays must indeed be probable, but why should this, the scheme of man's redemption be probable".
> WITTGENSTEIN: "I am glad to hear that I had the same thought as one of the Church Fathers. At one time I thought that the epistles of St. Paul were a different religion to that of the Gospels. But now I see clearly that I was wrong. It is one and the same religion in both the Gospels and the Epistles".

M. O'C. DRURY, PR, pp. 177–8

---

[43] Ch.8: 2–11.
[44] Lactantius (c.250–c.325).

1949
Another day walking in Phoenix Park.

> WITTGENSTEIN: "Drury, you have lived a most remarkable life. First those years in Cambridge studying philosophy; then as a medical student; then the war experiences – and now all this new work in psychiatry".
>
> DRURY: "There is one thing about it that I feel is all wrong with me: I have not lived a religious life".
>
> WITTGENSTEIN: "It has troubled me that, in some way I never intended, your getting to know me has made you less religious than you would have been had you never met me".
>
> DRURY: "That thought has troubled me too".
>
> WITTGENSTEIN: "I believe it is right to try experiments in religion. To find out, by trying, what helps one and what doesn't. When I was a prisoner of war in Italy, I was very glad when we were compelled to attend Mass. Now why don't you see if starting the day by going to Mass each morning doesn't help you to begin the day in a good frame of mind. I don't mean for one moment that you should become a Roman Catholic. I think that would be all wrong for you. It seems to me that your religion will always take the form of desiring something you haven't yet found".
>
> DRURY: "You remember a long time ago when we talked about Lessing – Lessing saying that he would choose the gift in the left hand, the striving after truth, rather than the possession of absolute truth".
>
> WITTGENSTEIN: "That might be all right for Lessing to say. But I can see that there is a much deeper state of mind than Lessing expressed there".
>
> DRURY: "I don't think what you suggest about Mass would help me. I still prefer the English Liturgy, with which I have been familiar since childhood, to the inaudible service in Latin".
>
> WITTGENSTEIN: "Yes I can understand that".
>
> DRURY: "However, I think a child brought up in the colourful symbolism of the Roman Catholic Liturgy would get a stronger and deeper impression of religious awe than one brought up in the plainer Protestant tradition".
>
> WITTGENSTEIN: "I don't agree with you at all. I would much prefer to see a child educated by a decent Protestant pastor than by a greasy Roman Catholic priest. When I look at the faces of the clergy here in Dublin, it seems to me that the Protestant ministers look less smug than the Roman priests. I suppose it is because they know that they are such a small minority".

Later, on the same walk.

> WITTGENSTEIN: "I am glad that you raised that point about the education of children. I see the matter quite clearly now. I have recently been

reading a book, in which the author blames Calvin for the rise of our present bourgeois civilization. I can see how easy it would be to make such a thesis plausible; but I, for my part, wouldn't dare to criticize a man such as Calvin must have been".

DRURY: "But Calvin had Michael Servetus burnt for heresy!"

WITTGENSTEIN: "Tell me about that".

So I told him at some length the story of Servetus's heretical book about the Trinity;[45] and how he had deliberately come into the church at Geneva in the middle of Calvin's sermon.

WITTGENSTEIN: "Whew! He deliberately courted his own death. What else could Calvin, believing as he did, have done than have Servetus arrested".

M. O'C. DRURY, PR, pp. 178–80

1949

After he had some time on treatment he expressed himself as feeling much stronger and no longer troubled by the pain in his arm. He told me that he had had an invitation to spend a long visit with a former pupil[46] and friend of his in America, and that he had decided to spend the summer there and return to Ross's hotel for the coming winter. I went down, the evening before he was due to leave Dublin, to help him to pack and decide what he would take with him. He was packing his large pile of notebooks, manuscripts and typescripts.

WITTGENSTEIN: "I have had a letter from an old friend in Austria, a priest. In it he says he hopes my work will go well, if it should be God's will. Now that is all I want: if it should be God's will. Bach wrote on the title page of his *Orgelbuchlein*, 'To the glory of the most high God, and that my neighbour may be benefited thereby'. That is what I would have liked to say about my work".

M. O'C. DRURY, PR, pp. 181–2

---

45 Drury is surely referring here to the work *Christianismi Restitutio*, published anonimously in 1553, though Servetus had previously published (1531) another one titled *De Trinitatis Erroribus*. Given that Servetus's condemnation provoked a major controversy, Calvino wrote his work *Defensio Ortodoxae Fidei* (1554) justifying the right to kill heretics.

46 Norman Malcolm.

Letter to Roy Fouracre[47]
03.01.1950
Vienna
TEL. U 40 402
IV. ARGENTINIERSTRASSE 16

Dear Roy,

The letter you sent off to America reached me here yesterday. I was very sorry to hear about all your trouble. Just before leaving England a fortnight ago I sent you a Christmas card with a letter to your old address. I hope they'll forward it to you. Please see to it that they do. I hope your wife is better now & that you find your new flat moderately convenient. – I intend to stay here for a couple of months & then to return to England. – My health is still very wobbly. I want to see you when I come back & have a long chat with you – preferably at the Strand Corner House. – Give Miss Wilkinson my good wishes; I think I forgot to write her a Christmas card, I'm sorry.
I'm looking forward to seeing you. – God bless you.

As always,
Ludwig

WTB

Spring 1950

317. When someone who believes in God looks around him and asks "Where did everything that I see come from?" "Where did everything come from?" he is *not* asking for a (causal) explanation; and the point of his question is that it is the expression of such a request. Thus, he is expressing an attitude towards all explanations. – But how is this shown in his life? It is the attitude that takes a particular matter seriously, but then at a particular point doesn't take it seriously after all, and declares that something else is even more serious.

In this way a person can say it is very serious that so-and-so died before he could finish a certain work; and in another sense it doesn't matter at all. Here we use the words "in a profounder sense".

What I actually want to say is that here too it is not a matter of the *words* one uses or what one is thinking when using them, but rather of the difference they make at various points in life. How do I know that two people mean the same

---

47 Wittgenstein met Fouracre – a man quite far from Wittgenstein's intellectual interests – in 1941 while he was working as a laboratory assistant at Guy's hospital.

when both say they believe in God? And one can say just the same thing about the Trinity. Theology which insists on the use of *certain* words and phrases and bans others, makes nothing clearer (Karl Barth). It, so to speak, fumbles around with words, because it wants to say something and doesn't know how to express it. *Practices* give words their meaning. (**CV** 1950).
ROC

28.08.1950
Today I walked with W. – along the canal and under the willows. I am thoroughly exhausted.

As we walked, he said that if there was something I should like to talk about I should bring it up. I suggested that some professor was to lecture on: the nature of religious truth – what would he say? Religious truth? He went on puzzling, thinking this way. Of course it isn't botany, it isn't anything about eclipses, it isn't economics or history. That is clear enough. Negatively it is easy to say something. But what is one to say besides that? The man in Christ Church will very likely talk about Christian dogmas. And one might make some sense in this way, each believer talking about what he believes. But there is no sense talking about religious truth in general. What religious? What truth? To illustrate this he cited a story of Gottfried Keller's[48] about a young man and woman in conversation. The young woman told about her falling in with three women who lived together in a small house. The one woman lived by herself in one room, by herself, could get along with no one, was hard and mean. The two lived in the other room and were noted for their sweetness and kind natures. They were also pious, went to church regularly, etc. She – the young woman – once made bold to enquire into the secret of their lives. And they told her, giving her a dry account of what one must believe – something like the Apostle's Creed. The young woman was disappointed. The conversation ends with the young man's saying: "This is my religion – the consciousness, the recognition – that I am at present doing well but that it may not always be so".

This, according to W., was actually Keller's view, his religion. Keller had apparently been brought up a Christian – Zwingli, perhaps – and later was interested in Feuerbach. So this was the shrunken, truncated Christianity.

Now then if this is religion, what will the man at Christ Church say about it? For see how much this is like what is said – namely that religion is a man's sense of dependence. For although this is "nonsense", one can see how one would come to say this.

---

48 Gottfried Keller (1819–90), Swiss writer, painter, and critic. Studied philosophy at the University of Heildeberg. Author of *Der Grüne Heinrich* (1854–5), an autobiographical work.

This is all it is in some cases and is part of it in most cases: Schleiermacher[49] was a serious man and not stupid, and Keller too was "A deeply grounded religious" man.

I suggested that one would not gather this merely from this sentence of Keller's. He allowed this and when I asked whether he spoke of Keller's being serious in the same that he spoke of some other men's being serious, he explained. He meant by serious a man who endured conflict and struggle, who came back again and again to these matters. He wrestled. This is not too plain to me.

The point is, in any case, that religion takes many forms, there are similarities, but there is nothing common to all religions.

I asked him for an explanation of the sentence: God is a spirit.

Well, first it means that God is not a human being, or like a tree. He cannot be seen, heard, etc. At first it seemed to him that this was all. Then it occurred to him that one might also say these things about a number. But one would not say that a number was a spirit. One means further then that God sees, hears prayer, forgives, speaks, etc. He allowed that he did not understand. The Gospel of John bothered him. But he was not criticizing. But if someone said that he did understand, then such a one must give an account. Let a man surrender and admit that he doesn't understand.

I quoted the rest of the sentence: "And they that worship him must worship him in spirit and truth". Of course this meant that man must not worship in mere words and forms without any fervor. I suggested that it involved a rebuke to those who supposed that God was to be worshipped only in a certain place. He objected to this. "Rebuke? How could it be a rebuke? The Jews were taught to worship in a certain place. And Jesus said he came not to destroy the law, but to fulfil".[50]

("This was to Nicodemus, wasn't it?" I didn't know. Anyhow, Saint John).

Believe whatever you can. I never objected to a man's religious beliefs, Mohammedan, Jew, or Christian. (To the Samaritan woman).[51]

A peculiarity of religious beliefs is the great power they have over men's lives.

(*Not lehrt uns Beten*). (Misery teaches us to pray).

CB, pp. 54–6

09.09.1950

W. says he doesn't understand everything. He says this particularly speaking of religious languages. This now may mean any of several things. It may mean

---

49 Friedrich Daniel Ernst Schleiermacher (1768–1834), German philosopher and theologian. Indebted to Kant, Schlegel and Schelling, he was one of the most relevant German theologians of the nineteenth century.
50 The Gospel According to Matthew, ch. 5, v. 17.
51 The parable of the Samaritan woman. The Gospel According to John, ch. 4, vv. 5–42.

something like: "I have no use for such language. I cannot pray". He once said, I remember, that he could make nothing of the dogma of the Incarnation. And the Gospel of John puzzles him. He does not "understand" it. But he does not say that some other people do not understand it. The question then is about *their* use of these sentences. And here one thing is clear. Whatever this use is, it is different from the use of ordinary sentences describing the world. But this difference then must be recognized by both those who have a use for them and by those who do not. Those who have no use for them are not to disparage all use of them simply because they cannot deal with them as they deal with: "Pussy says meow". But likewise those who have use for them are not to resort to proofs and evidence as they too might with: "Pussy says meow". But neither will it do to suggest as Waismann seems to, that this language is vague. For there is here no contrast with some other language which is clear. But I hadn't better attribute this to Waismann. Of course there are religions which are frankly anthropomorphic. The Greeks certainly did believe that there was a company of man-like creatures – taller – stronger – more handsome, etc. – who lived up there on Mount Olympus.

CB, pp. 57–8

14.09.1950

By this time we had begun walking back. I asked him again: You said that you did not understand – and they didn't either – such sentences as: God is a spirit. I meant to go on, but he took me up. I had apparently misunderstood him. To understand such a sentence one must note the context in which it is used. It is perhaps introduced among idolators – worshippers of sticks and stones. (Are there such worshippers?) To them this says: God is not sticks and stones, God has no body. So far then we understand this; but there is more. God is prayed to, he is like a person. He hears and answers prayer.

We walked along for some way and he came back to the subject. There is an independent use of the phrase "The Spirit of the Lord": What is the passage in Luke where Jesus reads from Isaiah? (I was stupid as usual). "The spirit of the Lord is on me."[52] (I looked it up last night after we returned from the Bucks' where we had dinner). Here, of course, the use of the phrases is the same as the Inspirer. What Inspires?

I imagine that the religious, the fervent in prayer, etc., understands these phrases.

It amazes me how eager and how grasping and tightly he must be when he reads. How lazy I always am. In all the years of going to church how lazily I've

---

52 Luke 4:18. Cf. Isaiah 61:1–2.

listened. But he, when he reads, what he reads is in bright gold and shining and it is for so long imprinted and ready in his mind.
CB, pp. 61–2

02.10.1950
HERE ARE a few sentences from W.:

The sense of the world must lie outside the world. In it there is no value, it must lie outside all happening and being-so. It must lie outside the world.

Ethics and aesthetics are one.

The world of the happy is quite another than that of the unhappy.

The solution of the riddle of life in space and time lies outside space and time.
CB, p. 68

1950

If the believer in God looks around & asks "Where does everything I see come from?" "Where does all that come from?", what he hankers after is *not* a (causal) explanation; and the point of his question is that it is the expression of this hankering. He is expressing, then, a stance towards all explanations. – But how is this manifested in his life?

It is the attitude of taking a certain matter seriously, but then <u>at a certain point</u> not taking it seriously after all, & declaring that something else is still more serious.

Someone may for instance say that it is a very grave manner that such & such a person has died before he could complete a certain piece of work; & in another sense that is not what matters. At this point one uses the words "in a deeper sense".

Really what I should like to say is that here too what is important is not the *words* you use or what you think while saying them, so much as the difference that they make at different points in your life. How do I know that two people mean the same thing when each says he believes in God? And just the same thing goes for the Trinity. Theology that insists on *certain* words and phrases & prohibits others makes nothing clearer. (Karl Barth)

It gesticulates with words, as it were, because it wants to say something & does not know how to express it. *Practice* gives the words their sense.
CV

1950

A proof of God ought really to be something by means of which you can convince yourself of God's existence. But I think that *believers* who offered such proofs wanted to analyse & make a case for their 'belief' with their intellect, although they themselves would never have arrived at belief by way of such proofs. "Convincing someone of God's existence" is something you might do by means of a certain upbringing, shaping his life in such & such a way.

Life can educate you to "believing in God". And *experiences* too are what do this but not visions, or other sense experiences, which show us the "existence of this being", but e.g. sufferings of various sorts. And they do not show us God as a sense experience does an object, nor do they give rise to *conjectures* about him. Experiences, thoughts, – life can force this concept on us.

So perhaps it is similar to the concept 'object'.

CV

1950

How God judges people is something we cannot imagine at all. If he really takes the strength of temptation & the frailty of nature into account, whom can he condemn? But if not, then these two forces simply yield as a result the end for which a person was predestined. In that case he was created so as either to conquer or succumb as a result of the interplay of forces. And that is not a religious idea at all, so much as a scientific hypothesis.

So if you want to stay within the religious sphere, you must *struggle*.

CV

01.01.1951 (?)

The sequence of events in an image (Film) and in the reality that it represents.

121. Causality in reality, and in the image of reality. (Theology)

122. "But you surely cannot deny that an inner procedure takes place when you remember." –

MS 235, 7 *121

15.03.1951

God may say to me: "I am judging you out of your own mouth. You have shuddered with disgust at your own actions when you have seen them in other people".

CV

27.03.1951

We are often bewitched by a word, for example the word "know".

Is God bound by our knowledge? Might many of our expressions be wrong? That is what we want to say.

I am inclined to say: "That <u>cannot</u> be wrong". That is interesting but what consequences does it have?
MS 176, 25r–25v

06.04.1951
Is the sense of belief in the Devil this, that not everything that comes to us as an inspiration is good?
CV

1951
On my way back from my honeymoon in Italy I went up to Cambridge to see Wittgenstein, who was now living in Dr. Bevan's house.[53] He looked very ill, but was alert and lively as ever.

> WITTGENSTEIN: "It was such a relief to me when the doctors told me that there was now no use continuing the hormone and X-ray treatment; and that I could not expect to live more than a few months. You know that all my life I have been inclined to criticize doctors. But now at the end of my life I have had the good fortune to meet three really good doctors. First, the professor you introduced me to in Dublin, then the doctor Malcolm got me to see in America, and now Dr. Bevan".

"Isn't it curious that, although I know I have not long to live, I never find myself thinking about a 'future life'. All my interest is still on this life and the writing I am still able to do".

We talked for a time about my visit to Italy; and he told me about Goethe's visit to Italy and the deep impression it had made on him. Somehow – I can't remember quite how – the conversation came around to talk about the Bible.

> DRURY: "There are some passages in the Old Testament that I find very offensive. For instance, the story where some children mock Elisha for his baldness: 'Go up, thou bald head'.[54] And God sends bears out of the forest to eat them".
> WITTGENSTEIN: (very sternly) "You mustn't pick and choose just what you want in that way".
> DRURY: "But I have never been able to do anything else".
> WITTGENSTEIN: "Just remember what the Old Testament meant to a man like Kierkegaard. After all, children have been killed by bears".

---

53 Wittgenstein spent the last days of his life living with Dr. Bevan and his wife in Cambridge.
54 2 Kings 2:23–5.

DRURY: "Yes, but we ought to think that such a tragedy is a direct punishment from God for a particular act of wickedness. In the New Testament we are told the precise opposite – the men on whom the Tower of Siloam fell were not more wicked than anyone else".
WITTGENSTEIN: "That has nothing to do with what I am talking about. You don't understand, you are quite out of your depth".

I did not know how to reply to this. It seemed to me that the conversation was distasteful to him, and I did not say anything further.

After a pause we began to talk about more trivial matters. When the time came for me to go to the station, Wittgenstein insisted on coming with me although I tried to persuade him he should not do anything to tire himself. On the way to the station he suddenly referred to our dispute over the Old Testament.

WITTGENSTEIN: "I must write you a letter about that".

Just before the train pulled out he said to me, "Drury, whatever becomes of you, don't stop thinking". These were the last words I ever had from him.
M. O'C. DRURY, PR, pp. 182–4

I had only been back in Dublin a few days when I had a telephone message from Dr. Bevan to say that Wittgenstein was dying and had asked me to come. I started at once. When I arrived at the house, Dr. Bevan met me at the door, and told me,

"Miss Anscombe,[55] Richards and Smythies are already here. Smythies had brought with him a Dominican priest whom Wittgenstein already knew. Wittgenstein was already unconscious when they came, and no one will decide whether the priest should say the usual office for the dying and give conditional absolution".

I remembered the occasion when Wittgenstein had said he hoped his Catholic friends prayed for him, and I said at once that whatever was customary should be done. We then all went up to Wittgenstein's room, and, kneeling down, the priest recited the proper prayers. Soon after, Dr. Bevan pronounced Wittgenstein dead.

There was much hesitation about what arrangements should be made about the funeral. No one seemed ready to speak up.

DRURY: "I remember that Wittgenstein once told me of an incident in Tolstoy's life. When Tolstoy's brother died, Tolstoy, who was then a stern critic of the Russian Orthodox Church, sent for the parish priest and had

---

55 Elizabeth Anscombe (1919–2001). One of Wittgenstein's closest friends and literary executor of his testament. She was a renowned analytic figure and allegedly "the greatest English philosopher of her generation" (obituary in *The Guardian*).

his brother interest according to the Orthodox rite. "Now", said Wittgenstein, "that is exactly what I should have done in a similar case".

When I mentioned this, everyone agreed that all the usual Roman Catholic prayers should be said by a priest at the grave side. This was done the next morning. But I have been troubled ever since as to whether what we did then was right.
M. O'C. DRURY, PR, p. 184

Other Sources

REMARK'S ON FRAZER'S GOLDEN BOUGH

INTRODUCTORY NOTE

Dr. M.O'C. Drury writes: "I think it would have been in 1930 that Wittgenstein said to me that he had always wanted to read Frazer but hadn't done so, and would I get hold of a copy and read some of it out loud to him. I borrowed from the Union Library the first volume of the multi-volume edition and we only got a little way through this because he talked at considerable length about it, and the next term we didn't start it again" – Wittgenstein began writing on Frazer in his manuscript book of June 19th, 1931, and he added remarks during the next two or three weeks – although he was writing more about other things (such as Verstehen eines Satzes, Bedeutung, Komplex und Tatsache, Intention ...). He may have made earlier notes in a pocket notebook, but I have found none.

It was probably in 1931 that he dictated to a typist the greater part of the manuscript books written since July 1930; often changing the order of remarks, and details of the phrasing, but leaving large blocks as they stood. (He rearranged the material again and again later on.) This particular typescript runs to 771 pages. It has a section, just under 10 pages long, of the remarks on Frazer, with a few changes in order and phrasing. Others are in different contexts, and a few are left out.

The typed sections on Frazer begin with three remarks which are not connected with them in the manuscript. He had begun there with remarks which he later marked S (='schlecht') and did not have typed. I think we can see why. The earlier version was:

> "Ich glaube jetzt, daß es richtig wäre, mein Buch mit Bemerkungen über die Metaphysik als eine Art von Magie zu beginnen.

Ludwig Wittgenstein: The Meaning of Life, First Edition. Edited by Joaquín Jareño-Alarcón.
© 2023 John Wiley & Sons Ltd. Published 2023 by John Wiley & Sons Ltd.

> Worin ich aber weder der Magie das Wort reden noch mich über sie lustig machen darf.
> Von der Magie müßte die Tiefe behalten werden.–
> Ja, das Ausschalten der Magie hat hier den Charakter der Magie selbst.
> Denn, wenn ich damals anfing von der ‚Welt' zu reden (und nicht von diesem Baum oder Tisch), was wollte ich anderes als etwas Höheres in meine Worte bannen".[1]

I

We must begin with the mistake and transform it into what is true.

That is, we must uncover the source of the error; otherwise hearing what is true won't help us. It cannot penetrate when something is taking its place.

To convince someone of what is true, it is not enough to state it; we must find the *road* from error to truth.

I must plunge again in the water of doubt.

Frazer's account of the magical and religious notions of men is unsatisfactory: it makes these notions appear as *mistakes*.

Was Augustine mistaken, then, when he called on God on every page of the *Confessions*?

Well – one might say – if he was not mistaken, then the Buddhist holyman, or some other, whose religion expresses quite different notions, surely was. But *none* of them was making a mistake except where he was putting forward a theory.

Even the idea of trying to explain the practice – say the killing of the priest-king – seems to be wrong-headed. All that Frazer does is to make this practice plausible to people who think as he does. It is very queer that all these practices are finally presented, so to speak, as stupid actions.

But it never does come plausible that people do all this out of sheer stupidity.

When he explains to us, for example, that the king must be killed in his prime because, according to the notions of the savages, his souls would not be kept fresh

---

[1] "I think now that the right thing would be to begin my book with remarks about metaphysics as a kind of magic.

But in doing this I must neither speak in defence of magic nor ridicule it.
What it is that is deep about magic would be kept. –
In this context, in fact, keeping magic out has itself the character of magic.

For when I began in my earlier book to talk about the 'world' (and not about this tree or table), was I trying to do anything except conjure up something of a higher order by my words?"

otherwise, we can only say: where that practice and these views go together, the practice does not spring from the view, but both of them are there.

It may happen, as it often does today, that someone will give up a practice when he has seen that something on which it depended is an error. But this happens only in cases where you can make a man change his way of doing things simply by calling his attention to his error. This is not how it is in connexion with the religious practices of a people; and what we have here is *not* an error.[2]

Frazer says it is very difficult to discover the error in magic and this is why it persists for so long – because, for example, a ceremony which is supposed to bring rain is sure to appear effective sooner or later.[3]

But then it is queer that people do not notice sooner that it does rain sooner or later anyway.

I think one reason why the attempt to find an explanation is wrong is that we have only to put together in the right way what we *know*, without adding anything, and the satisfaction we are trying to get from the explanation comes of itself.

And here the explanation is not what satisfies us anyway. When Frazer begins by telling the story of the King of the Wood at Nemi, he does this in a tone which shows that something strange and terrible is happening here. And that is the answer to the question "why is this happening?": Because it is terrible. In other words, what strikes us in this course of events as terrible, impressive, horrible, tragic, &c., anything but trivial and insignificant, *that* is what gave birth to them.

We can only *describe* and say, human life is like that.

Compared with the impression that what is described here makes on us, the explanation is too uncertain.

Every explanation is an hypothesis.

But for someone broken up by love an explanatory hypothesis won't help much. – It will not bring peace.

---

2 Cf. *The Golden Bough*, p. 264: "But reflection and enquiry should satisfy us that to our predecessors we are indebted for much of what we thought most our own, and that their error were not wilful extravagances or the ravings of insanity, but simply hypotheses, justifiable as such at the time when they were propounded, but which a fuller experience has proved to be inadequate. It is only by the successive testing of hypotheses and rejection of the false that truth is at last elicited. After all, what we call now truth is only the hypothesis which is found to work best. Therefore in reviewing the opinions and practices of ruder ages and races we shall do well to look with leniency upon their errors as inevitable slips made in the search for truth, and to give them the benefit of that indulgence which we ourselves may one day stand in need of: *cum excusatione itaque veteres audiendi sunt*."

3 Cf. p. 59: "A ceremony intended to make the wind blow or the rain fall, or to work the death of an enemy, will always be followed, sooner or later, by the occurrence it is meant to bring to pass; and primitive man may be excused for regarding the occurrence as a direct result of the ceremony, and the best possible proof of its efficacy."

The crush of thoughts that do not get out because they all try to push forward and are wedged in the door.

Put that account of the King of the Wood at Nemi together with the phrase "the majesty of death", and you see that they are one.

The life of the priest-king shows what is meant by that phrase.

If someone is gripped by the majesty of death, then through such a life he can give expression to it. – Of course this is not an explanation: it puts one symbol in place of another. Or one ceremony in place of another.

A religious symbol does not rest on any *opinion*.

An error belongs only with opinion.

One would like to say: This is what took place here; laugh, if you can.

The religious actions or the religious life of the priest-king are not different in kind from any genuinely religious action today, say a confession of sins. This also can be "explained" (made clear) and cannot be explained.

Burning in effigy. Kissing the picture of a loved one. This is obviously *not* based on a belief that it will have a definite effect on the object which the picture represents. It aims at some satisfaction and it achieves it. Or rather, it does not *aim* at anything: we act in this way and then feel satisfied.

One could also kiss the name of the loved one, and here the representation by the name would be clear.

The same savage who, apparently in order to kill his enemy, sticks his knife through a picture of him, really does build his hut of wood and cuts his arrow with skill and not in effigy.

The idea that one can beckon a lifeless object to come, just as one would beckon a person. Here the principle is that of personification.

And magic always rests on the idea of symbolism and of language.

The description [*Darstellung*] of a wish is, *eo ipso*, the description of its fulfilment.

And magic does give representation [*Darstellung*] to a wish; it expresses a wish.

Baptism as washing. – There is a mistake only if magic is presented as science.

If the adoption of a child is carried out by the mother pulling the child from beneath her clothes, then it is crazy to think there is an *error* in this and that she believes she has borne the child.[4]

We should distinguish between magical operations and those operations which rest on a false, over-simplified notion of things and processes. For instance, if someone says that the illness is moving from one part of the body into another, or

---

4 "The same principle of make-believe, so dear to children, has led other peoples to employ a simulation of birth as a form of adoption. A woman will take a boy whom she intends to adopt and push or pull him through her clothes; ever afterwards he is regarded as her very son, and inherits the whole property of his adoptive parents" (*The Golden Bough*, pp. 14, 15).

if he takes measures to draw off the illness as though it were a liquid or a temperature. He is then using a false picture, a picture that doesn't fit.

What narrowness of spiritual life we find in Frazer! And as a result: how impossible for him to understand a different way of life from the English one of his time!

Frazer cannot imagine a priest who is not basically an English parson of our times with all his stupidity and feebleness.

Why should it not be possible that a man's own name be sacred to him? Surely it is both the most important instrument given to him and also something like a piece of jewelry hung around his neck at birth.

Just how misleading Frazer's accounts are, we see, I think, from the fact that one could well imagine primitive practices oneself and it would only be by chance if they were not actually to be found somewhere. That is, the principle according to which these practices are ordered[5] is much more general than Frazer shows it to be and we find it in ourselves: we could think out for ourselves the different possibilities. – We can readily imagine that, say, in a given tribe no-one is allowed to see the king, or again that every man in the tribe is obliged to see him. And then it will certainly not be left more or less to chance, but the king will be *shown* to the people. Perhaps no-one will be allowed to touch him, or perhaps they will be *compelled* to do so. Think how after Schubert's death his brother cut certain of Schubert's scores into small pieces and gave to his favourite pupils these pieces of a few bars each. As a sign of piety this action is *just* as comprehensible to us as the other one of keeping the scores undisturbed and accessible to no-one. And if Schubert's brother had burnt the scores we could still understand this as a sign of piety.

The ceremonial (hot or cold) as opposed to the haphazard (lukewarm) is a characteristic of piety.

And Frazer's explanations would be no explanations at all if finally they did not appeal to an inclination in ourselves.

Eating and drinking have their dangers, not only for savages but also for us; nothing more natural than wanting to protect oneself against these; and we could think out protective measures ourselves. – But what principle do we follow in imagining them? Clearly that of reducing the various forms of danger to a few very simple ones that anyone can see. In other words, the same principle that leads uneducated people in our society to say that the illness is moving from the head into the chest &c., &c. In these simple images personification will of course play a large part, for men (spirits) can become dangerous to a man and everyone knows this.

---

5 I.e., how they stand related to one another and what this depends on.

That a man's shadow, which looks like a man, or that his mirror image, or that rain, thunderstorms, the phases of the moon, the change of seasons, the likeness and differences of animals to one another and to human beings, the phenomena of death, of birth and of sexual life, in short everything a man perceives year in, year out around him, connected together in a variety of ways – that all this should play a part in his thinking (his philosophy) and his practices, is obvious, or in other words this is what we really know and find interesting.

How could fire or fire's resemblance to the sun have failed to make an impression on the awakening mind of man? But not "because he can't explain it" (the stupid superstition of our time) – for does an "explanation" make it less impressive?

The magic in *Alice in Wonderland*, trying to dry out by reading the driest thing there is.[6]

In magical healing one *indicates* to an illness that it should leave the patient.

After the description of any such magical cure we'd like to add: If the illness doesn't understand *that*, then I don't know *how* one ought to say it.

I do not mean that it is especially *fire* that must make an impression on anyone. Fire no more than any other phenomenon, and one will impress this person and another that. For no phenomenon is particularly mysterious in itself, but any of them can become so to us, and it is precisely the characteristic feature of the awakening human spirit that a phenomenon has meaning for it. We could almost say, man is a ceremonious animal. This is partly false, partly nonsensical, but there is also something in it.

In other words, one might begin a book on anthropology in this way: When we watch the life and behaviour of men all over the earth we see that apart from what we might call animal activities, taking food &c., &c., men also carry out actions that bear a peculiar character and might be called ritualistic.

But then it is nonsense if we go on to say that the characteristic feature of *these* actions is that they spring from wrong ideas about the physics of things. (This is what Frazer does when he says magic is really false physics, or as the case may be, false medicine, technology, &c.).

What makes the character of ritual action is not any view or opinion, either right or wrong, although an opinion – a belief – itself can be ritualistic, or belong to a rite.

If we hold a truism that people take pleasure in imagination, we should remember that this imagination is not like a painted picture or a three-dimensional model, but a complicated structure of heterogeneous elements: words and pictures. We shall then not think of operating with written or oral signs as something to be contrasted with the operation with "mental images" of the events.

We must plough over the whole of language.

---

6 Chapter III, the remark of the mouse.

Frazer: "... That these observances are dictated by fear of the ghost of the slain seems certain ..." (p. 212). But why does Frazer use the word "ghost"? He evidently understands this superstition well enough, since he uses a familiar superstitious word to describe it. Or rather, he might have seen from this that there is something in us too that speaks in support of those observances by the savages. – If I, who do not believe that somewhere or other there are human-superhuman beings which we might call gods – if I say "I fear the wrath of the gods", then this shows that with these words I can mean something or express a feeling that need not be connected with that belief.

Frazer might just as well believe that when a savage dies he is in error. In primary-school reading books it says that Attila undertook his great campaigns because he believed he possessed the sword of the god of thunder.

Frazer is much more savage than most of his savages, for these savages will not be so far from any understanding of spiritual matters as an Englishman of the twentieth century. His explanations of the primitive observances are much cruder than the sense of the observances themselves.

An historical explanation, an explanation as an hypothesis of the development, is only *one* kind of summary of the data – of their synopsis. We can equally well see the data in their relations to one another and make a summary of them in a general picture without putting it in the form of an hypothesis regarding the temporal development.

Identifying one's own gods with the gods of other peoples. One becomes convinced that the names have the same meaning.

"And all this point to some unknown law" is what we want to say about the material Frazer has collected. I *can* set out this law in an hypothesis of development,[7] or again, in analogy with the schema of a plant I can give it in the schema of a religious ceremony, but I can also do is just by arranging the factual material so that we can easily pass from one part to another and have a clear view of it – showing it in a "*perspicuous*" way.

For us the conception of a perspicuous presentation [a way of setting out the whole field together by marking easy the passage from one part of it to another][8] is fundamental. It indicates the form in which we write of things, the way in which we see things. (A kind of "*Weltanschauung*" that seems to be typical of our time. Spengler).[9]

---

7 Or evolution?
8 Introduced in translation, not in Wittgenstein's texts.
9 Oswald Spengler (1880–1938). German thinker. Best known for his influential work: *The Decline of the West*.

This perspicuous presentation makes possible that understanding which consists just in the fact that we "see connections". Hence the importance of finding *intermediate links*.

But in our case an hypothetical link is not meant to do anything except draw attention to the similarity, the connection, between the *facts*. As one might illustrate the internal relation of a circle to an ellipse by gradually transforming an ellipse into a circle; *but not in order to assert that a given ellipse in fact, historically, came from a circle* (hypothesis of development)[10] but only to sharpen our eye for a formal connection.

But equally I might see the hypothesis of development as nothing but a way of expressing a formal connection.

[The remarks up to this point form the "selection" Wittgenstein had typed as though forming a separate essay. The passages which follow now were not included in this, although they come – at various points – in the same large manuscript and in the revision and typing of it].

I wish to say: nothing shows our kinship to those savages better than the fact that Frazer has at hand a word as familiar to us as "ghost" or "shade" to describe the way these people look at things.

(For this is something different from what it would be if he described, say, how savages imagine that their heads fall when they have slain an enemy; where our *description* would have nothing superstitious or magical about it).

What is queer in this is not limited to the expression "ghost" and "shade", and too little is made of the fact that we include the words "soul" and "spirit" in our own civilized vocabulary. Compared with this, the fact that we do not believe our soul eats and drinks is a minor detail.

A whole mythology is deposited in our language.

To cast our death or to slay death; but he is also represented as a skeleton, as in some sense dead himself. "As dead as death". "Nothing is so dead as death; nothing is so beautiful as beauty itself". Here the image which we use in thinking of reality is that beauty, death &c. are the pure (concentrated) substances, and that they are found in the beautiful object as added ingredients of the mixture. – And do I not recognize here my own observations on "object" and "complex"?

What we have in the ancient rites is the practice of a highly cultivated gesture-language.

And when I read Frazer I keep wanting to say: All these processes, these changes of meaning, – we have them here still in our word-language. If what they call the "Corn-wolf" is what is hidden in the last sheaf; but also the last sheaf itself and

---

10 Or evolution?

also the man who binds it, we recognize in this a movement of language with which we are perfectly familiar.[11]

I could imagine that I had had to choose some being on earth as my soul's dwelling place, and that my spirit had chosen this insignificant creature as its seat and point from which it has to view things. Perhaps because a beautiful dwelling would be an exception and this repelled him. Certainly the spirit would need to be very sure of itself to do this.

We might say "every view has its charm", but this would be wrong. What is true is that every view is significant for him who sees it so (but that does not mean "sees it as something other than it is"). And in this sense every view is equally significant.

It is important also that the contempt each person feels for me is something I must make my own, an essential and significant part of the world seen from the place where I am.

If a human being could choose to be born as a tree in a forest, then there would be some who could seek out the most beautiful or the highest tree for themselves, some who would choose the smallest and some who would choose an average or below-average tree, and I do not mean out of philistinism, but for just the reason, or the kind of reason, for which the other man chose the highest. That the feeling we have for our life is comparable to that of a being who could choose his own standpoint in the world, is, I believe, the basis of the myth – or belief – that we choose our body before birth.

The characteristic feature of primitive man, I believe, is that he does not act from *opinions* he holds about things (as Frazer thinks).

I read, amongst many similar examples, of a rain-king in Africa to whom the people appeal for rain *when the rain season* comes.[12] But surely this means that they do not actually think he can make rain, otherwise they would do it in the dry periods in which the land is "a parched and arid desert". For if we do assume that it was stupidity that once led the people to institute this office of Rain King, still they obviously knew from experience that the rains begin in March, and it would have been the Rain King's duty to perform in other periods of the year.

---

11 "In various parts of Mecklenburg, where the belief in the Corn-wolf is particularly prevalent, everyone fears to cut the last corn, because they say the Wolf is sitting in it; ... the last bunch of corn is itself commonly called the Wolf, and the man who reaps it ... is himself called Wolf" (*The Golden Bough*, p. 449).

12 "... the Kings of the Rain, *Mata Kodou*, who are credited with the power of giving rain at the proper time, that is, in the rainy season. Before the rains begin to fall at the end of March the country is a parched and arid desert; and the cattle, which form the people's chief wealth, perish for lack of grass. So, when the end of March draws on, each householder betakes himself to the King of Rain and offers him a cow that he may make the blessed waters of heaven drip on the brown and withered pastures" (*The Golden Bough*, p. 107).

Or again: towards morning, when the sun is about to rise, people celebrates rites of the coming day, but not at night, for then they simply burn lamps.

II

Simple though it may sound, we can express the difference between science and magic if we say that in science there is progress, but not in magic. There is nothing in magic to show the direction of any development.

Page 617ff. (in Chapter LXII, "The Fire Festivals Of Europe").

The most noticeable thing seems to me not merely the similarities but also the differences throughout all these rites. It is a wide variety of faces with common features that keep showing in one place and in another. And one would like to draw lines joining the parts that various faces have in common. But then a part of our contemplation would still be lacking, namely what connects this picture with our own feelings and thoughts. This part gives the contemplation its depth.

In all these practices we see something that is similar, at any rate, to the association of ideas and related to it. We could speak of an association of practices.

> So soon as any sparks were emitted by means of the violent friction, they applied a species of agaric which grows on old birch-tress, and is very combustible. This fire had the appearance of being immediately derived from heaven, and manifold were the virtues ascribed to it.
> *(The Golden Bough, p. 618)*

There is nothing to explain why the fire should have such a nimbus surrounding it. And what a queer thing, what does it actually mean, "it had the appearance of being derived from heaven"? From what heaven? No, it by no means goes without saying, that the fire is regarded in this way – but that is how it is regarded.

> The person who officiated as master of the feast produced a large cake baked with eggs and scalloped round the edge, called *am bonnach bealtine* – i.e., the Beltane cake. It was divided into a number of pieces, and distributed in great form to the company. There was one particular piece which whoever got was called *cailleach beal-tine* – i.e., the Beltane *carline*, a term of great reproach. Upon his being known, part of the company laid hold of him and made a show of putting him into the fire …. And while the feast was fresh in people's memory, they affected to speak of the *cailleach beal-tine* as dead. (p. 618)

Here it seems as though it were the hypothesis that gives the matter depth. And we may remember the explanation of the strange relationship between Siegfried and Brunhilde in our *Nibelungenlied*. Namely that Siegfried seems to have been

Brunhilde before. It is clear that what gives this practice depth is its *connection with the burning of a man*. If it were the custom at some festival for men to ride on one another (as in horse-and-rider games), we would see nothing more in this than a way of carrying someone which reminds us of men riding horses. But if we knew that among many peoples it had been the custom, say, to use slaves as mounts and to celebrate certain festivals mounted in this way, we should then see in the harmless practice of our time something deeper and less harmless. The question is: is what we may call the sinister character of the Beltane fire festival as it was practised a hundred years ago – is this a character of the practice in itself, or only if the hypothesis regarding its origin is confirmed? I think it is clear that what gives us a sinister impression is the inner nature of the practice as performed in recent times, and the facts of human sacrifice as we know them only indicate the direction in which we ought to see it. When I speak of the inner nature of the practice I mean all those circumstances in which it is carried out that are not included in the account of the festival, because they consist not so much in particular actions which characterize it, but rather in what we might call the spirit of the festival: which would be described by, for example, describing the sort of people that take part, their way of behaviour at other times, i.e. their character, and the other kinds of games that they play. And we should then see that what is sinister lies in the character of these people themselves.

> In ... western Perthshire, the Beltane custom was still in vogue towards the end of the eighteenth century. It has been described as follows by the parish minister of the time: "... They put all the bits of the cake into a bonnet. Every one, blindfold, draws out a portion .... Whoever draws the black bit is the *devoted* person who is to be sacrificed to *Baal* ..."
>
> Thomas Pennant, who travelled in Perthshire in the year 1769, tells us that "... every one takes a cake of oatmeal, upon which are raised nine square knobs, each dedicated to some particular being ..."
>
> Another writer of the eighteenth century has described the Beltane festival as it was held in the parish of Logierait in Perthshire. He says: "... These dishes they eat with a sort of cakes baked for the occasion, and having a small lumps in the form of *nipples*, raised all over the surface." ...We may conjecture that the cake with knobs was formerly used for the purpose of determining who should be the "Beltane carline" or victim doomed to the flames (pp. 618, 619).

Here something looks like the ruins of a casting of lots. And through this aspect it suddenly gains depth. Should we learn that the cake with the knobs in a particular case had originally been baked, say, in honour of a button-maker on his birthday and the practice had been persisted in the district, it would in fact lose all "depth", unless this should lie in the present form of the practice itself.

But in a case like this we often say: "this practice is obviously age-old". How do we know that? Is it only because we have historical evidence regarding ancient practices of this sort? Or is there another reason, one that comes through interpretation? But even if its ancient origin and its descent from an earlier practice is established by history, it is still possible that there is nothing sinister at all about the practice today, that no trace of the ancient horror is left on it. Perhaps it is only performed by children now, who have contests in baking cakes and decorating them with knobs. So that the depth lies solely in the thought of that ancestry. Yet this ancestry may be very uncertain and one feels like saying: "Why make what is so uncertain into something to worry about?" (like a backwards-looking Kluge Else). But worries of that kind are not involved here.

Above all: whence the certainty that a practice of this kind must be age-old (what are the data, what is the verification)? But *have* we any certainty, may we not have been led into a mistake because we were over-impressed by historical considerations? Certainly, but that still leaves something of which we are sure. We would then say: "Very well, the origin in this case may be different, but as a general rule certainly it is age-old". It is our *evidence* for it, that holds what is deep in this assumption. And this evidence is again non-hypothetical, psychological. For when I say: what is deep in this practice lies in its origin, if it *did* come about like that, then either the depth lies in the idea (the thought) of [its descent] such an origin, or else the depth is itself hypothetical and we can only say: *if* that is how it went, then it was a deep and sinister business. What I want to say is: What is sinister, deep, does not lie in the fact that that is how the history of this practice went, for perhaps it did not go that way; nor in the fact that perhaps or probably it was that, but in what it is that gives me reason to assume it.

What makes human sacrifice something deep and sinister anyway? Is it only the suffering of the victim that impresses us in that way? All manner of diseases bring just as much suffering and do *not* make this impression. No, this deep and sinister aspect is not obvious just from learning the history of the external action, but *we* impute it from an experience in ourselves.

The fact that for the lots they use a cake has something especially terrible (almost like betrayal through a kiss), and that this does seem especially terrible to us is of central importance in our investigation of practices like these.

If I see such practice, or hear of it, it is like seeing a man speaking sternly to another because of something quite trivial, and noticing in the tone of his voice and in his face that on occasion this man can be frightening. The impression I get from this may be a very deep and extremely serious one.

The *environment* of a way of acting.

There is one conviction that underlies [or is taken for granted in] the hypotheses about the origin of, say, the Beltane festival; namely that festivals of this kind are not so to speak haphazard inventions of one man but need an infinitely broader basis if they are to persist. If I tried to invent a festival it would very soon die out or else be so modified that it corresponded to a general inclination in people.

But what makes us unwilling to assume that the Beltane festival has always been celebrated in its present (or very recent) form? We feel like saying: it is too meaningless to have been invented in this form. Isn't it like this when I see a ruin and say: that must have been a house once, for nobody would have built up hewn and irregular stones into a heap constructed like this one. And if someone asked, how do you know that? I could only say: it is what my experience of people teaches me. And even where people do really build ruins, they give them the form of tumbled-down houses.

We might put it this way: Anyone who wanted to impress us with the story of the Beltane festival would not need to explain the hypothesis of its origin anyway; he would only have to lay before us the material (which leads him to this hypothesis) and say nothing more. Here one may be inclined to say: "Of course, because the listener or reader will draw the conclusion himself!" But must he draw the conclusion explicitly? i.e., draw it at all? And what sort of conclusion is it? That this or that is *probable*? And if he can draw the conclusion himself, how should the conclusion make an impression on him? What makes the impression must surely be something *he* has not done. Is it only the hypothesis when expressed by him or by someone else that impresses him, or is he already impressed by the material for it? But could I not just as well ask: When I see someone being killed – is it simply what I see that makes an impression on me or does this come with the hypothesis that someone is being killed here?

But it is not just the idea of the possible origin of the Beltane festival that makes it impressive, but what we call the overwhelming probability of this idea. What we get from the material.

The Beltane festival as it has come down to us is the performance of a play, something like children playing at robbers. But then again it is not like this. For even though it is prearranged so that the side which saves the victim wins, there is still the infusion of a mood or state of mind in what is happening which a theatrical production does not have. And even if it were a perfectly cool performance we should be uneasy and ask ourselves: What is this performance trying to do, what is its point? And apart from any interpretation its queer pointlessness could make us uneasy. (Which shows the kind of reason that an uneasiness of this sort can have.) Suppose some harmless interpretation; perhaps that they cast lots just so that they can have the fun of threatening to throw someone in the fire, which would be disagreeable; then the Beltane festival becomes much more like one of those practical jokes in which one of the company has to submit to cruel treatment and which satisfy a need just in this form. Such an explanation would take all mystery from the Beltane festival, were it not that the festival is something different in action and in mood from those familiar games of robbers &c.

In the same way, the fact that on certain days children burn a straw man could make us uneasy, even if no explanation [hypothesis] were given. Strange that they should celebrate by burning a *man*! What I want to say is: the solution is not any more disquieting than the riddle.

But why should it not really be (partly, away) just the *idea* that makes the impression on me? Aren't ideas frightening? Can I not feel horror from the thought that the cake with the knobs once served to select by lot the victim to be sacrificed? Hasn't the *thought* something terrible? – Yes, but that which I see in those stories is something they acquire, after all, from the evidence, including such evidence as does not seem directly connected with them – from the thought of man and his past, from the strangeness of what I see in myself and in others, what I have seen and have heard.

PHILOSOPHICAL INVESTIGATIONS

373. Grammar tells what kind of object anything is. (Theology as grammar).

Part II
"I believe that he is not an automaton", just like that. So far makes no sense.

My attitude towards him is an attitude towards a soul. I am not of the *opinion* that he has a soul.

Religion teaches that the soul can exist when the body has disintegrated. Now do I understand this teaching? – Of course I understand it- I can imagine plenty of things in connexion with it. And haven't pictures of these things been painted? And why should such a picture be only an imperfect rendering of the spoken doctrine? Why should it not do the *same* service as the words? And it is the service which is the point.

If the picture of thought in the head can force itself upon us, then why not much more that of thought in the soul?

The human body is the best picture of the human soul.
P. 178e

REMARKS ON THE PHILOSOPHY OF PSYCHOLOGY VOL. I

139. The picture "He knows – I don't know" is one that makes our lack of knowledge appear in an especially irritating light. It is like when one looks for an object in various drawers, and tells oneself that God knows the whole time *where* it actually is, and that we are searching this drawer quite futilely.

198. But it is true: with mental defectives we often feel as if they talked more automatically than we do, and if someone were what we called 'meaning-blind', we should picture him as making a less lively impression than we do, behaving more 'like an automaton'. (One also says: "God knows what goes on in his mind", and one thinks of something ill-defined, disorderly).

213. What must the man be called, who cannot understand the concept 'God', cannot see how a reasonable man may use this word seriously? Are we to say he suffers from some *blindness*?

475. The way you use the word "God" shews, not *whom* you mean, but what you mean. (**CV** 11.09.1946)

492. Suppose someone said "I wish – but I don't want my wish to be fulfilled". – (Lessing: "If God in his right hand ...") Can one then ask God to give the wish, and *not* to fulfil it?

816. But consider this: After all I sometimes take someone else's word, -so I would surely at least sometimes have to take my own word too, that I have such and such a conviction. But when I report my observation in a quasi-automatic fashion, then this report has nothing at all to do with my conviction. On the other hand I might have confidence in myself, or in my observing self, just as another person does. So I might say "I say 'It's raining', so it will presumably be true" Or: "The observer in me says 'It's raining', and I am inclined to believe him". – For isn't this – or something like this- how it is, when a man says that God has spoken to him or through his mouth?

REMARKS ON THE PHILOSOPHY OF PSYCHOLOGY VOL. II

648. Only God sees the most secret thoughts. But why should these be all that important? And need all human beings count them as important? (*Zettel* *560).

ON CERTAINTY

107. Isn't this altogether like the way one can instruct a child to believe in a God, or that none exists, and it will accordingly be able to produce apparently telling grounds for the one or the other?

236. Is someone said "The earth has not long been ..." what would he be impugning? Do I know?
   Would it have to be what is called a scientific belief? Might it not be a mystical one? Is there any absolute necessity for him to be contradicting historical facts? Or even geographical ones?

239. I believe that every human being has two human parents; but Catholics believe that Jesus only had a human mother. And other people might believe that there are human beings with no parents, and give no credence to all the contrary evidence. Catholics believe as well that in certain circumstances a wafer completely changes its nature, and at the same time that all evidence proves the contrary. And so if Moore said "I know that this is wine and not blood", Catholics would contradict him.

361. But I might also say: It has been revealed to me by God that it is so. God has taught me that this is my foot. And therefore if anything happened that seemed to conflict with this knowledge I should have to regard *that* as deception.

436. Is God bound by our knowledge? Are a lot of our statements *incapable* of falsehood? For that is what we want to say.

554 [it refers to 553]. In its language-game it is not presumptuous. There, it has no higher position than, simply, the human language-game. For there it has its restricted application.
But as soon as I say this sentence outside its context, it appears in a false light. For then it is as if I wanted to insist that there are things that I *know*. God himself can't say anything to me about them.

ZETTEL

144. How words are understood is not told by words alone (Theology).

560. Only God sees the most secret thoughts. But why should these be all that important? Some are important, not all. And need all human beings count them as important?

717. "You can't hear God speak to someone else, you can hear him only if you are being addressed". – That is a grammatical remark.

G.E.M. ANSCOMBE: "LUDWIG WITTGENSTEIN" *Philosophy*, voL 70 (1995)

"The father, Karl, was a Protestant, the mother a Catholic. The Jewish blood was sufficient to bring the family later on into danger under Hitler's Nuremberg Laws. They did not think of themselves as Jews or belong to the Jewish community in Vienna. The children were brought up sort-of Catholic though so far as I know only the eldest, Hermine, towards the end of her life, took this seriously and made a profession of

faith before friends and household. At 9 years of age Ludwig and Paul, a year or two older than Ludwig, talked together and decided that their religion was all nonsense".
p. 395

M. O'C. DRURY

When he was working on the later part of the *Philosophical Investigations* he told me: "It is impossible for me to say in my book one word about all that music has meant in my life. How then can I hope to be understood". And about the same date: "My type of thinking is not wanted in this present age, I have to swim so strongly against the tide. Perhaps in a hundred years people will really want what I am writing". Again in the same conversation: "I am not a religious man but I cannot help seeing every problem from a religious point of view".

Now these remarks at once raise for me the question as to whether there are not dimensions in Wittgenstein's thought that are still largely being ignored. Have I seen that the *Philosophische Bemerkungen* could have been inscribed 'to the glory of God'? Or that the problems discussed in the *Philosophical Investigations* are being seen from a religious point of view?
PR, 94

In the first serious conversation I ever had with Wittgenstein I told him I had come up to Cambridge with the intention of being ordained as a priest in the Anglican Church.

> WITTGENSTEIN: I don't ridicule this. Anyone who ridicules these matters is a charlatan and worse. But I can't approve, no I can't approve. You have intelligence, it is not the most important thing, but you can't neglect it. Just imagine trying to preach a sermon every Sunday, you couldn't do it, you couldn't possibly do it. I would be afraid that you would try and elaborate a philosophical interpretation or defence of the Christian religion. The symbolism of Christianity is wonderful beyond words, but when people try to make a philosophical system out of it I find it disgusting. At first sight it would seem an excellent idea that in every village there should be one person who stood for these things, but it hasn't worked out like that. Russell and the parsons between them have done infinite harm, infinite harm.

He then went on to say that there had been only two European writers in recent times who really had something important to say about religion, Tolstoy and Dostoievsky. (It is of interest that on this occasion he did not mention Kierkegaard.) He advised me in the coming vacation to read *The Brothers Karamazov*, *Crime and Punishment*, and the short stories of Tolstoy collected under the title *Twenty Three Tales*.

We met again after the vacation and he asked me what impression I had got from this reading.

> WITTGENSTEIN: When I was a village schoolmaster in Austria after the war I read the *Brothers Karamazov* over and over again. I read it loud to the village priest. You know there really have been people like the Elder Zosima who could see into people's hearts and direct them.
> DRURY: I found Dostoievsky more to my liking than Tolstoy.
> WITTGENSTEIN: I don't agree with you. Those short stories of Tolstoy's will live for ever. They were written for all peoples. Which one of them was your favourite?
> DRURY: The one entitled *What Men Live By*.
> WITTGENSTEIN: My favourite is the story of the three hermits who could only pray, 'You are three we are three have mercy upon us'.

It was soon after this conversation that he mentioned to me that when Tolstoy's brother died, Tolstoy, who by then was very far from being an Orthodox believer, sent for the parish priest and had his brother buried according to the full Orthodox rite. Now, said Wittgenstein, "that is exactly what I would have done in the same circumstances". (Years later on the evening on which Wittgenstein died, his friends whom he had sent for, Miss Anscombe, Mr. Smythies, Dr. Richards, and myself, had to decide what should be done about Wittgenstein's burial. No one would speak up. I then mentioned the above conversation and it was unanimously agreed that a Roman Catholic priest should say the usual committal prayers at the grave side. This later gave rise to false rumours and I have been troubled ever since as to whether what we then did was right.)
PR, pp. 100–2

During a discussion after a meeting of the Moral Sciences Club at Cambridge Wittgenstein mentioned the name of Søren Kierkegaard. I had already come across some quotations from this author in the writings of the Baron Von Hügel. These quotations had so impressed me that I had anxiously searched the catalogues of the University Library to see if anything by Kierkegaard had been translated into English. My search had been fruitless. So the next day when we were alone I asked Wittgenstein to tell me more about Kierkegaard.

> Wittgenstein: "Kierkegaard was by far the most profound thinker of the last century. Kierkegaard was a saint".

He then went on to speak of the three categories of life style that play such a large part in Kierkegaard's writing. The aesthetic, where the objective is to get the maximum enjoyment out of this life: the ethical where the concept of duty demands renunciation; and the religious where this very renunciation itself becomes a source of joy.

> WITTGENSTEIN: "Concerning this last category I don't pretend to understand how it is possible. I have never been able to deny myself anything, not even a cup of coffee if I wanted it. Mind you I don't believe what Kierkegaard believed, but of this I am certain that we are not here in order to have a good time".

[...]

Again at a later date Wittgenstein told me that one of his pupils had written to him to say that he had become a Roman Catholic, and that he, Wittgenstein, was partly responsible for his conversion because it was he that had advised the reading of Kierkegaard. Wittgenstein told me he had written back to say: "If someone tells me he has bought the outfit of a tight-rope walker I am not impressed until I see what is done with it".
PR, pp. 102–3

I had begun to attend Professor Moore's lectures. At that time I was unable to appreciate what could be learnt from Moore. At the commencement of his first lecture Moore had read out from the University Calendar the subjects that his professorship required him to lecture on, the last of these was 'the philosophy of religion'. Moore went on to say that he would be talking about all the previous subjects except this last concerning which he had nothing to say. I told Wittgenstein that I thought a Professor of Philosophy had no right to keep silent concerning such an important subject. Wittgenstein immediately asked me if I had available a copy of St. Augustine's *Confessions*. I handed him my Loeb edition. He must have known his way about the book thoroughly for he found the passage he wanted in a few seconds.

> WITTGENSTEIN: You are saying something like St. Augustine says here. "Et vae tacentibus de te quoniam loquaces muti sunt". But this translation in your edition misses the point entirely, it reads "And woe to those who say nothing concerning thee seeing that those who say most are dumb". It should be translated, "And woe to those who say nothing concerning thee just because the chatterboxes talk a lot of nonsense". "Loquaces" is a term of contempt. I won't refuse to talk about God or about religion.

He went on to say that he considered St. Augustine's *Confessions* as possibly the "most serious book ever written". He had tried to read *The City of God* but had been unable to get on with it.
PR, pp. 104–5

A short time after this I mentioned Wittgenstein that I was reading Dr. Tennant's book entitled *Philosophical Theology* which had just been published.

> WITTGENSTEIN: A title like that sounds to me as if it would be something indecent.
> DRURY: Tennant tries to revive in a complicated way the 'argument from design'.
> WITTGENSTEIN: You know I am not one to praise this present age, but that does sound to me as being 'old fashioned' in a bad sense.
> DRURY: Tennant is fond of repeating Butler's aphorism. 'Probability is the guide of life'.
> WITTGENSTEIN: Can you imagine St. Augustine saying that the existence of God was 'highly probable'!

PR, p. 105

Soon after this conversation he sent me a copy of the Vulgate New Testament advising me to read the Latin text. He said that in reading the Latin he thought I would get an entirely new impression. He also told me that at one time he and Moore had planned to read St. Paul's Epistle to the Romans. But after a very short time they had had to give it up. (Many years later when he was living in Dublin he told me that at one time he thought the religion of the Gospels was entirely different from that found in St. Paul's epistles but that now he saw that he had been wrong, it was the same religion in each.)

PR, p. 105

Secondly this. For Pascal there was only one true religion, Christianity; only one true form of Christianity, Catholicism; only one true expression of Catholicism, Port Royal.[13] Now although Wittgenstein would have respected this narrowness for its very intensity, such exclusiveness was foreign to his way of thinking. He was early influenced by William James' *Varieties of Religious Experience*. This book he told me had helped him greatly. And if I am not mistaken the category of *Varieties* continued to play an important part in his thinking.

> WITTGENSTEIN: The way in which people have had to express their religious beliefs differ enormously. All genuine expressions of religion are wonderful, even those of the most savage peoples.

---

13 Cistercian monastery which became the center of the Jansenist Movement. Jansenism remitted to St. Augustine with regard to the gratuity of divine grace and Augustine's conception of human freedom (a pessimistic view of human condition), challenging scholastic theology and modern humanism. Its views were strongly criticized as they seemed to be close to some Protestant principles, though in fact they remained within the Catholic order.

In the "Remarks on Frazer's Golden Bough" he writes:

> Was St. Augustine mistaken then, when he called on God on every page of the *Confessions*? Well – one might say- if he was not mistaken, then the Buddhist holy man, or some other, whose religion expresses quite different notions, surely was. But none of them was making a mistake except where he was putting forward a theory.

Thirdly and most important this. Pascal has been accused by some of 'fideism'.[14] And there are places in the *Penseés* where this accusation might seem justified: "Il faul s'abetir": "Le pyrrhonism est le vrai": Wittgenstein could never have written that.

> WITTGENSTEIN: "Drury, never allow yourself to become too familiar with holy things".

PR, p. 108

I have been trying to give some indication of the conversations I had with Wittgenstein concerning ethics and religion. I do not think I could end this attempt in a better way than by quoting a letter he once wrote me. It was at a time when I was doing my first period of residence in hospital and was distressed at my own ignorance and clumsiness. When I mentioned this to him he at first dismissed it with the remark that all I lacked was experience, but the next day I received the following letter from him.

> Dear Drury,
>
> I have thought a fair amount about our conversation on Sunday and I would like to say, or rather not to say but write, a few things about these conversations. Mainly I think this: Don't think about yourself, but think about others, e.g. your patients. You said in the Park yesterday that possibly you had made a mistake in having taken up medicine: you immediately added that probably it was wrong to think such thing at all. I am sure it is. But not because being a doctor you may not go the wrong way, or go to the dogs, but because if you do, this has nothing to do with your choice of a profession being a mistake. For what human being can say what would have been the right thing if this is the wrong one? You didn't make a

---

14 Point of view according to which we can have access to religious truths by means of faith alone.

mistake because there was nothing at the time you knew or ought to have known that you overlooked. Only this one could have called making a mistake; and even if you had made a mistake in this sense, this would now have to be regarded as a datum as all the other circumstances inside and outside which you can't alter (control). The thing now is to live in the world in which you are, not to think or dream about the world you would like to be in. Look at people's sufferings, physical and mental, you have them close at hand, and this ought to be a good remedy for your troubles. Another way is to take a rest whenever you ought to take one and collect yourself. (Not with me because I wouldn't rest you). As to religious thoughts I do not think the craving for placidity is religious; I think a religious person regards placidity or peace as a gift from heaven, not as something one ought to hunt after. Look at your patients more closely as human beings in trouble and enjoy more the opportunity you have to say 'good night' to so many people. This alone is a gift from heaven which many people would envy you. And this sort of thing ought to heal your frayed soul, I believe. It wont rest it; but when you are healthily tired you can just take a rest. I think in some sense you don't look at people's faces closely enough.

PR, pp. 109–10

Many of these conversations are concerned with religion. So here it must be said that he frequently warned me that he could only speak from his own level, and that was a low one. He sometimes used in this connexion a vulgar French proverb which is perhaps too coarse to print here. It will be seen that as the years developed his views on some religious matters changed and deepened, so that some remarks in the earlier part of this essay he would later repudiate. Once, near the end of his life, I reminded him that in one of our first conversations he had said that there was no subject as 'theology'; and he replied, "That is just the sort of stupid remark I would have made in those days".
PR, p. 113

PAUL ENGELMANN

III. Religious matters

Was Wittgenstein religious? If we call him an agnostic, this must not be understood in the sense of the familiar polemical agnosticism that concentrates, and prides itself, on the argument that man could never know about these matters.

The idea of a God in the sense of the Bible, the image of God as the creator of the world, hardly ever engaged Wittgenstein's attention (as G.H. von Wright rightly points out in his *Biographical Sketch*), but the notion of a last judgment was of profound concern to him. 'When we meet again at the last judgment' was a recurrent phrase with him, which he used in many a conversation at a particularly momentous point. He would pronounce the words with an indescribably inward-gazing look in his eyes, his head bowed, the picture of a man stirred to his depths.

The key to an understanding of the many self-accusations uttered by Wittgenstein at that time and in his later schoolmastering period lies in the fact that *he was not a penitent*. To cast himself in any role even remotely like it would have seemed to him a gross case of religious hypocrisy, for which he had a mortal hatred. What prompted him was an overpowering – and no doubt long-suppressed – urge to cast off all encumbrances that imposed an insupportable burden on his attitude to the outside world: his fortune as well as his necktie. The latter (I remember having been told) he had in his early youth selected with particularly care, and no doubt with his unerring taste. *But he did not discard it in order to do penance* (I am sure he remembered it without any compunction). He simply had for years led a life out of harmony with all this, and so he eventually decided to shed all the things, big or small, that he felt to be petty or ludicrous. So when from that time on he went about without a tie in an open-necked shirt, he was not *donning a new garb* (say, that of a penitent); on the contrary, he was trying (unsuccessfully) to go about without any garb at all.

I have truthfully reported here what religion meant to me, at any rate in the first year of our acquaintance; what my entirely subjective and personal feelings about it were; how religion, together with art, fashioned my spiritual life during the war and for many years afterwards; and how I have striven – unsuccessfully on the whole, yet earnestly – to change my everyday life according to its demands.

Yet, I fear that this account will be misunderstood, and that in particular the image of Wittgenstein will be affected and falsified as a result. I have described his lively and deep interest in what I told him and, even more, in what he perceived himself. But in doing so, I never intended in the least to make propaganda for the feelings and thoughts that moved me at the time. I confine myself to the most essential points, so as to elucidate some passages in his letters which I consider important. First of all, to clear up some of the most likely misconceptions, a few words about how *not* to visualize Wittgenstein's attitude to religion:

Above all, he was never a mystic in the sense of occupying his mind with mystic-gnostic fantasies. Nothing was further from his mind than the attempt to paint a picture of a world beyond (either before or after death), about which we cannot speak. (He says in the *Tractatus* that the fact of a life after death could explain nothing).

The conclusions, however, which Wittgenstein and I drew, each of us from his own religious concepts, were different, in keeping with the difference in both magnitude and direction of our talents and abilities. He 'saw life as a task', and on that I agreed with him. Moreover, he looked upon all the features of life as it is, that is to say upon all facts, as an essential part of the conditions of that task; just as a person presented with a mathematical problem must not try to ease his task by modifying the problem. But – it may be asked – could it not be that for an individual of a suitable disposition such a modification of the data of the task may actually form *part of the task*, indeed may be felt in his conscience as vital to the task itself? Yet, the person who consistently believes that the reason for the discrepancy lies in himself alone must reject the belief that changes in the external facts may be necessary and called for.

3

Wittgenstein felt unreserved admiration and respect for Tolstoy, at least when I knew him. Among Tolstoy's writings he had an especially high regard for *The Gospel in Brief* and the Folk Tales. One story is about two old Russian peasants who in fulfilment of a vow made long ago set out on a pilgrimage to Jerusalem. During the journey one of them pulls his snuff-box out of his pocket and snuffs. His companion reproaches him for such behaviour unfitting for a pilgrim. 'Sin got the better of me', the other replies.

Such self-knowledge – Wittgenstein thought – was a sign of true religious feeling: instead of trying to excuse his action before himself and others as 'not really sinful', the peasant confessed having succumbed to sin.

And often he quoted, full of enthusiasm, the words spoken by the convicted officer and libertine Dmitri Karamazov in full awareness of his guilt: 'Hail to the Highest – also within me!'

In Tolstoy's tale only one of the two pilgrims, the one who admonished his friend, reaches Jerusalem. The other never got beyond a famine-stricken area in the Ukraine which they had passed on their way. There, in a miserable hovel, he found a family of cottagers starving and on the point of death. He could not tear himself away until he had saved them and nursed them back to health, spending in the process all the money he had saved up for the journey. So he returned home by himself.

The first peasant, though in Jerusalem, finds it impossible, among the bustling throngs of pilgrims and under constant threat from pickpockets, to concentrate his thoughts on devotion. At the Holy Sepulchre he sees at the head of the crowd his lost companion surrounded by a halo. But he cannot reach him.

Back home he finds his companion attending to the beehives in his garden. Lit up by a shaft of sunlight, the bees seem to float around his head like the halo in Jerusalem. But when the returning pilgrim tells his friend what he saw and asks about his stay with the starving, the other hushes him with some alarm: 'That is God's business, my friend, God's business. But come into the house and taste some of my honey'.

Significantly, Tolstoy chose a passage from the Gospel of St. John (IV, 19–23) as a motto for this tale. It will not be amiss, I believe, to place it at the end of this section:

> The woman saith unto him, Sir, I perceive that thou art a prophet. Our fathers worshipped in this mountain and ye say, that in Jerusalem is the place where men ought to worship. Jesus said unto her, Woman, believe me, the hour cometh, when ye shall neither in this mountain, nor yet at Jerusalem, worship the Father. Ye worship ye know not what; we know

what we worship; for salvation is of the Jews. But the hour cometh, and now is, when the true worshippers shall worship the Father in spirit and in truth.

LPE, pp. 77–81

4

I believe it was during a tram ride into town from the Olmütz railway station that Wittgenstein told me he had now for the first time read the Latin version of the Bible, the Vulgate. He was enthusiastic. Only here, he said, had the text revealed to him his true shape and greatness. I understood precisely what he meant: in contrast with versions such as the German or the Greek (the Hebrew original he was unable to read) in which the emotions accompanying the rational text are conveyed with much greater immediacy, Latin is the language where reason dominates and *all* emotional aspects become manifest without words. As a result the text assumes in that language a different and new, monumental stature akin to the mode of expression Wittgenstein himself endeavoured to achieve in the *Tractatus*.

Incidentally, on the subject of Bible translations: Much later, in Vienna, I once read to him some specimen passages of the Buber-Rosenzweig translation into German. In my view this version does unnecessary violence to the German language in places, whereas I have always had the highest respect for Luther's translation as a work of literature which reproduces the spirit of the original no less faithfully in the garb of his own time than do Rembrandt's etchings. Wittgenstein agreed with me on the whole, but judged Buber's translation somewhat more favourably than I, as he felt that in spite, or possibly because, of the liberties taken with the German language it conveyed to him the exotic and 'barbaric' aspect of the original text. This amounts to a recognition, though qualified, of the value of that translation.

LPE, pp. 111–12

RAY MONK

In the autumn Wittgenstein asked Anscombe if she could put him touch with a 'non-philosophical' priest. He did not want to discuss the finer points of Catholic doctrine; he wanted to be introduced to someone to whose life religious belief had made a practical difference. She introduced him to Father Conrad, the Dominican priest who had instructed Yorick Smythies during his conversion to Catholicism. Conrad came to Anscombe's house twice to talk to Wittgenstein. He wanted, Conrad recalls, 'to talk to a priest as a priest and did not wish to discuss philosophical problems':

> He knew he was very ill and wanted to talk about God, I think with a view to coming fully to his religion, but in fact we only had, I think, two conversations on God and the soul in rather general terms. (*Father Conrad to the author, 30.08.1986*)

Anscombe, however, doubts that Wittgenstein wanted to see Conrad 'with a view coming back fully to his religion', if by that Conrad means that Wittgenstein wanted to return to the Catholic Church. And, given Wittgenstein's explicit statement that he could not believe certain doctrines of the Catholic Church, it seems reasonable to accept her doubt.
TDG, pp. 573–4

NORMAN MALCOLM

At this point I should like to say what I can on the difficult subject of Wittgenstein's attitude towards religion. He told me that in his youth he had been contemptuous of it, but that at about the age of twenty-one something had caused a change in him. In Vienna he saw a play that was a mediocre drama, but in it one of the characters expressed the thought that no matter what happened in the world, nothing bad could happen to *him* – *he* was independent of fate and circumstances. Wittgenstein was struck by this stoic thought; for the first time he saw the possibility of religion. He said that during his service in the First War he came across Tolstoy's writings on the Gospels, which made a great impression on him.

Wittgenstein says in the *Tractatus*: 'Not *how* the world is, is the mystical, but *that* it is' (*6.44). I believe that a certain feeling of amazement that *anything should exist at all*, was sometimes experienced by Wittgenstein, not only during the *Tractatus* period, but also when I knew him. Whether this feeling has anything to do with religion is not clear to me. But Wittgenstein did once say that he thought that he could understand the conception of God, in so far as it is involved in one's awareness of one's own sin and guilt. He added that he could *not* understand the conception of a *Creator*. I think that the ideas of Divine judgement, forgiveness, and redemption had some intelligibility for him, as being related in his mind to feelings of disgust with himself, an intense desire for purity, and a sense of the helplessness of human beings to make themselves better. But the notion of a being *making the world* had no intelligibility for him at all.

Wittgenstein once suggested that a way in which the notion of immortality can acquire a meaning is through one's feeling that one has duties from which one cannot be released, even by death. Wittgenstein himself possessed a stern sense of duty.

I believe that Wittgenstein was prepared by his own character and experience to comprehend the idea of a judging and redeeming God. But any cosmological conception of a Deity, derived from the notions of cause or infinity, would be repugnant to him. He was impatient with 'proofs' of the existence of God, and with attempts to give religion a *rational* foundation. When I once quoted to him a remark of Kierkegaard's to this effect: 'How can it be that Christ does not exist, since I know that He has saved me?' Wittgenstein exclaimed: 'You see! It isn't a question of *proving* anything!' He disliked the theological writings of Cardinal Newman, which he read with care during his last year at Cambridge. On the other hand, he revered the writings of St. Augustine. He told me he decided to begin his *Investigations* with a quotation from the latter's *Confessions*, not because he could not find the conception expressed in that quotation stated as well by other philosophers, but because the conception *must* be important if so great a mind held it. Kierkegaard he also esteemed. He referred to him, with something of awe in his expression, as a 'really religious' man. He had read the *Concluding Unscientific Postscript* – but found it 'too deep' for him. The *Journal* of George Fox, the English Quaker, he read with admiration – and presented me with a copy of it. He praised one of Dickens' sketches – an account of the latter's visit on board a passenger ship crowded with English converts to Mormonism, about to sail for America. Wittgenstein was impressed by the calm resolution of those people, as portrayed by Dickens.

I do not wish to give the impression that Wittgenstein accepted any religious faith – he certainly did not – or that he was a religious person. But I think that there was in him, in some sense, the *possibility* of religion. I believe that he looked on religion as a 'form of life' (to use an expression from the *Investigations*) in which he did not participate, but with which he was sympathetic and which greatly interested him. Those who did participate he respected – although here as elsewhere he had contempt for insincerity. I suspect that he regarded religious belief as based on qualities of character and will that he himself did not possess. Of Smythies and Anscombe, both of whom had become Roman Catholics, he once said to me: 'I could not possibly bring myself to believe all the things that they believe'. I think that in this remark he was not disparaging their belief. It was rather an observation about his own capacity.

NML, pp. 70–2

GEORG HENRIK VON WRIGHT[15]

The period of the war was a crisis in Wittgenstein's life. To what extent the turmoil of the time and his experiences in war and captivity contributed to the crisis, I cannot say. A circumstance of great importance was that he became acquainted with the ethical and religious writings of Tolstoy. Tolstoy exercised a strong influence on Wittgenstein's view of life, and also led him to study the Gospels.

NML, pp. 9–10

---

15 (1916–2003): Professor of Philosophy at Cambridge University (1948–51) after Wittgenstein. One of his literary executors.

Wittgenstein's most characteristic features were his great and pure seriousness and powerful intelligence. I have never met a man who impressed me so strongly in either aspect.

It seems to me that there are two forms of seriousness of character. One is fixed in 'strong principles'; the other springs from a passionate heart. The former has to do with morality and the latter, I believe, is closer to religion. Wittgenstein was acutely and even painfully sensitive to considerations of duty, but the earnestness and severity of his personality were more of the second kind. Yet I do not know whether he can be said to have been 'religious' in any but a trivial sense of the word. Certainly he did not have a Christian faith. But neither was his view of life un-Christian, pagan, as was Goethe's. To say that Wittgenstein was not a pantheist is to say something important. 'God does not reveal himself *in* the world', he wrote in the *Tractatus*. The thought of God, he said, was above all for him the thought of a fearful judge.

Wittgenstein had the conviction, he sometimes said, that he was doomed. His outlook was typically one of the gloom. Modern times were to him a dark age. His idea of the helplessness of human beings was not unlike certain doctrines of predestination.

NML, pp. 19–20

Wittgenstein received deeper impressions from some writers in the borderland between philosophy, religion, and poetry than from the philosophers, in the restricted sense of the word. Among the former are St. Augustine, Kierkegaard, Dostoievsky, and Tolstoy. The philosophical sections of St. Augustine's *Confessions* show a striking resemblance to Wittgenstein's own way of doing philosophy. Between Wittgenstein and Pascal there is a trenchant parallelism which deserves closer study. It should also be mentioned that Wittgenstein held the writings of Otto Weininger in high regard.

NML, p. 21

Index

a

abstinence   100
Adam   17, 74, 107, 141
aesthetics   28, 49, 57, 95–97, 194
agnosticism   220
altar   103
analogy   61, 92, 99, 100, 183, 205
Angel   149
Anglican Confession (Anglican Church, Anglicanism, Anglican Reformation)   91, 104, 181, 215
Anglican Prayer-Book   76
Anscombe, Gertrude Elizabeth Margaret   155, 197, 214–215, 223–225
anthropology   204
anthropomorfism   174
apologetic   140
apostle   85, 113, 149, 149, 191
Apostle's Creed   191
a priori (experience)   48
argument   93, 182, 218, 220
art   30, 35, 68, 70, 149, 221, 222
asceticism (ascetic)   1, 76
atheism   66
atheist   137, 180
Attila   205
attitude   1, 3, 4, 36, 79, 118, 130, 140, 146, 158, 172, 179, 180, 183, 186, 190, 194, 212, 221, 224

Augustine of Hippo (St. Augustine)   158, 217–219, 225, 226
Ayer, Alfred Julius   80, 176

b

Bach, Johann Sebastian   189
Barth, Karl   77, 157, 165, 191, 194
Beethoven, Ludwig van   72, 84
belief, religious (believer)   106, 133, 135, 137–138, 173, 182, 192, 223, 225
Beltane Festival, the   97, 209, 211, 212
Bevan, Edward   155
Bevan, Joan   5, 156
Bible, the
  Buber-Rosenzweig translation of   223
  The English Authorised Version of the Bible   148
  The Scriptures   127, 149
  The Vulgate   218, 223
blasphemy (blasphemous)   91, 126, 139
Book of Ecclesiastes, the   149
Book of Genesis, the   74, 186
Book of Revelation, the   149, 186
Borgia, Cesare   178
Bosch, Hieronymus   64
Brothers Karamazov, The   66, 74, 151, 215, 216
Buddhist holyman   200

Ludwig Wittgenstein: The Meaning of Life, First Edition. Edited by Joaquín Jareño-Alarcón.
© 2023 John Wiley & Sons Ltd. Published 2023 by John Wiley & Sons Ltd.

c

Calvin 149, 180, 189
Calvinism 104
cannon 149
Catholic
   Anglo-Catholic 65
   Catholicism 44, 65–66, 84, 104, 155–156, 218, 223
   Roman Catholic 74–75, 159, 162, 181, 187–188, 198, 216–217, 225
   Roman Church 75
cause (causal explanation, causal nexus, causality) 34, 36, 59, 108, 165, 169, 174, 224, 190, 194, 195
ceremony (ceremonial) 100, 159, 181, 201–205
Christ (Jesus, Savior, Son of God) 73, 75, 78, 85, 86, 90, 99, 101, 113, 122, 165, 185, 191, 224–225
Christianity 16, 76, 86–87, 90–91, 111, 116, 124, 127, 130, 136, 151, 168, 177, 191, 215, 218
Church 65, 66, 75, 76, 91, 100, 102, 125, 126, 158, 159, 181, 186, 187, 189, 191, 193, 197, 215, 224
Church Fathers 186, 187
City of God, the 217
civilization 70, 167, 189
Claudius, Matthias 88, 130
Cleopatra 179
Comforter, the (the Holy Spirit) 102
command (commandment) 53, 105, 118, 120, 183
Concluding Unscientific Postscript 225
condemnation 65
confession 83, 87, 90, 100, 101, 128, 158, 172, 200, 202, 217, 225, 226
Confessions 83, 200, 219, 225, 226
confidence 165, 213
conscience 17, 27, 32, 55, 105, 132, 153, 174, 180, 184, 222
consecrated Host 75
convert 84, 165
Copleston, Frederick (S. J.) 176
corn-wolf 206
creation 116, 117, 141
Crime and Punishment 215
Cross 91, 175

d

Darwin, Charles 94, 97, 98
definition 57, 83, 99, 163, 183, 184
Descartes, René 91
Devil (Satan) 8, 44, 74, 88, 91, 105, 165, 168, 170, 174, 196
Dickens, Charles 225
divine right 67
death (life) 1, 22, 23, 27, 50, 108, 111, 153, 155–156, 177, 202–204, 221
description 58, 59, 62, 71, 72, 79, 85, 99, 124, 136, 178, 202, 204, 206
devoutness 129
doctrine 102, 104, 105, 120, 121, 124, 129, 130, 155, 168, 177, 212, 223, 224, 226
dogma 75, 125, 136, 191, 193
Dostoievsky, Fyodor 26, 66, 151, 216, 226
Drury, Maurice O'Connor 64–66, 73–77, 91, 99–100, 102–105, 123, 128, 132, 148–149, 156–159, 161–162, 169, 176, 186–189, 196–199, 215–216, 218–219

e

Easter time 100
Eastern Orthodox Church (Orthodox rite) 66, 198, 216
Elisha 196
Engelmann, Paul 38, 41, 44, 46, 220–222
Epistle of James 149
Epistle to the Hebrews 149
Epistle to the Romans 77, 218
eternity (future life) 23, 26–27, 50, 103, 108, 196
ethics
   ethical judgment 30, 58
   ethical law (moral law) 30, 49, 84
   ethical principle 178–179
   ethical proposition 59, 85
Euthydemus 184
evidence 1, 36, 90, 135–140, 193, 210, 212, 214
evil 21, 25, 27–31, 38, 90, 113, 125–126, 170, 174, 185
Ewing, Alfred Cyril 184
experience 2, 4, 33, 37, 44, 48, 50, 52, 55, 60–62, 70, 72, 98, 108, 122, 124, 136, 138–139, 141, 142, 147, 157–158, 188, 195, 207, 210–211, 219, 225

explanation   57, 69, 71–72, 87, 92–93, 97, 99, 133, 135, 140, 157, 178, 181, 190, 192, 194, 201–205, 208, 212

f

faith   1, 2, 29, 38, 42, 112, 113, 118, 121, 124, 131, 134, 136, 155, 158, 168, 171, 174, 179, 185, 215, 223, 225, 226
fate   11, 17, 25, 27, 33, 48, 118, 166, 172, 224
Father O'Hara   136
Faust   4, 108, 170
Feuerbach, Ludwig   191
Ficker, Ludwig von   3, 14, 17, 19, 39
fideism   219
Final Judgment   220
Fox, George   225
Francis of Assisi, Saint   148
Frazer, James George   93, 96, 97, 199, 200, 201, 203–207, 219
Freud, Sigmund   96, 104

g

game (language game)   107, 115, 168, 214
Gnostic   221
Goethe, Johann Wolfgang von   4, 196, 226
God
    Creator   116, 220, 224
    Deity   139, 141, 224
    God's essence   177
    God's existence   194, 195
    Godhead   73
    Lord   23, 77, 114, 125, 131, 166, 193
    The Perfect One   117, 121, 127
    Proof of God   194
    Will of God   27, 117, 118
god of thunder, the   205
gods (Olympus)   178
ghost   123, 131, 205, 206
Golden Bough, The   93, 96, 97, 199–226
Good Friday   100, 120
goodness (good)   94, 95, 167, 177
Gospel According to John, the   102, 192
Gospel According to Luke, the   11, 149
Gospel According to Matthew, the   192
Gospel in Brief and What I Believe, The   3, 19, 222
Gospel/Gospels   3, 7, 10, 19, 45, 65, 73, 126, 130, 157, 187, 192, 193, 218, 222, 224

grace (election by grace, predestination)   126, 129, 176
grammar (grammatical remark, grammatical sense)   147, 214
Grammar of Assent, the   181
Greek myths   181
guilt   4, 59, 61, 111, 183, 184, 222, 224

h

Hamann, Johann Georg   83
Hänsel, Ludwig   66, 100, 131
happiness (being happy, happy life)   16, 27, 30–32, 53, 112, 170
heaven (eternal bliss)   87, 88, 98, 101, 107, 119, 124, 127, 131, 132, 179, 208, 220
Hebrews   149
hell (eternal damnation, unending torment)   44, 74, 87, 103, 107–108, 114, 119, 122, 131, 177
heresy (heretical)   186, 189
hierarchy   126
Hitler, Adolf   80–81, 164, 214
hypothesis   90, 136, 195, 201, 205–206, 208–209, 211–212
Holy Communion   102
Holy Week   100
Horus   158
Hooker, Richard   104
Hügel, Friedrich von   74, 216
human being   33, 48, 58, 61, 67, 69, 73, 84, 86–87, 89, 93, 96, 101, 105, 106, 108, 109, 113, 114, 117, 118, 125, 126, 130–132, 147, 158, 174, 176, 192, 204, 207, 213, 214, 219, 220, 224, 226
humanity   21, 55, 153, 167

i

idea   2–3, 28, 31, 35–36, 41, 45, 58, 60, 70, 75–76, 80, 83–85, 89, 94, 100, 110, 117, 142–146, 155, 195, 202, 210–212, 215, 220, 224, 226
idealism   35
idolators   193
immortality   50, 146, 182, 224
impurity   126
inexpressible, the   88
interpretation (of Scriptures)   3, 43, 71, 104, 140, 149, 210, 211, 215

Interpretation of Dreams, the 104
Isaiah, the prophet 179, 193

j

James, William 2, 4, 40, 73, 149, 218
Jesuit 176
Jews 81, 90, 180, 183, 192, 214, 223
John of the Cross, Saint 175
Johnson, Samuel 163, 164, 185
Judaism 1, 180

k

Kant, Immanuel 74
Keller, Gottfried 98, 191, 192
Kempis, Thomas à 99
Kierkegaard, Sören 2, 40, 53, 83, 85, 110, 116, 127, 168, 185, 196, 215–217, 224–226
King David 111
Kingsley, Charles 181
knowledge (life of knowledge) 32, 33
Koder, Rudolf 63

l

Lactantius 187
language 18, 25, 46, 47, 50, 60–63, 72, 79, 87, 93, 98, 107, 113, 115, 135, 141, 168, 178, 192, 193, 202, 204, 206, 207, 214, 223
Latin mass (mass) 75
Laws of Ecclesiastical Polity 104
Leavis, Frank Raymond 77
Lenau, Nikolaus 170
Lessing, Gotthold Ephraim 54
Life of Pope 163
liturgy 188
logic (logical connexion, laws of logic) 25, 28–29, 31, 46, 48, 57, 67, 161
Loos, Adolf 14

m

magic 97, 113, 200–202, 204, 208
Martin Luther 83–84, 92, 115, 148–149
McTaggart, John McTaggart Ellis 182
meaning of life (purpose of existence, purpose of life) 3, 24–26, 53, 58, 63, 80
Mendelssohn, Moses 83
Mendelssohn Bartholdy, Felix 106
Mercy 107, 121, 179, 216
metaphor 59, 72, 148

metaphysics (metaphysical) 30, 31, 33, 37, 48, 52, 200
Michelangelo Buonarroti 141
microcosm 34, 47
mind 38, 42, 46, 53, 58–60, 63, 72, 90, 92, 103, 105, 112, 115, 118, 123, 130–131, 133, 134, 142–143, 157, 170, 181, 188, 194, 204, 211, 213, 217
miracle (miraculous phenomenon) 14, 16, 35, 62, 85, 116, 139, 162, 168, 181, 187
misdeed 101
Modernist movement 74
monk 2, 40–41, 74, 155
Monk, Ray 2, 80, 223–224
Moore, George Edward 57, 69, 77, 79, 96, 141, 150, 156, 169, 214, 217–218
Mormons (Mormonism) 161, 179, 185, 225
Morrell, Lady Ottoline 2
mortification 120
Moses 92
mysticism (mystical) 2, 40–41
myth 181, 207
mythology 206

n

Napoleon Bonaparte 136, 181
natural reason 75
Newman, John Henry Cardinal 102, 161, 181–182, 225
New Testament 65, 108, 164, 184, 187, 197, 218
Nibelungenlied, das 208
nonsense 60–62, 72, 80, 96, 138, 165, 173, 186, 191, 204, 215, 217
Nuremberg Laws 214

o

offense 90
Old Testament 65, 149, 196–197
opinion 52, 63, 101, 107, 113, 118, 119, 125, 136, 165, 186, 202, 204, 207, 212
Origen 186
Oxford Movement 181

p

paradise 121
paradox 62, 66, 83, 90, 122, 130
paragon 131

parson   65, 100, 203, 215
Pascal, Blaise   218–219
Paul of Tarsus (Saint Paul)   180
Peer Gynt   108
penitent (penance)   221
Penseés   219
Pepler, Father Conrad (O.P.)   155
perspicuous presentation   205–206
Peter, Saint   149
   Second Epistle of   149
Philebus   184
Philosophische Bemerkungen   215
Philosophical Investigations   80, 92, 153, 154, 212, 215
philosophy   3, 12, 32, 37–38, 43, 45, 48, 52, 68, 70, 73, 79–80, 83, 87, 116, 151, 153–155, 166, 169, 173, 177, 188, 204, 217, 226
picture (image)   204, 221
pilgrim   157, 177, 222
Pilgrim's Progress, the   157, 177
Pinsent, David Hume   5, 11, 12, 15
Pius IX, pope (Giovanni Maria Mastai Ferreti)   75, 102
piousness (piety)   130
Plato   94, 98, 184, 186
Pope, the   102, 181
practice   42, 77, 94, 125, 143, 144, 181, 194, 200, 201, 203, 204, 206, 208, 210
prayer   75–77, 107, 151, 156, 163–165, 180, 183, 185, 192, 193, 197, 198, 216
preacher   65, 75, 102
priest   3, 44, 65, 66, 70, 75, 76, 84, 139, 155, 183, 187–189, 197, 198, 200, 202, 203, 215, 216, 223
priest-king   200, 202
primitive
  people   70, 97
  religion   69–70
  tribes   66, 70
proof   65, 75, 93, 130, 133, 146, 147
prophet   183, 222
Protagoras   184
Protestantism (Protestant Tradition)   84
providence   117, 118
psalms   111, 112
psychoanalysis   104

psychology   2, 4, 48, 50, 60, 95, 153, 155, 212–213
punishment   30, 49, 50, 73, 93, 108, 111, 127, 130, 134, 135, 176, 177, 197, 215

q
Quakers   76

r
rain-king   207
realism   33, 35, 48
redemption   124, 131, 187, 224
reference   18, 41, 45, 72, 144, 174, 184
relief   53, 103, 110, 158, 196
religion (irreligious/ness)
  religiosity   66, 83
  religious   1–2, 44, 54–55, 61–62, 66, 69, 72, 75–77, 79–80, 83–84, 86, 90, 100, 106, 118, 120, 125–126, 130, 132–138, 145, 155, 157, 159, 162, 166, 173–175, 186–188, 191–193, 195, 200–202, 205, 215, 217–223, 225–226
religious statements   79, 137
Rembrandt Harmenszoon van Rijn   223
Renan, Ernest   69, 70
Republic   184
Respinger, Marguerite   68, 83
responsibility (duty)   101, 145, 146
resurrection   105, 107, 131, 133, 136
reward (retribution)   30, 49, 50, 73, 108, 130, 134, 138
Richards, Ben   197, 216
right/wrong   40, 95, 111, 204
Rilke, Rainer Maria   17
ritual (rite, ritualism, ritualistic)   70, 181, 204
rule (following a rule)   93
Rusell, Bertrand   22

s
sacraments   165, 181
sacred gesture   168
sacrifice   29, 94, 110, 111, 113, 116, 118, 119, 120, 122, 180, 181, 209, 210
saint   4, 21, 148, 162, 180, 192, 216
salvation   29, 89, 107, 113, 121, 223
savages   181, 200, 203, 205, 206
sceptic   145
science
  natural law   177
  natural science   37, 50, 52
  scientific explanation   69

Schlick, Moritz 71
Schopenhauer, Arthur 24, 31
Schubert, Franz 63, 203
Schweitzer, Albert 73
sentence (proposition) 31, 37, 39, 43, 53, 61, 88, 94, 98, 116, 137, 138, 142, 144–146, 165, 172, 192–194, 214
sermon 5, 65, 102, 106, 150, 189, 215
Servetus, Michael 189
Silesius, Angelus 2, 40
sin (sinner) 4, 24, 29, 32, 38, 87, 89, 119, 124, 222, 224
Smythies, Yorick 143, 144, 146, 147, 150, 155, 159, 161, 197, 216, 223, 225
Solipsism 18, 33, 35, 47, 48
soul 17–18, 20, 23, 33, 48, 50, 67, 89, 92, 96, 101, 114, 119, 124, 130, 131, 133, 145, 155, 157–158, 167, 170, 172, 176, 182, 200, 206, 207, 212, 220, 223
Spengler, Oswald 205
Spinoza, Baruch 8, 88
spiritualist 145–146
state of affairs (fact) 59
states of mind 58–59, 134
spirit (spiritual) 2, 7–9, 11–18, 24, 27, 34, 41, 45, 54–56, 70, 85–86, 113, 120, 123, 127, 142, 148, 175, 180, 192–193, 203–207, 209, 221, 223
Sraffa, Piero 81
sub specie aeterni 51, 68
subject (willing subject/metaphysical subject/thinking subject/philosophical subject/I) 18, 23, 31, 33, 35–37, 47–48, 50, 56–57, 59, 106, 161, 183, 193, 217, 220, 223–224
suicide 1, 12, 38, 42
superstition 31, 64, 70, 114, 138, 174, 178, 204–205
synagogue 180
system 44, 62, 66–67, 98, 137, 173–174, 215

t

temple 64, 158, 180
temptation 83, 86, 122, 136, 195
Tertullian 186
theology (theological) 71, 92, 115, 160, 165, 191, 194, 195, 212, 214, 220, 225
theory 72, 124, 126, 200, 219
Tolstoy, Leo 3, 7, 10, 19, 41, 44, 66, 81, 151, 157, 164, 197, 215–216, 222, 224–226

Trakl, Georg 12–14
transubstantiation 148
Trinity, the Holy 91, 189, 191, 194
Truism 204
truth 16, 18, 47, 62, 63, 103–105, 110, 126, 130, 167, 172, 174–175, 177, 188, 191–192, 200, 223
Turing, Alan 147
Twenty Three Tales 151, 215

v

Vanity 52, 70, 90, 105, 107, 110, 114, 116, 118, 125, 128, 167
Varieties of Religious Experience, the 2, 40, 73, 218
verification 85, 94, 145, 148, 210
vice 91
Virgin Mary, the 11, 149
virtue 20, 89, 106, 179, 208
value (judgment of value) 58

w

Wagner, Richard 55
Waismann, Friedrich 72, 79, 193
Weininger, Otto 226
Whitehead, Alfred North 4
will (alien, metaphysical, psychological) 26–27, 59
wisdom 14, 118, 121, 131, 168, 171, 172
witches 86, 121
Wittgenstein, Gretl (Margarethe Stonborough) 164, 173
Wittgenstein, Hans 12
Wittgenstein, Helene 63
Wittgenstein, Hermine 24, 164, 214
Wittgenstein, Karl 2
Wittgenstein, Kurt 6, 12
Wittgenstein, Leopoldine 1
Wittgenstein, Ludwig 1–2, 6, 19, 40–42, 63, 66, 80, 132, 150, 151, 157, 160, 161, 163–164, 190, 214–215
Wittgenstein, Paul 2, 12, 113, 149, 215
Wittgenstein, Paul (uncle) 12
Wittgenstein, Rudi 1–2, 12

z

Zionism 180
Zwingli 148, 191